Oh, Carol!

CAROL McGIFFIN

Oh, Carol!

life, love and telling it like it is

HODDER &
STOUGHTON

First published in Great Britain in 2010 by Hodder & Stoughton
An Hachette UK company

1

A CIP catalogue record for this title is available from the British Library.

Hardback ISBN 978 1 444 72506 3
Trade Paperback ISBN 978 1 444 70945 2

Typeset in Bembo by Ellipsis Books Limited, Glasgow

Printed and bound in the UK by CPI Mackays, Chatham ME5 8TD

Hodder & Stoughton policy is to use papers that are natural, renewable and recyclable products and made from wood grown in sustainable forests. The logging and manufacturing processes are expected to conform to the environmental regulations of the country of origin.

Hodder & Stoughton Ltd
338 Euston Road
London NW1 3BH

www.hodder.co.uk

I am dedicating this book to the memory of Heather, my beautiful, dear, departed Mum. I only wish she were here to read it. On second thoughts, if she were still here, then given some of the content, I probably wouldn't have written it . . .

ACKNOWLEDGEMENTS

First and foremost I want to thank ITV and the programme that I am hugely privileged to be a part of, *Loose Women*. The success of that show has undoubtedly played a very large part in my being able to get a book all about me published by a major publishing house.

Hodder and Stoughton have afforded me that opportunity and, somehow, they've managed to inspire and extract from me a volume of work that I would never have thought possible. Rowena Webb, Ciara Foley and all the team, I thank you. But special thanks must go to Fenella Bates, my Editor, who has been so positive, patient and encouraging throughout despite my doubts and misgivings about myself and my ability to deliver.

And to Craig Latto and KT Forster, my agent and literary agent, who both had what I thought was way too much undeserved and unwarranted faith all along. Thank you.

Of course I must thank my family, especially my brother Mark for his unofficial editing – invaluable when you don't want to sound like a twat for getting things wrong. But also my sisters, Kim and Tracy, for their help with memories, pictures and family matters.

Most of all, I want to thank Mark, my gorgeous fiancé, because while I have been spending my weekends in a Slanket® staring at a blank screen, he's been taking care of the business of cleaning, cooking, shopping and generally facilitating my project with minimal 'mithering' (Northern term for hassle and bother) and entirely without complaint despite hardly seeing me for the best part of six months.

I want to also mention Apple Inc.© here too for making the MacBook Air – the supermodel of laptops – so slim and light. The job of transporting a computer everywhere in preparation for impromptu inspiration has been a joy, not a chore.

And finally, Neil Sedaka. Thank you so much for writing the song, 'Oh, Carol'. It is because of that song that I have Carol as my first name and not something beginning with D that is my second (don't ask), and indeed the title of my book.

Oh, and thank *you* for reading it.

CONTENTS

INTRODUCTION

I always knew I *wanted* to write a book. I always knew I *would* write a book. I just didn't know how, or when, or if I could. I used to buy books about writing books and never read them, and I've got a folder on my computer called 'Books', full of weak, unfinished attempts at novels or memoirs. I've spent hours online looking at websites for literary agents and publishers, and for years, every time I walked by my local bookshop I fantasised about seeing a book with my name on it in the window. My plan was to retire to the South of France and write books in front of a window with a nice view. Whenever we had authors on *Loose Women* I'd question them about their first experience, how they got published, how long it took, where they go to write, at what time of day and for how long. The fascination was there but the trouble was that the drive, the determination and the need wasn't. I obviously didn't want it enough to sit there and write for hours a day, perfecting a manuscript that I was prepared to persuade someone to publish.

Then, somewhere along the line, *Loose Women* became very popular indeed and a couple of the other Loose Women brought out their own books. The show itself also had three very successful books, two of them No.1 Bestsellers – all published by Hodder & Stoughton, who then thought it might be a good idea if I wrote one. I agreed and said, 'Yes, I'd love to', but in the way that you do when you're not sure if you can and so you start to wonder if maybe you might have exceeded your limitations.

But I needed that challenge, that deadline, and I needed to scare myself into doing something difficult. Something that would inspire me to work harder than I'd had to in many years due to my preference for an easy life and, lacking in drive and ambition as I am, choosing to say no to things that might cause consternation and stress.

This time I went for it because writing a book has been my only real ambition in my whole life. In fact, it's been on my list of New Year's resolutions since about 1979. Trouble was, where did I start? All those words and all those pages – where were they going to come from? 'Don't be afraid to ask for help', they said. 'No', I said. 'If I'm going to have a book out there with my name on the cover, that's all about me, it has to be written by me and not by someone else. It might be the way for others in my profession but it's not for me.'

So I bought myself a Slanket® (blanket with sleeves) that you wrap around your whole body – feet and all – so that if you try to get up to either put the telly on or search for a snack or alphabeticise your CD collection in order to procrastinate, you fall over. And all winter I sat there, staring at a screen with the internet turned off in case I was tempted by the class A cyberdrug that is Twitter.

I knew it wouldn't be easy but I hadn't reckoned on quite how hard it would be, and I admit, I was tempted to dial 0800-GHOST-WRITER more than once but I stuck it out and cancelled holidays, snubbed my friends, ignored Christmas and even stayed in on New Year's Eve on my own for the first time since 1973.

Then, while skiving one day, I read something (via Twitter...oops) by Stephen Fry. He was giving notice to his followers that he'd not be around for a while because he was off to write a book. On his blog, he wrote that the only way he could do it was to lock himself in a dark room and speak to no one, and he quoted someone's advice to him on the subject: '*"It is almost impossibly hard," he told me. "It is supposed to be. But once you truly understand how difficult it is," he added, with signature paradoxicality, "it all becomes a lot easier."*' Now, I have no idea who said that to him, nor did I have the first clue what paradoxicality meant but I loved reading about how writing troubled him so, and it made me feel better. Not that I'm comparing myself to the great man himself but surely if that clever dick finds it hard then what chance was there for me with my undisciplined 'alphabetti spaghetti' thought processes. As a result, it was probably at least six weeks before I wrote the first word.

I used that time to start familiarising myself with myself. And, of course, my past. Luckily I'd kept boxes of memorabilia – diaries, journals, music and mementoes – which ended up being permanently scattered all over the floor for easy access. And my music collection was a great way of transporting myself back to certain times. Playing vinyl records relative to the period I was writing about really helped to restore deleted elements of my cerebral hard drive. Because the human brain is exactly like a computer hard drive in that it can't possibly retain every little event and detail as there's only a finite amount of space. So when it becomes full, old stuff gets deleted to make room for the new stuff. Recovering data isn't always possible though, however many times you find a trigger. It was fascinating realising that even after I'd recalled something, I still had no recollection of it ever happening proving that though my memory isn't too bad, it is, like everyone's I suppose, selective.

Eventually, and thankfully, it became an enjoyable, pleasant and enlightening experience, especially given that I've not had that much misery or trauma in my first fifty years. Although writing about the harrowing experiences I have had, like my mum dying, and surviving the Asian tsunami, have brought me as many tears as the rest of it has laughs.

So, it's done and I did it. The first time I wrote a book. Now I hope you'll enjoy reading about some of the other things I did in my life for the first time, most of which I probably won't or can't ever do again. I'm keeping my fingers crossed that writing a book isn't one of them.

CHAPTER 1

The First Time I: Came second

(The Family and my Place in it Chapter)

The first born was Kim. Two years and four days before me, she was born on St Valentine's Day at St Barts in London – within the sound of Bow Bells, which makes her a real gorblimey guvner cockney. Well it would have, but between 1941 when the bells were destroyed in the Blitz and 1961 when they were replaced, no real cockneys could officially be born but don't tell her that, she's proud of her cockney status.

It's rubbish being born second. Especially when you have three siblings where one is the eldest, one the youngest and the other the only boy. Where do I fit into that little list of specialties apart from being the glaringly insignificant 'number two'? Great. I'm nothing but a big old 'number two'. I couldn't even call myself a cockney being born as I was in the Whittington in North London. I can hear my mum now introducing the family. 'This is Kim, she's the eldest. And that's Tracy, she's my youngest. Ah, and Mark, he's the only boy. And that's Carol.' See?

I think I definitely suffered from second or middle child syndrome as they call it, especially as I've now looked into it in detail. So many of the traits explain so much about why I am like I am and why I turned out like I did. I found that the most notable ones were:

S/he will often do almost anything for parental attention, even if that means being naughty. (Spot on.)
They may be the loud, boisterous child in school. (100% correct.)
The second child may feel out of place because they aren't over achievers.

Instead, the middle child usually just goes with the flow. (Explains my lack of ambition.)
They have a history of starting projects and never finishing them. (My worst trait. Believe me, the fact that I've actually written and finished this book on time is a miracle.)
When choosing a career, most middle or second children would be best suited for something where they could freely express themselves. (Like *Loose Women*?)

So it's a good job Kim was born first; she was a born leader. Looking at pictures of us when we were little she always has a protective arm around us and a reassuring yet slightly worried look on her face. She was so tall as a kid, Kim. And skinny. Really skinny. Whenever she looked at photos of herself she always commented, 'Bleedin 'eck, I look like a right streak o' piss!' Well, she was a cockney. I never once fell out with Kim. I think it was because as the number two, I always looked up to her for guidance; she was like a second mum to me really. Still is. She is extremely hardy, our Kim. She's had quite a tough time with her choices of men, just like Mum. And she's like her in that she never stops worrying about her kids: Daniel, who's now 27 and Emma, who's 25. They are both a credit to her resilience and tenacity. Kim lives and works in Kent for a major supermarket in a freezer, not literally but it is a cold storage facility which makes it feel like one, inspecting fruit (she's a Q&A inspector). She does 12-hour night shifts, four on, four off, for very little money. But she'd rather struggle and work than not. It's that work ethic that we've luckily inherited from my mum.

Mark was born a mere 21 months after me. He was the cutest baby of all of us. We all had bright white-blond hair to start with but Mark was the only one who retained it. I can still see him in his old-fashioned Mary Poppins pram in the sunshine with his little sunburnt face (a sunburnt baby, when was the last time you saw one of those!?!?). For some reason, aged five, I took a spiteful dislike to Mark. There was no reason for it, nothing behind it, I just 'hated' him. Middle child syndrome again I guess. But how could I? In his little shorts, looking like a miniature replica of my old grandad. I felt a bit sorry for him being the only boy, surrounded by girls. He had no real male role models growing up but mercifully he wasn't really affected by that fact and out of all of us was probably the best behaved growing up. He never smoked or broke the law and he did really well at school compared to us girls. In fact, I don't even remember him ever getting told off by Mum. We used to tease him being the only boy, calling him 'Mummy's little soldier' although it was her that coined the phrase. It was never malicious though, we were never jealous of him for it. Mark's a civil engineer/project manager and specialises in the construction of very tall chimneys for power stations. He's been an expat for the best part of 25 years and has worked in some fairly exotic places. The Falkland Islands, Iraq, Ghana, Bahrain, Taiwan, Malaysia, Singapore and now the Philippines – great for cheap accommodation if I fancy a holiday. With the magic of the internet and Skype, I probably talk to him more than if he lived here and I definitely talk to him more than to my sisters, who, compared to him, live just down the road. Mark's the only one of us who has never married, although he has a girlfriend of six years, Nani, whom he met while working in Malaysia.

Tracy is the baby of the family and she always looked like the baby. Every photo that she's in, she has that worried, cute, slightly distressed look. It might have been because she was the last to get the hand-me-down clothes which almost never fitted and always looked so urchin-like. She was born four days after my birthday. (All three girls are February babies 14th, 18th and 22nd respectively – how weird is that?) This meant that when Mum went off to give birth, she disappeared on my birthday, an event that had far-reaching effects on my psyche as you will find out. I also went through a phase of not getting on with Tracy, though it wasn't at the same time as Mark. We would really fight, never more so than when she'd borrow my clothes as a teenager without asking and put them back with her teenage hormonal whiff all over them. Mum never reprimanded her either, because being the youngest Mum quite enjoyed indulging her as she'd not been able to with us. She was the lucky one too because as Kim, Mark and I all went off to work for anything we wanted, as well as needed, Mum had the chance to mildly spoil her. She always admitted it was a mistake but she said she couldn't help herself. I could understand it. Tracy's certainly not lazy and is very capable but she doesn't quite have the work ethic that us three have, so hasn't minded spending the last 14 years just bringing up her daughter Holly although she's looking for work now. To her credit, Holly has grown up a very well adjusted and intelligent girl and is doing very well at school.

So that meant that between 14 February 1958 and 22 February 1963 Mum had given birth to four children. I don't know how she did that, she must have been pregnant constantly for almost the whole five years. That was always her plan though. She came from a very stable background – her parents, Len and Mary Ellen, or Nell as she was known to her friends, were together until death did them part. Visiting them was like going back in time and sitting in the kitchen there while Grandma baked cakes and made jam on the 1950s freestanding cooker is a lovely memory. While Grandma cooked and cleaned, Grandad played golf or was in the garden. He loved his garden and should have won prizes for it, it was so beautiful. They married in 1932 and Grandad died in 1986. I remember going to their golden wedding anniversary party at the golf club of the course near to where they'd retired to in Sanderstead, Surrey. One of my favourite photos is from that day – my grandma and grandad at the head of the table, looking so proud, surrounded by their children and grandchildren. Grandma died in 2000.

They did a very good job of bringing up Heather, my mum. She had exceptional manners, was quiet but headstrong and extremely stoical. She was tall, slim and elegant and always took immense pride in her appearance, even if she wasn't working, although at home she was never out of her Dot Cotton style housecoat overalls. And beautiful too, with natural auburn hair and bright blue eyes that lit up the room when she laughed. She loved a good laugh and when she did it, so did everyone else, they couldn't help it, it was so infectious. She worked so hard all her life but she had no sense of entitlement whatsoever and for someone who ended up fairly poor, she had zero wealth envy. It was a truly admirable quality of hers. She so loved my dad that when they got married she described it as 'the best day of her life' until of course, it all went wrong. Then, despite having the odds stacked right against her and without ever complaining, blaming or asking for sympathy, and rarely asking for help, she in turn did a marvellous job bringing up her four kids each of whom she was immensely proud of in one way or another. She had a lot to be proud of, my mum.

My dad, John, was from proper East End stock. His mother lived in the City of London all of her life, in an old tenement on the Sutton Estate just off the City Road. He was another one of four children and also a second born. He was a real 'number two' in more ways than one, especially to my mother at one point. He was very tall, dark and handsome and had been in the RAF. He and my mum got together when they were both working at Unilver House, just by Blackfriars Bridge in London, right across the river from where I work now. Mum worked in the typing pool and Dad was the post boy. My grandma never approved of him but then she was a bit of a snob and he was just a cockney Londoner. Mum had her father on her side though and even though he probably saw trouble ahead, he backed my mum because he knew how happy she was with him.

Oh, and then there's me, Carol.

CHAPTER 2

The First Time I: Went out for an ice cream and came back with a mouth organ

(The Childhood Homes Chapter)

We had moved five times by the time I was five years old although being so young it never really occurred to me that this wasn't normal. In fact, I probably didn't even know what was happening. I just lived where we lived.

My dad was a manager for the food store chain David Greig's. This meant we lived in town centre shopping streets, above the shop. The first one was in Hornsey High Street, not far from where I live now in North London. I have absolutely no recollection of it at all, now, but when searching through my stuff I found a passage I'd written in a school book about moving house which describes it as being huge with a playground with swings and a paddling pool.

Funny how I remembered that when I was 13 but I don't now. I was studying *Jane Eyre* at the time but I also have no recollection of reading that either.

So when I was only a year old, we had to up sticks and relocate to the Garden of England and its county town, Maidstone. The shop was on Week Street, still the main shopping drag to this day except that where it used to be full of grocers, open-air greengrocers and shops where you bought things you needed, it's now full of mobile phone shops, jewellers and fashion chains like River Island and Next. Marks and Spencer's is now on the site of the old David Greig's. Again, I thought the flat was huge but I was still very small, so it

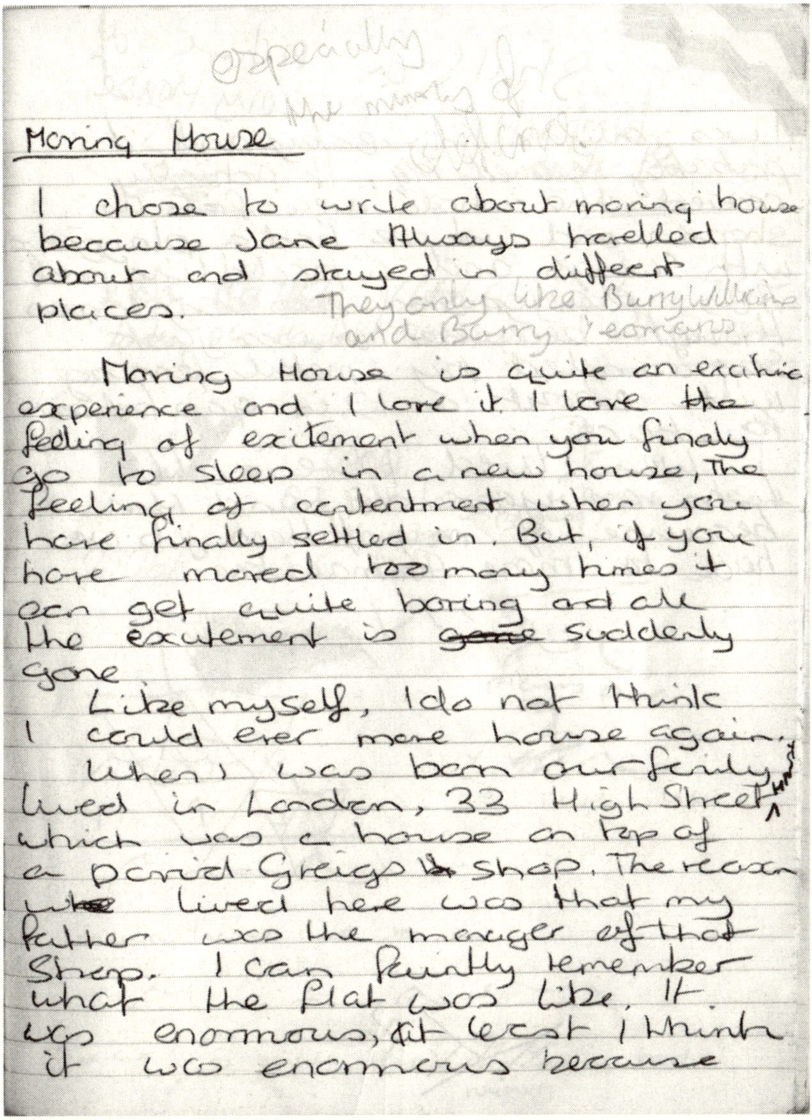

Moving House

I chose to write about moving house because Jane Always travelled about and stayed in different places. They only like Barry Williams and Barry Yeomans

Moving House is quite an exciting experience and I love it. I love the feeling of excitement when you finaly go to sleep in a new house, The feeling of contentment when you have finally settled in. But, if you have moved too many times it can get quite boring and all the excitement is ~~gone~~ suddenly gone

Like myself, I do not think I could ever move house again.

When I was born our family lived in London, 33 High Street which was a house on top of a David Greigs shop. The reason we lived here was that my father was the manager of that shop. I can faintly remember what the flat was like. It was enormous, at least I think it was enormous because

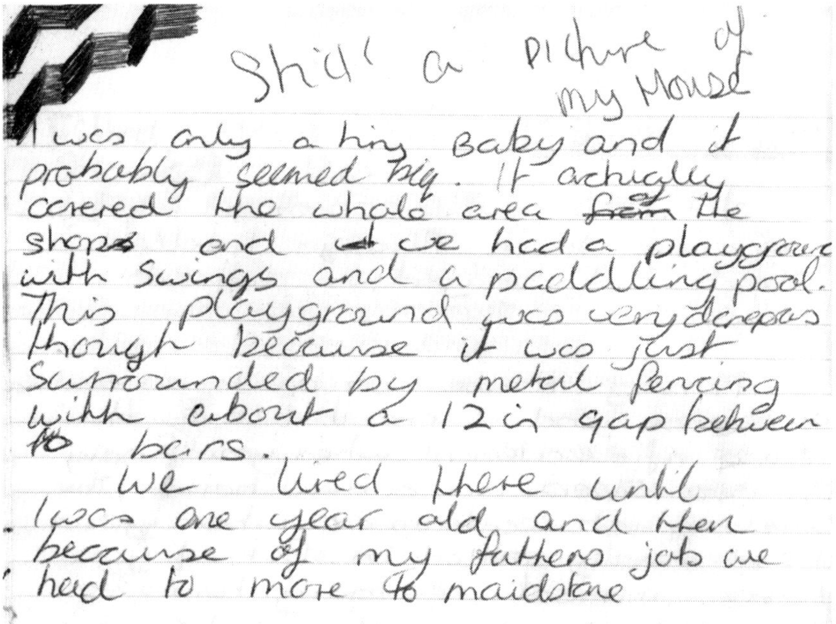

Sketch a picture of my House

I was only a tiny Baby and it probably seemed big. It achugly covered the whole area ~~from~~ the shops and we had a playground with Swings and a paddling pool. This playground was very dangerous though because it was just Surrounded by metal fencing with about a 12in gap between to bars.

We lived there until I was one year old and then because of my fathers jobs we had to move to maidstone would have been like *The Land of the Giants* (TV show from the late 1960s where some little people land on a planet full of really big people, or giants). I can mostly only piece together what it was like from photographs – quite grand with posh gold curtains and silk panelled wallpaper; an expensive looking grey velour three-piece suite. The kitchen seemed huge too and had a big yellow cabinet with a little bowl of sweets on the top that was kept for treats. One of my earliest memories involved those sweets. I was having a mild fit one day after realising I couldn't actually run away from my own shadow and to calm me down and shut me up, Mum gave me a fruit gum from the stash. I was so hysterical that the sweet left my mouth and ended up stuck to my forehead, freaking me out even more because obviously I thought this was a monster alien invading my space. Apparently I didn't shut up until I got another one. Then there was the time when I decided to help Mum with the chores by 'cleaning' the pristine white door to the living room with brown boot polish. Mum went bananas and, thinking about it now, was I really trying to be helpful or was I being surreptitiously naughty?

In the kitchen there was a big white butler's sink where we used to have our baths. There was no garden with it being a flat, just another lethal flat rooftop that we called a playground, where we'd play handstands and have water fights. The only way down was the imposing wrought iron spiral staircase which was missing a vital 'health and safety' feature – a gate preventing us from playing on it so one day, obviously feeling lazy, I decided to ride my little tricycle down it. Of course I don't remember anything about it but obviously it was carnage. My head was so badly damaged, Mum thought I might never look normal again. She told me one side of my head was extended to the point of looking like the Tefal man (a man featured in an ad for Tefal® in the '70s where, because he was so brainy for inventing non-stick pans, his forehead was elongated and stretched to about 12 inches high), but only half of him. My head is still quite sensitive there as I found out later during an argument with my younger sister, Tracy. She threw a hard-centre chocolate at me which hit me on the forehead and a lump the size of a giant hard-centre chocolate appeared within seconds. Everyone was panicking; 'Don't let her go to sleep!' they were all shouting because such an injury might have caused a blood-clot-induced coma due to the serious accident on the stairs all those years before. It is still quite sensitive, if I get a spot there and try to squeeze it, it comes up like a pus-filled bee sting. Luckily I don't get many spots. Another legacy of that good idea is that I still have a slightly more receding hairline on that side where the hair never grew back, which makes it look (now, at my age) like I'm going bald. Oh well, at least there was no brain damage, although that's debatable too. A nice wooden gate was installed soon after that little incident.

In the early 1960s there were no supermarkets as such but David Greig's was a forerunner, along with Sainsbury's who were their big rivals. It was a fine store. A real old-fashioned grocer's with white brick-tiled walls and tins stacked up like they do at the fair for you to shoot and win a crap teddy bear. It had a different counter for different produce around the edges and in the middle a stand for the bread. It had a beautiful black and white parquet-style tiled floor. And for everything you bought you were served by a real person, wearing a bonnet and an apron, with their own counter and till. Living above it was handy for shopping, because you didn't have to do any. Mum used to send one of us downstairs for whatever she needed. Usually a loaf of bread. Even if she didn't need it, I'd take it, spending ages deciding which colour Wonderloaf to get. Blue was medium sliced, maroon was thick sliced and yellow was thin sliced. Or was it the other way round?

It was an endless source of amusement and having the run of it was a kid's dream come true. My favourite part was the giant fridge-freezer at the back with its rows and rows of dead animals hanging from big lethal hooks and swinging from side to side. I was fascinated and would get in there and observe them whenever I could. I think it taught me very early on a valuable lesson about the food chain and it obliterated any soppy thoughts I might have had about eating cute animals or becoming a vegetarian. It never disturbed me even though you could see they were still cows, pigs and sheep; they just didn't have their coats on and they'd all lost their heads. I was aware of one of the butchers imposing time limits, telling me I couldn't stay in any longer without a coat or I'd die too. I didn't believe him, it didn't even seem that cold to me. What fun it was being a kid then, you could perform daredevil stunts on spiral staircases, steal food whenever you felt like it and hang out with dead meat in sub-zero temperatures. Oh, how things have changed.

Perhaps the lack of parent paranoia and Health and Safety measures was the reason I used to get into all sorts of scrapes but then maybe it was simply because I was three and it was the early 1960s, a time when kids could and would walk just about anywhere, even on their own. Or maybe it was that second child syndrome playing up again. But still, as small as I was, I was free to leave the shop, walk down the road, which although pedestrianised now, then had very narrow pavements and two-lane traffic with buses, to get a Mister Softee ice cream from the stall right at the front of Woolworths about four shops down (also a Marks and Spencer's now, the men's clobber and food bit). I wonder where I got the money from.

Woolies was an absolute wonder. The shop was arranged by islands in those days with people serving from inside each one, again with their own till. I'd spend ages in there, wandering around, eyeing up things I couldn't possibly buy. At Christmas time there were always two or three islands tinselled, paper chained and baubled right up and I'd stand there for hours, transfixed. Same with the toys. But the fact that I couldn't buy things never stopped me acquiring them because for some reason, I started shoplifting mouth organs. Harmonicas. It might have had something to do with one-man-bands, they were big in the 1960s, they seemed to be all over the place. I can't think why else I would have taken a shine to such a weird musical instrument. Maybe because they were just easy to steal. After all, I might have liked trombones but I think I'd have been spotted leaving the shop with one of those. There was a whole section of them in different sizes and colours, always in weak, worn-looking boxes with a drawing of one on the outside. I stole loads of them but only one at a time. I don't know how I got away with it, maybe the assistants just thought I was cute and let me get on with it. I would go straight to that island, wait for the assistant to turn her back and then reach up and nab it. I'd make my way back home and hide it straight away in the big cupboard in the corner of the living room where the hoover and all the other cleaning paraphernalia was kept. The cupboard was my hiding place and when I could I'd go and sit in there, leaving the door ajar so I wasn't in total darkness, and inspect my haul, just like Fagin did with his jewels. I never played them in case Mum heard so I just took them out of the boxes, looked at them and put them back. I was rumbled one day after she enquired as to what I was doing in there and was apoplectic. She was so mad and her voice so loud that my fear must have turned to confusion and I suddenly felt like I was in a Tom and Jerry cartoon where you only see the legs of the woman who's always reprimanding the cat. I was the cat, being dragged down the stairs, along the road, by the ear, all the way back to Woolies with the contraband in tow. She made me return them all and apologise profusely, which I could hardly do through the shame and humiliation of being pulled down the road and the tears over the loss of my precious toys. A valuable lesson had been learned, or so I thought. But it was good enough for Woolies and the police were never involved. I often think about what would happen in that situation today, even at three you'd probably still be arrested, have your DNA taken and social services would no doubt take you away!

Our third home, No.4, Hayle Road, on the outskirts of town was probably the most depressing, awful house full of horrid memories. It was a fairly standard-looking semi-detached Edwardian house with a yellow door but it was grim. And dark. Although it's possibly the black and white photograph I have of us four kids standing by the window that makes me think it was. Apart from that, all I know is that it was infested with spiders – I remember freaking out after hiding in the curtain and emerging with a massive spider on me. No fruitgums at Hayle Road – and for some reason, we weren't allowed out in the garden.

It was where we were living in 1964 when my dad left. It's why we had to move there, because he knew he was going.

By then things had already gone horribly wrong between Mum

and Dad and they were on the verge of splitting. There was a lot of shouting and fighting between them, things were thrown frequently, I'll always remember the butter dish going across the room, but being very young I still didn't really register much of it. Sometimes I wonder if I subconsciously chose not to retain what was happening or if somehow I managed to block it right out, which for life purposes is a good thing, I think. For autobiography purposes, maybe not.

It must have happened quite quickly because one minute he was there and then he was gone. It wasn't exactly 'just like that', I'm sure there were all sorts of shenanigans going down but I wasn't aware of them. I know he went off to be with a family friend and I remember him leaving.

My dad, Kim and I had just been to visit our first school, East Borough Girls School in Maidstone, and post-visit we were standing on the pavement outside the new house. My dad was standing there telling Kim and me that he was going now and he wasn't coming back. I certainly didn't understand the magnitude of what he was telling us but I'm absolutely sure that's how it happened because it's a very clear memory and some things you retain and some you don't. Kim and I both remember the moment he got in his car and drove off. I can still picture and replay it now because as we were receiving this monumental earth-shattering news I could see the lollypop lady in the background, gently guiding children across the road. Kim was shattered, traumatised. I was confused. Mark and Tracy were too young to know what was going on. Mum, as far as I can remember, just carried on cleaning and cooking and putting on a brave face. So even if the house wasn't dark and bleak it felt it and there really was a sombre mood that even we small children must have picked up. I dealt with it by playing with a Sindy doll I'd had for Christmas, though interestingly, always on the table in front of the window, probably hoping to see his car and my dad coming home.

I was aware of the new woman in his life. I remember her as my mum's friend who babysat for us sometimes. She worked in the store. I don't know the details but according to Mum, Dad had been having an affair with her for a while.

I've got a photo of her with us kids and my mum on the sofa at

Week Street and I often look at it and wonder if it was already going on then. I asked my mum about it but she didn't like talking about it, she was angry though and she hated them both for a long time after he'd gone. When I saw my dad later in my life I also asked him what happened but his reply just annoyed me. He said, 'You can't help who you fall in love with' which may be so, but falling in love doesn't mean you can walk away from everything without taking full responsibility for what you've created like he did, as you'll find out in the next chapter.

I was four when he left and for the following five years he visited us regularly. He used to turn up in his brand new white Ford Anglia (BKE 873B – why do I remember that?) and take us out for the day. I have fond memories of those outings. I used to love going for Sunday roast in the restaurant that used to be in the Granada cinema complex on Gabriel's Hill. He would tell me off for putting ketchup on my food. We'd also go to the park and feed the ducks and he would always scare us by pretending to almost drive into the lake. Or we'd drive to the seaside, Sheerness usually because it was closest, and we'd get a tanner (sixpence in old or two and a half pence in new money) if we were the first one to see the sea. As soon as we shut the doors and pulled away, it was a constant chorus of 'I can see the sea', all the way there.

Sometimes we'd go up to London to see his mum, our nan, in her funny flat. She lived in a dreadful old tenement block just off the City Road roundabout. It was funny because, before it was modernised, the bath was in the kitchen under the worktop, hidden, when it wasn't in use, by a lovely floral curtain on a piece of wire. We were highly amused by this and would play hide and seek in it forever. My Auntie Alma lived there as well, and my Auntie Alice and Uncle Bert who never seemed to get any older but were just always really old. Even when I was a little girl they seemed to be 102. Bless them, they were an adorable couple, like two characters from *Tales of the Riverbank*.

Dad usually turned up at Christmas. One year he bought us a bike each from Halfords. We couldn't believe it. I had a maroon one with white tyres, Kim had a sophisticated navy blue one and Tracy was still on three wheels. Mark had a lookalike Chopper. Another time he came and took us all to one of the town's big department stores, Chiesemans in Maidstone where he shopped for toys, but not for us, probably for his new son, our half brother whom he never mentioned. He always said the toys were for Catherine, my cousin. Eventually he stopped coming altogether. Mum told me later that it was after he turned up unannounced one day and took us all out of school to go and do something or other. Mum was furious and told him she thought it'd be best if he stayed away and now, with hindsight, she was right. His visits confused us all. We didn't really understand why he was there or why he wasn't there, and bringing us expensive presents when Mum could only afford board games on tick just wasn't fair. She never stopped us seeing him when we got older though; she made sure we knew it was our choice if we wanted to and all of us, apart from Mark, did at various stages. The only contact Mum had with him though after that was at one of my cousins' wedding in London in 1977. That was the strangest thing with them being in the same room for the first time in so long and Dad being with his new wife and all. They didn't speak and I think it was quite difficult for her but she put on a brave face.

Hayle Road was always a temporary stop as it was a private rental and who was going to pay the rent? So before long we were on the move again, this time courtesy of Maidstone Borough Council.

46 Northumberland Court was above the shops in Northumberland Road on the Shepway Estate – an enormous 1950s sprawling landscape of terraced and semi-detached houses and flats. Mostly looking exactly the same. Ours was a maisonette but it only had two bedrooms so for Mum, three girls and a boy it was nowhere near big enough. It was on the end, right above the chip shop. Most of the shops are still there: the newsagents where Tracy, my younger sister, got her finger trapped in the door and almost bled to death, the dentist where we all had questionable treatment under hallucinagenic gas. I liked the gas, I loved the kaleidoscope dreams you had while the masked man with the pliers, probably unnecessarily, pulled your teeth out with all the care and consideration of a road digger with a pickaxe and a grudge. He was always yanking our teeth out, we hardly ever had fillings, just extractions of teeth that would never grow back again. No dentist in

my adult life has been able to work out why he took two of my bottom teeth away. They can't both have been rotten, they're the same ones on either side of my mouth. It's a nightmare because I'm getting older now and you do actually get 'long in the tooth' as they say, where your gums start to recede. Sometimes so much so that your teeth actually fall out. Mine aren't that bad but because I have these bloody gaps there's nothing to keep them together and I can see them slowly splaying out, a bit like Stonehenge. Perhaps he had a lucrative deal going on with the tooth fairy. Perhaps I could sue the bastard, if he's still alive.

The shops and their dingy, concrete staircase became our home and play area for the two years while we waited for a house. It was OK though, there was a green right opposite with swings, a see-saw, slide and roundabout. We spent hours there, again risking our little lives with its solid concrete floors. No cotton wool spongy landings for us.

We moved again just after my sixth birthday. I think it was my sixth. I say it was because Mum made a makeshift birthday celebration 'cake' using six mini swiss rolls with candles in them. Maybe I wasn't six, perhaps that was just to use up the whole packet so we could all have one each while I had two because it was my birthday. The Beatles were on the telly, probably the news, and Mum was telling us about the time she went to see them and was screaming in the audience. I was confused. Mum, The Beatles, screaming? She was so reserved and quiet. So sensible. 'What were you actually screaming?' I asked, trying to picture her leaning over railings and wailing with a tear-stained, scrunched up face. I still can't believe it. As she got older and grumpier though, she did actually deny it and said that she hated it because she couldn't hear the music for the screaming so it was a waste of time and money!

So finally we got our house. THE house. A WHOLE house! Our home for the next 14 years. It was on the same estate, about the same distance from the schools but in the opposite direction. It was 1966. It was small and typical of its type and time. Semi-detached. Three bedrooms, living room, dining room and kitchen. Bathroom and outside toilet. Coal shed and shed. Massive 100' garden that more or less backed onto Mote Park. We couldn't believe our luck and although we didn't have two ha'pennies to rub together we thought we were millionaires.

195 Plains Avenue, ME15 7BD, telephone 676428. There isn't much I don't remember about that house. From its pebbledash exterior and its coral coloured front door, to the little 9' x 9' dining room (how and why do I know it was nine feet square?) and the mishmash of carpets and paint, every detail is vivid almost beyond belief. Probably because it was our first proper house where we felt settled and it was where I really grew up. I was six when we moved in and nearly 20 when I moved out. It is, literally, the house of my dreams. Everything takes place there when my mind is doing its cleaning up or whatever it does when it's dreaming. Usually I can't draw the curtains or lock the door, or the gas fire won't turn off. Sometimes it's completely random situations with people from the present turning up there, always in that house. That's how I still know it so well. I quite often do a 'mind tour' of it. Where your mind, like a video camera, walks around taking in, noting and observing everything from the colours of the décor to the style of the blankets on the beds. I can even remember exactly what was in the drawers of my mum's dressing table and wardrobes. It is so predominant in my thoughts that sometimes I make an effort and think really, really hard to try and remember if there was anything really traumatic that happened there to make it so. But, although there were a few unpleasant incidents, they were few and far between and certainly not worthy of any long-term trauma. No, it must be that it was a happy time and place of real discovery with a feeling of belonging because up until that house, there was none of that.

The best thing about it was the three bedrooms so Mum could have her own room at last and so could Mark. We three girls still had to share, which we hated of course, it just didn't seem fair. But it was OK, there was plenty of room, or at least it seemed like there was after that flat.

The next best thing about it was the décor. Poor Mum, she did her best to keep the house and garden clean and tidy, decorating it, when she could, with whatever paint she could lay her hands on, which meant when she got some paint cheap, whatever the colour, it went everywhere. The living room was purple and I mean the whole living room. Walls, paintwork, ceiling, tiled fireplace, the whole room was purple. Including the carpet. Prince would have loved it. It looked especially good with the mustard floral nylon cover that hid the well-worn posh grey velour suite we had when we were rich and living at Week Street. Then when she'd finished Princing up the living room, she diluted what was left with some cheap white and painted her whole bedroom a paler version. Cupboards, walls, ceiling, headboard, everything. Our room had three blue walls and one yellow. Mark's room, however, was decorated like a proper boy's bedroom with expensive Thunderbirds wallpaper, a white ceiling and white gloss on the paintwork. I'm pretty sure that stuff didn't tumble off the back of the lorry but then it was always only the best for Mummy's little soldier, as we called him. Mark would like me to point out that he recalls that this perfect décor was in situ when we moved in, but then he would, wouldn't he? It wasn't but we didn't really mind, he'd spent the last two years sharing a room with my mum and he was the only boy so he deserved it.

Actually, she transformed that house. When we moved in it looked dull and nondescript, like all the other houses in the street, so Mum painted all the windowsills a bright red, like clay but brighter, then painted white stripes where the grouting would have been. It looked pretty. She also put pretty net curtains up at every window. My mum was obsessed with net curtains but I suppose on those cramped estates with the small gardens you needed them. They felt like a guard and they meant that what was inside was yours, safe from the outside world. They were also great for being nosey too. No one could see you peering, as long as you were careful with your twitching of the nets. I'm getting nostalgic for net curtains because I'm reminded of what a bloody good idea they are. No loss of light but total privacy. Especially as I live in very close proximity to my neighbours and the whole of the front of my living room is glass. And double especially because I do tend to forget this and walk around naked or semi-clothed most of the time.

She also managed somehow to carpet the whole house in the left-over, third-hand carpets that came from Week Street, via Hayle Road and Northumberland Court. Like a carpet jigsaw puzzle. And she singlehandedly dealt with the garden, a wild rambling mess of 2' high grass when we moved in and transformed that into a planted, well-manicured front and back lawn. We even had a swing.

The street was a proper old community. We knew everyone on our 'section' from the roundabout to the park entrance on both sides of the street. You always chatted to people at the bread van, or the Esso Blue van, the ice cream van or the fish and chip van. Lots of vans round our way.

Most of the neighbours were friendly enough. The ones to the right, Tom and Ann, were very close, helpful and friendly (I've been in their house a few times in my dreams too). We loved it because he was an ice cream man and she looked like a 1960s minx with a beehive hairdo that was almost as tall as her. But the other side weren't so, shall we say, agreeable. Suffice to say that if their front door was open in the summer, ours would have to be closed. Kim and Aggie would have had a field day in there. Occasionally, the obese mother would venture out to the Wonderloaf van, the milkman, the ice cream man or the lemonade man in order to stock up. We were always fascinated by her legs, and how they were like two giant white hams, with ankles that were so fat they almost covered her feet. She was actually a very pleasant woman – but we were only young so that's how we saw it.

Next door but one were 'The Spanishes' as we called them because they were Spanish, and then there were the Murphys. Mrs Murphy was nice. Mum got on well with her and she used to look after us on occasion. It was always lovely to see her, she had such a sunny disposition and she looked like she'd just stepped off the pages of a 1950s perfect housewife manual. She turned up one day when me and Mum were sitting outside enjoying the hot summer (remember those?) wearing the shortest of short mini dresses. I was shocked because although she must only have been about 30, I thought she was way too old to be wearing minis even though minis were all the rage. It was the 1960s after all. But Mrs Murphy in a thigh-skimming number, what was going on? Well, Marion was just popping round to show my mum this new invention that allowed her to wear such a short skirt and it was, tights! The great stocking liberator, what took them so long? I could tell Mum was also amused and feigning interest, 'Ooh yeah', she'd say with a wry smile while probably thinking, 'Pull your dress down love we don't wanna see what you 'ad for breakfast!' Now, every time I think about American tan tights I think of Mrs Murphy.

It felt good living in a street where everyone knew everyone else. It was, as they say, the good old days. The door was always open, everyone said hello, helped each other out, looked out for you. Sometimes they could be a bit nosey. Like if there was a police car in the street, everyone, usually the women, would come out and stand at the gate with their arms crossed, fags hanging out of their mouths, 1950s turbans on their heads . . . not really, but you get the picture. The thing was, a police car was rare then and it usually meant something really bad had happened. Also, you knew exactly who had done it because no one had cars so the road was always empty meaning plod could plonk his vehicle right outside, it was such a giveaway.

They came round to ours a couple of times. The one I was responsible for was when I was caught shoplifting in Woolworths again, obviously having not learnt my lesson from the mouth organ episode. Some school friends and I had been to the Christmas carol concert at All Saints Church and had methodically decided to go into town afterwards for a bit of a Christmas shoplifting spree. It wasn't my idea but I went along with it anyway. I had taken part in the service by playing the bongo drums and I was carrying them with me in a big plastic bag. Five of us headed for Woolies and set about doing some Christmas pilfering. I remember one girl stealing porcelain horses, the type you'd put on the mantelpiece. Others nicked Christmas cards and stuff like that. Me, ever aware of my mother's wrath, was careful only to put the booty into others' bags and the only thing that I ended up with was a roll of foil sticky tape. When we got caught, we were dragged into an office and made to give our addresses before they let us go home. I'm not sure I've ever felt such doom as then. On the bus on the way home, we could barely speak we were so terrified of what might happen. When the cops came the shame was unbearable. My mum sat there and cried while the dinner was ruined, the potatoes boiled dry, the peas were stuck to the pan and the fish fingers were cremated. They questioned me for hours about the horses; my friend had obviously told them I'd taken them because she didn't want to give them up. All I could say was 'I didn't', through floods of tears, over and over again. I remember it took me another hour to convince them that I hadn't stolen the bongo drums. They threatened me with court, a criminal record and God knows what else and scared me half to death. But the good thing was, it worked and I never stole another thing. The bad thing was, I'd almost ruined Christmas.

Luckily, nothing could ruin Christmas in that house. It was such a big thing, that not even a run-in with the rozzers could spoil it. Mum would get the same stuff out each year and every time the tree, a silver tinsel one that had less and less silver tinsel each time it emerged, looked more like just a tree-shaped piece of wire in the corner. The same paper chains would also come out, bedraggled and broken but sellotaped and fixed. All the cards would be hung up on string around the four walls, like washing. And with food, Mum would really push the boat out. On Christmas Eve she would lay out all the goodies that we couldn't have all year on the two sideboards in the dining room. Nuts, chocolates, sausage rolls, mince pies and beer. But we weren't allowed to touch any of it until a certain time. Mum was funny like that, I think she just enjoyed seeing food there and if we'd been allowed to get going as soon as we got up it would have been gone before 10am. That was when I probably had my first drink, which would have been a warm light ale in a can, a special treat because it was Christmas. Dinner was always the big event of the day, often we'd not have turkey because turkey tasted like chicken and we had that all year because it was cheap. So we'd have steak instead, which to our bored and conditioned palates tasted like nothing else on earth. It was so expensive and such a treat that we took photographs of it.

The most unbelievable thing about that house was the cold and the damp. In any room where there was heat, there was mould on the ceiling and the wallpaper resembled that hotel room in the film, *Barton Fink*. You could almost hear it creeping away from the walls. I'm sure winters were actually colder then or perhaps it was just that we had no proper, permanent central heating. There was a gas fire in the living room that only went on at night when we were watching telly – I'm sure that fire was a health hazard; it had big black carbon streaks all over it and we always used to fall asleep when it was on. Luckily, it was hardly on which is probably why it didn't kill us. We'd have to pull the sofa right up in front of it otherwise you couldn't feel it. There was a small two-bar electric wall fire in the dining room and the cooker in the kitchen. Life took place in those rooms in the winter. We got undressed, dressed, washed our hair, dried our hair, did our homework and ate in them because it was simply too cold in the rest of the house to do anything. The mornings were a nightmare. Four of us, all trying to wash hair, iron, get dressed, do homework, eat breakfast, clean shoes in a space the size of a small cupboard. I don't know how we did it. Mum would regularly scream at the top of her voice, 'Shut that bleedin' door!' if we left a door even ajar because what little heat there was would disappear. At bedtime we'd race upstairs with our hot water bottles, place them in the bed for 20 minutes and go back downstairs while they heated up slightly, then venture back up. It. Was. Freezing. So cold that if you spoke, your words literally froze as they came out your mouth so that people could read them. The inside of the windows were solid ice where the condensation would freeze on impact. Using the bathroom was another story. We could only have baths once a week on a Sunday, after listening religiously to the Top 20 or *Pick of The Pops* as it was known then with Alan Freeman on BBC Radio. As soon as the the Cliff Adams Singers went into their 'Sing Something Simple' mode, we were off, upstairs, fighting over the bath water. We could only afford enough hot water to fill it once so we had to share it between all four of us, taking turns over who got to get the fresh water as opposed to the fourth-hand scum-loaded stuff at the end. So during the week when we had to be at school, we'd probably spend no more than two minutes in the bathroom doing an impression of a film being speeded up while we tried to keep as clean as we possibly could. It was hell.

The cold could seriously have been the death of us when one super-freezing winter's night, because it was so cold, Mum left the paraffin heater on to take the chill off the house. I awoke at about 4am (why do these sort of things always happen at 4am?) not being able to breathe properly. Quite naturally, without knowing what was happening I scrambled to the windows, which were not only closed but also locked. The only bit I could open was the small middle opening at the top and I literally squeezed my nose and mouth out just trying to breathe. Next minute, Mum comes in, wakes up Kim and Tracy who were still asleep and is screaming at us to get downstairs where the front door is wide open. The house was full of thick black smoke and I mean thick. The paraffin heater had obviously developed a fault and exploded, nearly killing us all with toxic fumes. We all sat outside in minus temperatures in our pyjamas laughing at each other because we all had big, black soot marks round our noses and eyes and we looked like child chimney sweeps. We had no idea how close that was.

But despite the cramped conditions, the lack of heating and insulation, the peeling wallpaper and damp, the freezing bathroom and the icy windows, I loved that house. I loved the wellington boot that was stuck in the gutter for the whole time we lived there – Mark threw it up there when we first moved in and sparrows used to nest in it year after year. I loved the big metal dustbin that you'd just throw rubbish in, not in bags, that was never full even though we were a family of 5(!), and that got emptied by a man with big dirty gloves on who actually lifted it up on his back. I loved the garden and having the park as a virtual extension of it, the swing, sitting on the front porch in the summer. I loved living there because I was happy. It was our first proper family home and although we were poor, we didn't feel it and we certainly didn't know it.

CHAPTER 3

The First Time I: Walked to school in my socks

(The Poor Chapter)

During my very early years, I suppose we must have been quite well off, what with Dad being a manager and everything. My mum even had that 'rich' look about her: she was extremely well groomed, with immaculate hair, and always wore the beautiful pearls that her dad had bought her for her 21st birthday. So one minute we were being photographed in posh party frocks with big petticoats in front of expensive drapes and the next we're posing in second-hand jumpers in a dark rented house looking like urchins. Mum always got upset looking back at those photos, but if she was bitter about the change in lifestyle she kept it to herself.

We were kids so of course we didn't notice; it was Mum who had to make the biggest adjustment. Her background was certainly middle class and after marrying Dad, a working-class boy made good, it looked set to stay that way. Having been dragged from her roots in leafy Surrey to a strange town in Kent and then left – no, abandoned – with four kids under five and no way of going back, she just got on with it. She wasn't really cut out for life on a council estate but then going back to her parents and admitting that her mother was right about my dad wasn't an option. That's probably what spurred her on.

It was the mid 1960s, in the days before the convenience of automatic state benefits for single parents, when deserted families had to rely on the absent parent to send money, via the court, to be picked up. So if you didn't have that, no one paid your rent or your rates;

there was no free anything. The only benefit available was the Family Allowance, which everyone with kids received regardless of their situation. Compare that to what a single mother would get now: income support, child tax credit, lone parent benefit, housing benefit, council tax benefit, free prescriptions, free glasses, free school dinners and child benefit. We did eventually get free school dinners but I remember Mum had to fight tooth and claw to get them.

With no benefits, Mum had to rely on Dad to support us. He was supposed to pay £10 a week, but often it wasn't sent or didn't reach the court on time.

I only found this out after Kim and I had been down to the Magistrates' Court House in Maidstone to collect it. Mum usually went but it must have been the school holidays. I think I was about seven at the time, so Kim would have been nine. As young as we were, we'd gone on our own, unaccompanied, on the bus. Two little kids, clutching the white claim card, venturing down to the big, imposing building on Palace Avenue. The office was at the top of a grand sweeping staircase, all polished wood. Kim handed over the card and the attendant flicked through the well-thumbed and worn contents in the small index card boxes, one for each day of the week – ours was Friday. Those little boxes must have covered the whole town and most of the surrounding areas; that little office, the regional equivalent of the monster that is the CSA now.

The attendant took the little folded card with 'McGiffin' written on it and opened it up. It was empty. She shook her head and said sorry, even though it wasn't her fault. £10. It was virtually all we, a family of five, had to live on for the week. And it wasn't there. We walked back up to the High Street, got back on the bus and headed home to deliver the bad news – even though at this point I had no idea how bad it was.

There were quite a few firsts that day. Not only was it the day when I first realised how poor we were, but it was the first time I saw my mum cry and it was the first time I ever walked into a pub.

Mum had taken a bar job as soon as Tracy was at school and did two or three lunchtime shifts a week. I'd love to know what she earned but it couldn't have been much. Whatever it was, it went towards making ends meet – but the job wasn't just about the money. She also loved it, soldiering on even if she was ill, working as many hours as she could without ever causing any real disruption to our routine. She was never going to have us be latchkey kids – she needed to be there when we left for school and when we got back, always with our tea on the table – so the hours were ideal, because in those days they closed at 3pm and re-opened at 6pm.

The nearest pub was the Century on School Lane, about a twenty-minute walk round the corner from the house. It was one of those typical estate pubs, built at the same time as the houses to provide a social hub for the residents. There were about five of them in Shepway, all closed down now, which is sad. Most of the Shepway estate was built in the late 1940s/early 1950s and the pub, even though it tried to look old, was the same. Like most pubs then, it had two bars: the 'Public Bar' and the 'Saloon Bar'. The Public was the rougher side, where there were darts boards and snooker tables and calloused old benches covered in red vinyl. It was assumed that this was a more working-class bar where men drank pints of brown and mild or light and bitter. The Saloon was always seen as the posh, quiet side, with its velour seats and soft lighting. It was where the ladies went for their gin and tonics with 'ice and a slice' in small bubble wineglasses.

The pub also had an 'off-sales' where people bought booze to drink at home before there were giant Tescos or Threshers on every corner. Kim and I pushed the big door and walked up to the off-sales counter where we probably stood for a while before anyone saw us, not being tall enough to see over or reach the service bell. Kim knew we were delivering bad news but I still wasn't quite getting it.

'Was it there?' she said, with desperate hope written all over her face.

'No, Mum,' Kim admitted.

Mum immediately burst into tears and said, heartbreakingly, 'What am I gonna do?'As if we had the answer. I couldn't bear it and so I started crying too. She was so strong and you never knew anything was wrong even though it clearly was. Suddenly I knew we were poor.

But still, Mum did everything within her power to shield us from the horrible truth: that we were literally living on the breadline. We never really noticed. We had a house with three bedrooms and a garden and we weren't hungry – actually that's not true, we were *always* hungry, we were kids after all, but we never starved. We survived on a very basic diet of baked beans or tinned spaghetti on toast, egg and chips, sugar sandwiches, fishfingers, stews, and potatoes with everything. Chipped, mashed, roasted or boiled, all ways, any ways, because they filled us up and they were cheap. Mum used to buy half hundredweight (56lb!) sacks from the milkman and we'd get through at least one a week. It seemed like she was always peeling potatoes. It's one of those overriding memories of my mum in that house: always at the sink, scrubbing or peeling away. Then at weekends we'd have a roast or Mum would make steak and kidney pies. All good filling fare. There were never any treats though. We had a biscuit tin that on a good week had Rich Tea biscuits in it – but never for long. We never had puddings, cakes or sweets except on the occasional Sunday, so when we did, blimey, we could hardly contain ourselves. It was the only time we argued over who would go to the shop rather than who wouldn't. There were two shops: Richards, the newsagents on the corner, and its nameless competitor round the corner. We preferred 'round the corner' for treats as it had so many more jars on the back shelf and a much bigger selection of jamboree bags and 'four for a penny' sweets. When we got back, everything would be shared out exactly. If there was a packet of Jaffa Cakes and the number wasn't divisible by four then the odd biscuit would be carefully divided so everything was equal. No one ever deviated from this rule and if they did, there was hell to pay. Everyone always had the same.

She never said 'No' unless she had to; somehow she would find the money to facilitate as normal a childhood for us as possible. She even found the money at one point for me to have piano lessons; she was convinced I was going to be a concert pianist one day because I had long fingers. But, being the ungrateful idiot that I was, I protested and wouldn't go because it was like going to school at the weekends. This prompted her to chop up the old upright piano she'd acquired from somewhere into firewood in a semi-rage. She even sent me to ballet lessons once, but that was a real non-starter; I've always had the grace of a baby elephant.

We used to love going swimming but for four of us it was expensive so it wasn't always possible. She hated saying no and never said it was because of money, she just said no. Then I would go on and on as to why I couldn't go until she'd snap, get all upset and shout at me that she couldn't afford it. I'd feel really guilty then.

Sometimes you could see the stress getting to her and she'd lose her rag over something. Like one winter's day when I was about seven years old, I was designated to go to the shop for provisions. The remnants of snow and ice were still on the ground. I took a paper bag with me, as you always did, because there were no such things as plastic carriers doled out by the million for free. It was a paper carrier with the list and the money in a little red purse. That day, I got to the shop and handed over both to the bloke who ran the Spar up the road – we called him Denver Cream for some reason, and he looked a bit like Eddie Yates from *Coronation Street*. He gathered the stuff and packed the bag, took the money out of the purse and deposited the change in it. Anyway, on the way home I must have thought I'd save myself some energy and so dragged the bag instead of carrying it because it was difficult to carry, being almost as big as me and tricky to keep off the ground. When I got home, my mum picked up the bag and groaned. When she held it up towards me I saw that in the bottom there was nothing but a giant hole: no food, no purse and no money. She went mad. 'Where's the food? How could you not notice? Why didn't you carry it? Of course if you drag it it's going to break!'

Now, when I imagine how it must have looked, me, in my little coat and wellingtons, dragging a giant white carrier bag and depositing a trail of groceries behind me, it makes me laugh. I hadn't even noticed that the bag weighed nothing by the time I got home! But at the time it wasn't funny; I'd just lost a quarter of the week's budget and because of that we had no tea. With hindsight I can see why she went mad, but at the time I couldn't work out why she was so cross when I'd just done my good deed and gone to the shops. Anyway, I trudged all the way back up to the shops with my big sister and, thankfully, retrieved most of the items and, more importantly, the purse with the change in it.

A similar thing happened after I'd been sent down the town to get groceries. The note said '1½lb of st & k', Mum's abbreviation for steak and kidney. Unfortunately I misread her handwriting and came back with three ½lb packs of Stork margarine.

When she saw me, she screamed, 'What do you think I'm going to do with one-and-a-half pounds o' marge?' I didn't know. I didn't think about it like that.

God only knows how she got by. One thing was for sure, she'd beg, steal and borrow to make ends meet. If we ever got money from relatives for our birthdays or Christmas she'd always 'borrow' it. Right up until the day she died she still owed me £4 2s and Kim £6 12s. She even pawned her wedding and engagement rings to buy food. She had arrangements with everyone from the milkman to the Esso Blue man. They rarely got paid but people were sympathetic. The rent? Forget it. She was in hock to everyone, including her own children.

Everything else came from the catalogues. Or the shop in town known as Gordon Higgins. It didn't even look like a shop, it was more like a warehouse space, stacked up with cheap stuff, which was sold on extortionate tick to people who were so poor they couldn't get any kind of proper credit. A woman with bright red lipstick (we called her the Kettle Lady) came round every week for about four years collecting 4s (20p) to pay for a kettle that my mum bought there. That kettle must have cost about forty quid by the time she'd paid the exorbitant interest on it, which would be about £300 in today's money. How funny that forty years later you can buy one for a fiver in Poundstretchers. Sadly for my mum, nothing was cheap back then.

Saving electricity, or not wasting it, became an obsession. For years we had an electric bar fire in the living room that had ornamental logs at the front, lit by a flickering red light. Mum used to put the light on and try to fool us into thinking that it would keep us warm so she didn't have to put the heat elements of it on.

She even resorted to criminal measures to keep the lights on. There was an electric meter under the stairs that you had to put 10p or 5p coins in to get power and someone or something had conveniently dislodged the glass over the little wheel that registered your use, so to stop it going round and round, she stuck a PG Tips card into it, thereby removing the need to insert money. Then if they ever came round to check the meter, she'd somehow make it look normal again. So if ever there was a knock on the door we always had to check who it was first, because if it was the electric man we had to quickly whip out the card and put the glass back before we could let them in. Of course we all thought this was completely normal and if we went past the meter and saw the card had fallen out, we'd pick it up and put it back in its rightful place. We didn't know any different. As with ice on the inside of the window in winter? Didn't everyone have that? It didn't even seem odd that when we weren't eating the usual egg and chips or baked beans on toast with no butter, we scrimped about four good meals out of one small shoulder of lamb that we'd started on a Sunday. Never mind that Mum used to mince up the bones as well to make it go further. We used to call her shepherd's pie 'bone pie'. We weren't even phased when she confessed that the dog had somehow snaffled the freshly cooked joint off the cooker, mauled and munched most of it, and taken it out into the garden, only for Mum to find it, panic because there was nothing else to eat, then wash it under the tap and mince it up for one of her famous pies. We didn't notice and were none the wiser until she told us. She thought it was hilarious and it was, especially when you imagine the dog running off into the garden with a big joint in its jaws. It probably wasn't funny at the time though.

Yes, we had a dog, Penny, then Sindy. I do sometimes question that decision now, but we didn't get one until Mum was working. We'd all hounded her (sorry) to get one, so when she gave in she made sure that we took responsibility for it and did all the walking. Kim even contributed towards paying for the food out of her paper round money.

Having pets taught us important lessons about life and death and when they died we were heartbroken, but Mum felt it was important we dealt with that. Although she always swore she'd never get another one, we always did.

She was amazing in those days, my mum. Correction: she was always amazing. Improvisation was the name of the game. When things broke she fixed them. Or she adapted them. Nothing was ever thrown away.

One morning I woke up sandwiched between the bed and the wall. The bed had collapsed on a broken leg. After that, for as many years as I can remember, that bed was propped up on a hard-cased typewriter, the sort that they use in old *Superman* films for the journalists on *The Globe*: tap tap tap, zip, ting. One of those.

Everything was handed down. Even Mark had to wear hand-me-down clothes from the neighbours. And shoes. We only ever had one pair of shoes each, and no one got new shoes until the old ones had holes in them. Big holes. Beyond-repair holes. I remember one pair of slip-ons, they were tan colour with small heels and had holes punched in the leather. They were so worn out that they literally split in two. I was walking to school and the front of the shoe kept flipping over the end of my foot so I was walking in my socks, which, of course, also ended up with holes in them. Mum had to concede then that it was time for a new pair and when you bought new shoes, boy, did you have to make sure you got the right ones because that was it, every day, for the next couple of years. Mum even made us put Blakey's metal studs on the heels to make them last longer. We sounded like a gang of tap dancers coming down the road.

Of course, I would have loved to have had more than one pair of shoes but I still really enjoyed the excitement and the anticipation of getting that one new pair; it was almost too much to bear. The decision was crucial. I look at my shoe 'collection' now and it makes me cross. I'm angry with myself because I have so many I haven't had a pair repaired for donkey's years. Most of them just sit in their boxes waiting to be worn. Some of them I can't wear because I simply can't walk in them. What is the point of that? And most of the time I can't decide which ones to wear and so I end up wearing the same pair every day. See, it doesn't matter what you end up with, old habits die hard.

We had to improvise with our spare time too. Not having the luxury of money to pay for things to do, we had to amuse ourselves. We were always out, down Mote Park doing incredibly dangerous things like swinging on ropes across streams, or from trees with almighty drops, exploring deep caves that went under the estate, getting stuck in the hollow tree – anything that was free. It was good; we were never bored and it gave us a certain sense of adventure. I'd hate to be a kid now, they're never allowed out because everyone's a potential paedophile. They can't climb trees or explore caves because they've all been wired up by Health and Safety to prevent accidents. We had accidents: Kim broke her coccyx swinging from a tree once, but accidents teach you to be more careful. I'm so glad I'm not of the generation of bedroom-bound kids who seem to have everything but do nothing. We had virtually nothing but what we did have meant so much, everything was so exciting. Now, it seems even less-well-off kids often have a bedroom full of expensive gadgets – TVs, mobile phones, computers, computer games. The most gadgety thing I ever owned was a Petite typewriter and a plastic record deck that ran on batteries and ruined all our records while making them sound like radio programmes from the 1920s. If we couldn't go out, we'd create amusement out of everyday household objects. Like setting up a zoo in the living room. We had these dining chairs with wire backs that we'd put in front of the sofa then take turns being behind them pretending to be lions while being fed dry Weetabix by whoever was playing keeper.

For most of my childhood we didn't even have a telephone and when we finally got one it was one of those with a dial and a curly wire. It sat in the hall at the bottom of the stairs on a telephone table. When it rang, someone answered it and if you weren't in, they would call back later. No answering machine, no call-waiting, no chorus of various beeps and songs with five mobiles going off in the same house; just that one reassuring ring. It was on a 'party line'. This meant that the GPO (General Post Office – now BT) would only install one line, but then put a shared connection from the telegraph pole to two houses. We shared with one of the neighbours down the road that we weren't really that familiar with, which – considering you could eavesdrop on all of each other's conversations – was a bit strange. Often you would pick up the phone and there'd be someone else talking, so you'd have to put it down and try again later. Sometimes you didn't put it down though; instead you'd carry on listening to annoy them into getting off the phone. What a carry on! But it was cheaper that way.

Christmases were a nightmare, moneywise. Mum always paid into a Christmas Club and God only knows how much debt she would get into with Gordon Higgins at that time of year but there was always a pile of presents each. Nothing fancy, just games, selection boxes and always a *Guinness Book of Records*.

When Mum was working, or doing extra shifts, she'd really try and push the boat out. One year my brother got the present of his dreams, a Tommy Seven toy gun. I have a fantastic picture of him outside the house with it all set up for combat. It really makes me laugh because even at age six, if he did it now he'd be locked up as a potential terrorist. We didn't mind if we didn't get anything big though. As long as they were wrapped up and we had the excitement of wondering what they were and opening them, we were fine.

In 1970 we suddenly thought we were rich when Mum got herself a boyfriend and we got the best present ever. At last we could afford to upgrade the rented black and white telly to a colour one. *Top of the Pops* in colour, we almost exploded with joy.

And then we all went on our first summer holiday to Pontin's at Camber Sands which, for a whole week self-catering, cost the princely sum of £25.

So all in all it wasn't that bad. I mean we weren't living on the streets or begging for food and I never saw it as deprivation, no matter what we couldn't have. I saw it as one great big learning curve and I think I've benefited greatly from my upbringing. For a start, in our family there is a complete absence of wealth envy and I'm grateful to have inherited that. The other good thing is, it's made me appreciate things, and I value what I have because I've had to work hard for it. I also have a huge respect for money. I don't live beyond my means and I think that conspicuous displays of wealth are vulgar, no matter how rich you are. I'm not at all mean or tight, but I am careful and I like to save money where I can. However, I often pay for things when I don't necessarily have to. For example, because of my job on TV I could probably get paid to go on free holidays in exchange for a few photos, but I don't and I won't. I could get all the free clothes I want but I don't. But I don't like to waste money or throw it away and if I feel someone's ripped me off I'll go all out to get my money back. Also, much to the horror of some of my friends, I think nothing of using vouchers in restaurants and asking for discounts in shops. I'm not penny pinching and I can well afford to pay the full price for a pizza in Pizza Express but why should I if they're offering them at 50% off?

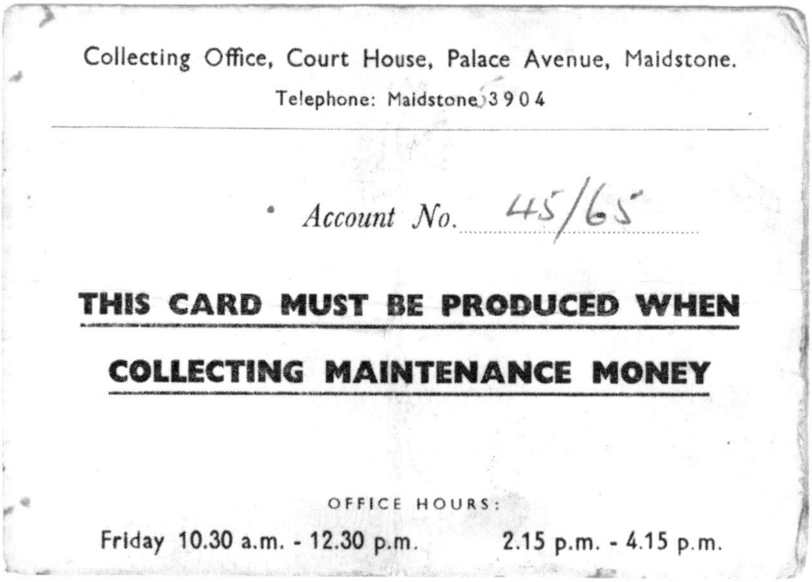
Collecting Office, Court House, Palace Avenue, Maidstone.

Telephone: Maidstone 3904

Account No. 45/65

THIS CARD MUST BE PRODUCED WHEN COLLECTING MAINTENANCE MONEY

OFFICE HOURS:

Friday 10.30 a.m. - 12.30 p.m. 2.15 p.m. - 4.15 p.m.

CHAPTER 4

The First Time I: Wasted five years learning nothing but the words to a Suzi Quatro song

(The School Chapter)

I'm not sure where it all went so horribly wrong. I left school aged 16 at the beginning of the long hot summer of 1976 with one O Level, and even that wasn't really an O Level – it was a CSE Grade 1 which made it equivalent to an O Level Grade 3 or above. But at least it was in Mathematics. Not that I could have done much better if I'd tried, because proper O Levels just weren't available in my school apart from English Literature. We had CSEs. Officially that stood for Certificate of Secondary Education, but unofficially they were lower-level O Levels and were fairly worthless, nothing more than a bit of paper proof that you'd been to school. I got four more of those: English Language (Grade 2), Sociology (Grade 3), Geography (Grade 2) and Art (Grade 4), but I cheated in that last one by flipping my paper over to my friend Clare who kindly painted me a decent picture. We switched back and she did hers. The teacher didn't even notice. Clare had arty parents and was really good at everything arty; she even looked arty because she had long curly Marc Bolan hair and wore an Afghan coat. She got a Grade 1.

But how did I end up with such a hopeless set of qualifications when it had all started so well?

Apparently I was quite bright from the off ('scuse my modesty!) but I can't recall ever sitting down with any grown-ups before school began and learning my ABC or doing sums. The only books I owned were *The Beano* and *Whizzer and Chips* annuals and *The Guinness Book of World Records* (favourite record: the woman with the twenty-three-stone cyst – rather disappointingly, no longer an entry) and the family medical book, but that was about it. The medical book was brilliant, but it was scary too. We used to pore over the pages, laughing at the staged pictures that demonstrated what you should do if an old lady falls down the stairs. The unfortunate old woman in question was slumped in an awkward position at the bottom of the stairs with her legs in the air and you could see her stocking tops. There was also a picture of a woman on fire and an old man chasing after her with a blanket. Not very funny, I know, but we thought it was hilarious. It also had a whole section on childhood illnesses which we studied over and over until we were convinced we were all going to get rickets and bow legs. We also had an encyclopaedia, a big red one with wafer-thin pages that I looked things up in sometimes because Mum was always too busy to answer our constant barrage of questions. 'Oh look it up!' she'd scream every time we'd ask her anything. She'd give the same answer even if we asked, 'Where's my red jumper?' But that was about it for books.

I was always curious and I know I did *want* to learn, so when I went to school I was all ears and tried really hard. I also spent hours working on my handwriting, although somewhere along the line that all went tits up, because it's completely atrocious now. I have the handwriting of a six-year-old. Not in an illegible way, but just in a sort of did-you-stop-learning-when-you-were-six kind of way. In fact, my handwriting was probably better when I was six.

My first school was Shepway Infants in Oxford Road on the Shepway Estate. I think I was dead lucky in that I always had a big sister there to help me out. Poor Kim, she must have really felt the pressure being the older sister to three little siblings but she was completely uncomplaining.

My first day at Shepway was only memorable because Mum sent us on the wrong day. We got all togged up in our new school clothes, looking our best (well, as best as Mum could manage with hand-me-downs and jumble sale finds) and trotted off. When we got there the gate was locked, causing confusion all round. Kim and I stood outside for a while, waiting for it to open and when it didn't we got quite distressed because we thought we were late and they'd locked us out. We went back home sobbing. Mum felt so guilty that the next day, the correct day, she actually walked us there – the first and last time ever in my whole life that my mum took me to school.

Perhaps the trigger for my educational nonchalance came from that first school. I really don't remember much about it or the teachers, all I know is I was very eager to please and really keen to impress. So the teacher was asking questions and because I knew all the answers, I stuck my hand up. Every question. And I didn't just *put* my hand up. I stretched it so high I almost elevated myself out of the chair. And I kept on doing that, getting the question right, while everyone else slumped in their seats. So in a real anti-competitive, offence-avoidance move, the teacher told me off. Reprimanded for trying. 'Give the others a chance and keep your hand down please, Carol.' Yes, I might have been showing off a bit, but I thought the point was to put your hand up if you knew the answer? That teacher ruined my education! I'm joking, of course, but who knows . . . maybe it did stick. Things like that do when you're five years old.

I first met my best friend Pauline at infant school. I remember thinking how much I wanted her name. I hated being Carol and thought Pauline was the best name I'd ever heard. Why the hell didn't my mum and dad call *me* Pauline? I hated my name, it was so big and clumsy and my middle name, well, I couldn't even spell it. I still can't. I don't like admitting what it is because whenever I do, it's greeted with gales of raucous laughter. It begins with D and it's the name of a character in *Coronation Street* who wears big glasses. See? Horrible name, sorry if it's yours . . . Anyway, Pauline was my first best friend and was gregarious, happy, smiley and blonde. I wanted her name, I wanted to be her, and I couldn't wait to get to school so we could catch up on the previous night's gossip but when you're five years old gossip's a bit thin on the ground. We stayed best friends right through senior school.

Shepway Juniors is more at the forefront of my mind. It was next door but one to the infant school; the Junior Boys school was in the middle. The whole of Oxford Road was dominated by schools. I used to walk past the junior school every day thinking how grown-up I'd be when I went there. It was an ugly 1960s monolith of a building with tilting glass panels along the main hall that faced the road. The classrooms were adjacent to that and could be seen from the road too. It was L-shaped, with a big grass front. It's not there anymore. In fact none of those schools are there now. Horrible buildings as they were, it's sad that they've gone. I wonder where the kids from that estate go now?

I remember my first day there because of the shoes I was wearing. They were black patent numbers from True Form with massive lace holes and big, chunky, convex heels. They were great shoes. When I was trying them on I knew they were about two sizes too small but I managed to convince Mum that they were perfect. I could hardly walk in them, but I had to have them. I wore them with white pop sox because in 1968 that's what you did. I might have been crippled but at least I was 'on trend'. Even the music teacher had patent wet-look shoes, but she had matching wet-look plastic socks as well so it looked like she was wearing boots. I *so* wanted that look. And anyway, if I'd put normal socks on the shoes were so small I wouldn't have got them on. I credit those shoes, which of course I had to wear until they wore out, with my prized bunion.

When I think about that school it's always the hall that springs to mind. It was the venue for assembly, school dinners, PE and bring-and-buy sales and it had this big curtain at the back with a mysterious space behind it that never got used. We never stopped peeping behind that curtain, dying to see something going on behind there. On the right side of the hall there was a massive sports climbing frame with ropes on that we had to climb up like monkeys during gym class. It was really high; there was no safety net or even a padded floor, so if we fell off the top of the rope that would have been it. Sport was quite important then. We did PE and gym work and also swimming at the local baths once a week on a Thursday. Those sessions were usually followed by recorder lessons, which always gave me crippling wind for some reason. Every week.

We also did field work and athletics regularly, in preparation for the annual school sports day and the Kent Games that all the schools took part in. I was always up for it, and was quite good at both long jump and high jump. I actually won the school sports day long jump once but my moment was ruined by my double-entendre obsessed mind. You know how it is when you're at school . . . like in assembly once, when the Headmistress said the word 'spunk' in the context of one of the new prefects being courageous and determined, the congregation literally collapsed on the floor in knicker-wetting giggles. Everything with even the slightest rude connotation was hilarious and very distracting. So when I won the long jump and the Head (who we used to joke was a lesbian) was standing right in front of me bellowing, 'Well done girl, now, can we see it?' my filthy little mind thought she meant, 'it' – you know, my thing! I know, pathetic and very, very childish. But the memory still makes me laugh.

Anyway, I was pretty – no totally – useless at everything else, especially running, which used to frustrate me terribly. I used to try so hard to run really, really fast but it just wouldn't happen. I run in real life like I run in dreams, using all my power and energy but getting absolutely nowhere. But why? I was tall, not overweight, why couldn't I run the hundred yards in ten seconds?

Maybe it was because I ate so much. Aside from the 1/3pt of milk (in the bottle, with a straw) at mid-morning, we also had free school dinners. Mum always told us to eat as much as we could because she never really knew where the next meal was coming from and how big it would be. As a result, I would forge through, ignoring the humiliation of having to stand in a different queue when giving in the tickets, and really go for it. One of the only times the school bullies tried to have a go was when a gang of them formed a human barrier and tried to stop me on my way to get second helpings of treacle pudding and custard. Nothing – not even a bunch of hard, spiteful, evil girls who were all bigger than me – was going to stop me. To get through it, I devised myself a little mantra and repeated it over and over as I attempted to walk through the barricade: 'There are some things in life you just have to face. There are some things in life you just have to face.' This was life or death after all; if I didn't get more pudding I would almost definitely die of starvation.

So, even though they were dead scary and intimidating and pushed me as I forged ahead, I won the day. I was quite pleased with myself and they never came near me again. It was my first lesson in sticking up for myself and I was only eight or nine years old. Mum had always said, 'You gotta learn to fight your own battles.'

I passed my 11 Plus. I don't even remember taking it but I passed it. When they read out the results in the class – 'McGiffin: Pass' – I was distinctly nonplussed, I suppose because I didn't really appreciate what it meant. Mum explained that it meant I had a choice of whether to go to Maidstone Grammar School for Girls or to the local comprehensive, South Borough Girls' School.

Now, how simple is that? Wouldn't most parents kill for that simple choice, rather than the ridiculous lottery that exists now. I thought it was a fairly good system, one where it didn't matter how rich or poor you were; if you could prove yourself and pass that test, you were in. What could be fairer than that? Didn't everyone accept that people were different and if you lump all children together, regardless of ability, the bright ones will be held back and hindered by the slower learners? It wasn't divisive or a class thing because I wasn't privileged, I was just a bit clever and the grammar school was going to be the best place for someone like me to flourish academically and gain a serious education. It was a no-brainer wasn't it? Well yes, it was – literally – because I didn't go. I quite obviously wasn't as clever as I thought because it was my decision. After weighing up the pros and cons Mum, rightly or wrongly, said it was entirely up to me. On reflection maybe it was wrong, and she should have dragged me kicking and screaming to that school. I'm certain that had my dad been around, he wouldn't have dreamt of letting me choose to go to the local comp. But then what would have happened? I often think about where I would be now and recoil at the thought of being a lawyer or something equally tedious where I'd be stuck in an office all day with a huge pile of paper in front of me. No, although it was a stupid decision I don't regret it at all.

My main criteria for not opting for the grammar school were: 1) The uniform was brown; 2) It would be full of posh, clever kids and I saw myself as neither (so maybe it was a class thing after all!);

3) My sister Kim was at South Borough; and 4) Pauline was going there. Mum's lenience probably stemmed from the fact that: 1) It was miles away and would have meant a bus fare that she couldn't afford; and, 2) The brown uniform was extremely expensive and there was no diverting from it.

And that's probably where it all began to go wrong.

South Borough Girls was the sort of school that now, I would imagine, no one would want to send their kids to. If they'd had league tables then, South Borough would probably have been right at the bottom. It was housed in a badly maintained Victorian building that had outside toilets. It was freezing in the winter and boiling in the summer.

The school was about a mile away from our house and I walked there and back every day. In the morning, Kim's friends all used to come round for her and they'd all walk en masse. They never asked if I wanted to join them but that was OK because I preferred to walk on my own, carrying my little brown leather satchel on my back and wearing Dr Scholl's. I swear that's why I have such well-developed footballers' calves now, because I wore 'exercise sandals' every day. My mum never allowed me to wear tights to school, not even in the evil winters we had then and that rule carried right through – I had to wear long socks right up until I left there at 16. Not only did my legs freeze but I always ended up looking like a schoolgirl, no matter how much I hitched up my skirt.

I didn't mind going to school, in fact I used to quite look forward to it. I never once played truant, skived off or feigned illness. I know that sounds hard to believe but it's true. I was way too worried that my mum would find out. There were, however, a few teething problems at South Borough. Some girls feebly tried to bully me in my first year so I told my sister. She got her mate Karen on to it and she picked up the bully and placed her neatly in the playground bin in front of the whole school. After she found out I had friends in hard places, she wanted to be my friend, but I never let her because she didn't smell very nice. Correction: she had a real personal hygiene problem. No, actually, she stank.

It was an all-girls school so it was big on DS (Domestic Science) which was very old fashioned in its approach. Mrs Goddard was our teacher and if you'd put her in a line-up of women and were asked to pick out the DS teacher, you'd have pointed straight at her. She was quite chinless with tightly curled, very 1940s hair and she wore long skirts, cardigans done up to the neck and (always) a pinnie. I've still got my old DS folder and the recipe in it for egg custard is absolutely foolproof.

Carol McGiffin.

Egg Custard

Recipie for Baked and pouring custard

1 egg — ½ oz Sugar — few drops of vanilla essence.
½ pint milk. — little nutmeg

Method for Baked Custard

1. Warm the milk to blood heat.
2. Beat the egg beat the egg and sugar together.
3. Strain into a greased pie dish, grate a little nutmeg on the top.
4. Place the pie dish in a tin and surround it with water.
5. Bake in a very moderate oven for 40 minutes. Reg 3 or 330°F

Method for Pouring custard

1. Beat the eggs with a little of the milk
2. Heat the rest of the milk and pour onto the egg.
3. Strain the egg and milk into the rinsed saucepan.
4. Cook over a moderate heat until the custard thickens and coats the back of

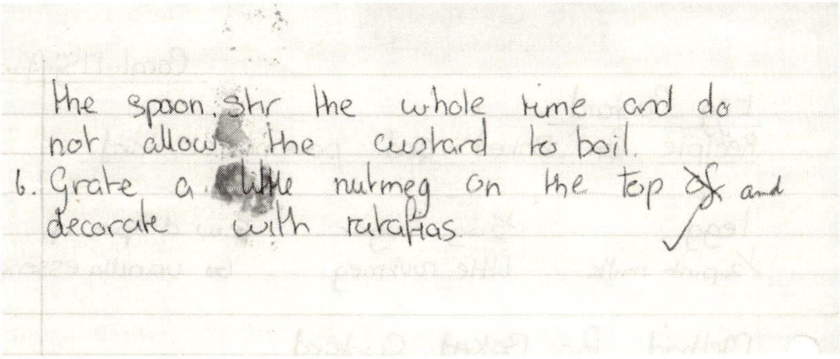
the spoon. Stir the whole time and do
not allow the custard to boil.
6. Grate a little nutmeg on the top and
decorate with ratafias.

We also did needlework. Mrs McMillan taught it, and she was just as you'd imagine a needlework teacher to be. Small, old and quite obviously wearing clothes that she'd made herself. It was really valuable learning all that stuff. I could sew on buttons, repair things, alter things. I went through a phase of completely transforming outfits at one point. And that was in the 1970s, before Gok Wan was even born.

It was a good job it was a girls school because this was the time when Pauline and I not only turned into teenagers but were becoming mildly obsessed by boys. If there'd been boys there, we'd have got even less done. Pauline remained my friend throughout but there was also a new bunch of girls that seemed interesting. Unlike the majority of the girls at the school, they hadn't come from Shepway and quite how they all ended up at South Borough when they lived all over town was a mystery. I thought they were all well posh coming, as they did, from Aylesford, Barming and East Peckham. The gang we formed consisted of Ann, Helen, Sally, Janice, Clare, Lorraine, Pauline, Gaynor, Dawn and me. We all bonded after a trip to Betws-y-Coed in Wales where we camped in the rain, climbed Mount Snowdon, made apple-pie beds and wound each other up. We were split down the middle by who liked The Osmonds and who preferred The Jackson Five. I liked both but The Osmonds had it by a nose. I bought Clare (the art cheat) the Jackson Five album *Lookin' Through the Windows* for her birthday from Woolworths but later on she admitted she didn't really like them, she just wanted to disagree with me, so she gave it back. I've still got it; the cover has a lovely picture of an unrecognisable Michael looking through a window, appropriately enough.

Reading my reports, it's quite clear that after the first year – where I was trying really hard, doing really well and achieving high grades, including As for French and Bs for pretty much everything else – I started to lose interest. The deterioration is stark. I still got Bs and Cs for achievement but for effort I got Ds or Es. There are constant comments about me disrupting class, misbehaving, being silly and distracting others. And they were right. I was bored. The classes weren't streamed by ability and so if people couldn't keep up the whole class had to slow down. That's how the comprehensive system worked. Except it didn't and still doesn't work. It just doesn't make sense.

During Art lessons we used to play Pink Floyd and Bonzo Dog Doo-Dah Band LPs and wear jeans; the teacher didn't give a shit. In Maths we used to amuse ourselves by writing disgusting poems while the teacher went out the back and smoked. In Science everyone rebelled because the teacher, Miss Piggy we called her, was so strict. Only in English did I pay attention. Mrs Clayton was very patient and even though she despaired sometimes, she soldiered on.

At break times I'd get up on the bench in the playground and sing Suzi Quatro songs like a proper show-off. 'COME ALIVE, COME ALIVE! DOWN IN DEVIL GATE DRIVE!'

When we made it to the fifth year we were given access to the common room. I managed to get everyone into trouble by taking in cans of light ale and cigarettes and, believe it or not, we would sit there smoking and drinking. We got rumbled one day when one of the girls grassed us up and we were summoned from our Art class by the headmistress, Miss Chadwick, and the deputy, Mrs Berkely. We were in double trouble as we were all wearing jeans and there was no time to change. As we walked in we could see the locker door open – the locker where we stashed the ash and the empty cans. On the top shelf there was literally a mountain of ash. On the bottom was an Andy Warhol-esqe display of old fashioned small beer cans. The Head's and Deputy's faces were like thunder and we could see we were in big trouble. So, of course, the only thing for it was to get the giggles. Every single one of us. Snorting, snotting, stifling, shoulder-shaking giggles. Mrs Berkley was roaring with rage, something about a letter and being expelled. That made us stand to attention! Actually we didn't get expelled – that was just an idle threat I think to make us stop laughing. But we were told that we were all going to be getting a letter sent home, so the best thing for us to do was to go home and tell our parents what we'd been up to and prepare them for the letter. Well, they didn't fool me. I told the other girls, 'Don't go home and tell your mum and dad, they're just saying that because they want you to confess to them.' I didn't say a word to my mum and sure enough the letter never arrived so she was none the wiser, which was good because she would have killed me for sure.

Thursday 25 March 1976
Today was a lot of TRUBBLE. The locker was full of fag butts and Miss Chadwick got information that we had been smoking. Helen, Clare, Beverly Bonny, Linda and me. We got into lots of trubble and a letter is going to be sent home. I don't care. Went to Blue Door. Very boring.

Friday 26 March 1976
Still got bragged about trubble. Very mysterious, common room is locked because some phantom beer cans appeared. 11.30. I went babysitting. Washed my hair again as well as Thursday.

I don't think the others got letters either but quite often I would get let off from crimes in school because, and I'm quoting the teachers here, I was 'from a broken home'. All the other girls had 'normal' two-parent families so being from a single-parent family was very rare in the 1970s. Child-sharing hadn't really caught on. What a sign of the times that was. I bet if you have two parents in school now, they place you in a glass box and the other kids pay 50p to stare at you. It was handy getting pitied for having no dad because I did get away with more. A couple of the girls used to try and think up ways of breaking their parents up so they could get away with stuff too. I thought they were mad. I used to love going round their houses and having tea with them, seeing their mums and dads getting on with each other. I didn't envy them, I just liked it. At school I never really felt different though. The only times I did, it was always about money. All the girls would come in with loads of cash which they'd either spend in the tuck shop or would go out to the shop at lunchtime to spend. I tried to keep up with the others as far as uniform went but on less than £1 a week from my paper round I had to be canny. Most of the time I didn't notice and I cared even less that I was different.

By the fifth year I'd just about given up and spent more time outside the classroom than in it. My reports reflect that totally. Most of the teachers said the same: 'Carol doesn't work to the best of her ability. She is a bad influence in class.' It probably wasn't a good thing for the other girls that I had a 100% attendance record. Anyway, the teachers may have been right but I just felt like I wasn't learning anything and I was desperate to leave so that I could get out there and earn some money. There was no careers advice at all; in fact, during my whole five years there, not one person asked me what I wanted to do when I left school. The last time I was asked that was in junior school when all I wanted to be was a bus conductor so I could swing round the pole without being told off – no wonder they gave up on me! My exam subjects were chosen in five minutes during a meeting with the form teacher and in the end, I just left as soon as I could. I didn't want to be wasting any more time, I needed to be out there working.

However, in one last burst of enthusiasm, I did a course at Maidstone Tech College on Commerce and gained both RSA and Pitman Qualifications in touch-typing. This was the most interesting thing I'd done in five years and I passed both exams with flying colours and in record time. See, I wasn't a total idiot. I couldn't have been because I wrote this:

The first choice of Bouquet of Barbed Wire came first on both counts. which means that Social Drama in this group has superseded historical drama and thrillers.

Mass media.

Mass Media is a term used for communication by press radio and television. These forms of communication influence the General Public (Masses) one way or another. In taste, opinion and conventional thinking [Before newspapers Public Opinion was not expressed except in Books and on the Stage. This only represented a few people.] When radio and television were invented more and more people were being educated so it has been the means of expressing general public opinion e.g. 1. The novelist John Galsworthy who wrote The Forsyte Saga suddenly became very popular after the television series when he wrote his novels in 1890 not many people could read. elections are won on the politicians tv personality.

OK the handwriting is shocking and it could do with a tidy up but it *was* written in a 'rough book'. Still, it's fairly astute don't you think and I don't *think* I copied it . . .

PARTING WORDS

Carol has not yet achieved a happy relationship with those in authority. I fear there will be difficult times ahead until she realises how important she really is.

Mrs B. Chadwick, Headmistress,
South Borough Girls' School. May 1976

Carol's work shows she has a lot of ability. Her lack of patience when amongst girls, some of whom work more slowly than she does makes her tiresome in a classroom and leads to bad behaviour she ought to be able to avoid.

Mrs F. M. Slaughter, Form Teacher. May 1976

AND IF IAN DURY HAD BEEN MY TEACHER

What a waste.

CHAPTER 5

The First Time I: Surrendered to a troll behind the church

(The Teenage Slut Chapter)

My first boyfriend was called Nigel and he lived down the road from us in Plains Avenue. I reckon I must have been about eight or nine. At the same time I also counted his cousin David as my boyfriend but I didn't like him really; he wore funny jumpers and had really red, rosy cheeks. I only went out with him because his surname was Jones and I was rather obsessed with The Monkees at the time. I even called him Davy.

Nigel and David didn't have a problem sharing me. We were so laid back then, but I suppose it *was* the 1960s. Well, not that laid back, I mean I never snogged either of them. All Nigel and I ever did was sit on the wall outside his or my house. David lived up the road in Kent Avenue and would also come down and sit on the wall. I wish I could remember what we talked about for all those hours. Probably a whole load of nothing.

No, in true 1960s free-love style, my first snog was with my sister Kim's boyfriend. He lived in the house on the roundabout with the huge garden that was open to the road, so you could always see what his family were doing. He had hair that seemed to be too big for him and an attractive gap in his teeth, with a really deep voice for a boy of ten. I don't know who instigated it but I do know that we were in my coal shed for ages and ages doing proper tongue-sarnie snogging and I remember thinking, 'Wow this is brilliant I never want it to stop,' while at the same time being mildly aware of the fact that I probably shouldn't be kissing my sister's boyfriend. I was having such a good time I wasn't even bothered by the army of spiders that inhabited the coal shed. Since we didn't use coal, there was piles of the stuff left there from the day we moved in until the day we left. In fact, the coal shed was only ever used for storing the giant sacks of spuds that stopped us from starving. Oh, and for snogging, of course.

There was no shortage of boys along Plains Avenue. The Parks family were a local dynasty, several related families of mostly boys. They seemed to be all over the place. The three brothers in our road were Paul, Stephen and Gary. Paul was too old for me, Gary was my age, and we were perfectly suited, but it was Stephen who was the best looking and even though he wasn't interested I decided he was my boyfriend. Really they were all just friends and we used to hang around with them.

They were co-conspirators in all things dangerous that constituted playing: negotiating swamps, walking to Sheerness (we never made it, it was too hot and we nearly died of dehydration before being rescued) and scrumping on local farms, which was nothing more than a fun way to steal fruit. Or we'd climb the giant haystacks that were stored in the barns and dare each other to jump off into a pile of hay before we'd checked how deep it was. Once the first one made their descent without breaking any bones or killing themselves, we'd all be doing it, for ages, or at least until we were caught. It was my favourite naughty thing to do and quite often the farmers would set geese on us or threaten us with air rifles for being on their land. We spent almost all of our time with those boys, them and a boy called Paul Winters (who was always referred to as 'Winners') who lived across the road from them.

When Mum was working nights in the Century she had an express rule: no boys around the house after she'd gone to work at six. Of course we always ignored her and they'd come round but nothing untoward ever happened. Obviously as kids we couldn't see that we were doing anything wrong; hanging about the house was better than sitting outside. I never knew how, but Mum always knew when we were disobeying orders and she'd go absolutely stark raving bonkers. We never went round their house because theirs was posher than ours – they had a glass door between the living room and the dining room.

I snogged Gary at some stage but I'm sure I was just using him as a stepping stone to get to Stephen. Much to my disappointment, it never worked.

Although I was completely aware that it was illegal, age fourteen seemed like a good time to lose my virginity. Pauline had dispensed with hers and we'd spent a great deal of time at school discussing the ins and outs of it, as it were. Pauline became our sex education teacher because, apart from one lecture from someone on getting pregnant, there was nothing like that on the curriculum. All the girls would gather round while Pauline held court, everyone preparing themselves for their big moment.

I never talked to my mum about sex. I just couldn't bear the thought of it. She did make one attempt to tell me about the 'birds and the bees', but I immediately went into non-registration, singing very loudly in my head so I couldn't hear her because I just didn't want to hear those words coming out of my mum's mouth. I don't know why, just that she was my mum and that's not what we talked about.

I learnt everything I needed to know from Pauline. We would sit around for hours, on a mattress on the floor of her bedroom, playing David Bowie records, particularly *Aladdin Sane*, and practising doing love bites on our own arms. God knows how I got that past Mum. Pauline also took me babysitting to a flat on the estate where, after rifling though their stuff, we found a load of soft porn magazines. After that, we kept going round, offering to babysit, because we couldn't stop looking at the magazines. It was just another aspect of my sex education.

When I felt prepared and ready to do it, I embarked upon a mission to lose my virginity. I was nervous, mainly because I was scared to death of Mum finding out. Pauline and I planned every detail and on the fateful night I arranged to stay the night with her. There was a disco on in St Martin's Hall next to the church on Northumberland Road. As soon as we got there we did some scouting for potential 'losers'. We didn't have to look far: they were everywhere and, shamefully, I wasn't particularly bothered who did it. David Bowie's 'Space

Oddity' came on; it was a slow song and enormously difficult to dance to, but everyone did anyway. I waited to be asked to dance, as you did, and a bloke came over. He was short, much shorter than me, and he had wild, dark hair that looked kind of synthetic and in need of a good brush. In fact, he looked exactly like a troll – like he should have been on the end of a pencil. We trod on each other's toes in a totally out-of-time fashion for about a minute when he asked, 'D'ya wanna go outside?' That was the question I'd been waiting for. So, we went outside, round the back of the church and that was it. Everything was over in seconds. It was horrible but it always is the first time. I went back into the disco, told Pauline, went home and didn't sleep a wink worrying that my mum would find out and know what I'd done.

I hated myself for being such a teenage slut for a while, especially because when I woke up the next day I found out that my mum's horrible ex-boyfriend had been round trying to get in and rough her up again. Mum had thrown him out a couple of weeks before because he'd become so violent when he was drunk. I've never felt as guilty as I did then in my whole life. I know it's illogical but I felt like I should have been there to protect her, rather than out having a knee-trembler round the back of the disco. I thought that if he had managed to do any real harm that night, I would never have forgiven myself.

I'd witnessed the violence one night while he was still living with us. He'd been in the pub all day and Mum had taken the precaution of sleeping in our room in Tracy's bed while Kim and I pushed our beds together for us and Tracy to share. But that didn't stop him beating down the door and charging around like a lunatic with a kitchen knife in his hand, screaming obscenities and accusing her of all sorts. You could tell he was so enraged that he really was on the verge of stabbing her but, at the same time, you could sense his tortured soul not wanting to. It was terrifying. Truly terrifying.

So it was no more one-night stands for me and I went back to being a good girl for a while. But then, later that year, I went on my first holiday as a 'grown-up'. Well, I thought I was grown-up because I was 14 and I'd lost my virginity. I was invited to join

Pauline, her mum Ellen and her partner Gerry for a week at Butlins holiday camp in Bognor Regis, West Sussex.

It wasn't my first time in a holiday camp. I had been to Pontin's when I was 10. 'Book Early!' was Fred Pontin's slogan when he advertised on the telly, with his thumb up and his cheeky little face. There were serious 'camp wars' between Pontin's and Butlins in the 1970s. Billy versus Fred. Pontin's was great, there was just so much stuff to do, but I went back there in 2008 with my sisters and nieces and it was just strange. Like it had been frozen in time. The chalets, I swear, looked like they had the same carpet and décor they had in 1970. It was hideous, but the best fun I'd had in ages.

And so, off to Butlins we went. First of all, I couldn't believe my mum was allowing me to go. If she'd known what had happened up the church hall a few months before she wouldn't have, but thank God she didn't and she still trusted me. It was a bit annoying that we still had to go with adults but in a family camp environment we could pretty much go off and do whatever we wanted. I was dying to get there, not least because we were going 'all inclusive' so we'd get to go in the restaurant instead of doing self-catering.

Butlins was a real rite of passage. It was the first time I did really feel grown-up. Age 13 I was still a child, but at 14 my hormones were raging and it was great to be on holiday without my mum, with my good friend Pauline. Overnight, too, I had become mildly obsessed with my appearance and was constantly brushing my hair which (because of the hormones) was greasy enough, but I was determined to make it greasier by my incessant grooming. I had it in a centre parting and it was long. I was also becoming much more aware of my clothes. But mostly I was interested in boys and I'd heard about the Redcoats and all the people who worked there, mainly young men who did so because they knew girls like us were there for the taking.

The year before we'd managed to get into the cinema to see the 15-rated *That'll be the Day* – the 1973 film starring David Essex. The film had such an effect on me; it was so indicative of its time and even though it shouldn't have been, and wasn't meant to be, it was kind of aspirational. David Essex plays the part of Jim McClaine perfectly, the slacker anti-hero who goes off to the seaside for a bit of adventure and rumpy-pumpy. He ends up working on the fairground and then a holiday camp, where he shags all the girls and treats them like shit. He's a total lothario but every single girl I knew fell in love with him and would absolutely have let him bed them too. I was convinced I was going to meet and get off with Jim McClaine at Butlins.

I was reminded of what we were like by my 12-year-old niece and her 13-year-old friend two years ago at Pontin's. They were just like Pauline and me, but way ahead in the maturity stakes. They had make-up and handbags and skipped around in denim shorts while we were in cardigans and loon pants. They spent a good deal of time smiling coyly at the handsome young Bluecoats, all the time checking to see if any grown-ups were noticing what they were doing. They didn't have any success but, in a fit of nostalgic madness, I did. I ended up snogging a 22-year-old children's entertainer. My nieces were 'well jealous', as they put it. Emma remarked, 'I'm 23 and I can't get off with anyone yet my 48-year-old auntie does!'

Anyway, back to 1974. The first night we were there we decided it was time to find out what it would be like to be drunk, and so headed straight for the Pig and Whistle bar. Doing our level best to look 18 as we walked in, we probably gave the game away by dithering at the top of the stairs and arguing over who was going to go to the bar. Eventually we went up to the bar and ordered two port and lemons; it was so obvious we weren't 18, but they didn't seem to care and served them up without question. Then we ordered another round. And another. By the time we were feeling tiddly we were getting chatted up by two old blokes. Uh oh. I think they bought us another couple of drinks and soon we were drunk. No so drunk though that we didn't have the good sense to dump the old gits and run away, which of course was a hilarious thing to do. Trying something for the first time is always hysterical, but this was doubly so. We laughed and laughed and when we left the bar we went into the photobooth and took pictures of ourselves to see what we looked like.

We hadn't been at the camp long when we spotted our prey. We were in the 'dining room' (a giant, heaving hall with long rickety tables and a horrendous racket coming from the kitchen) having our

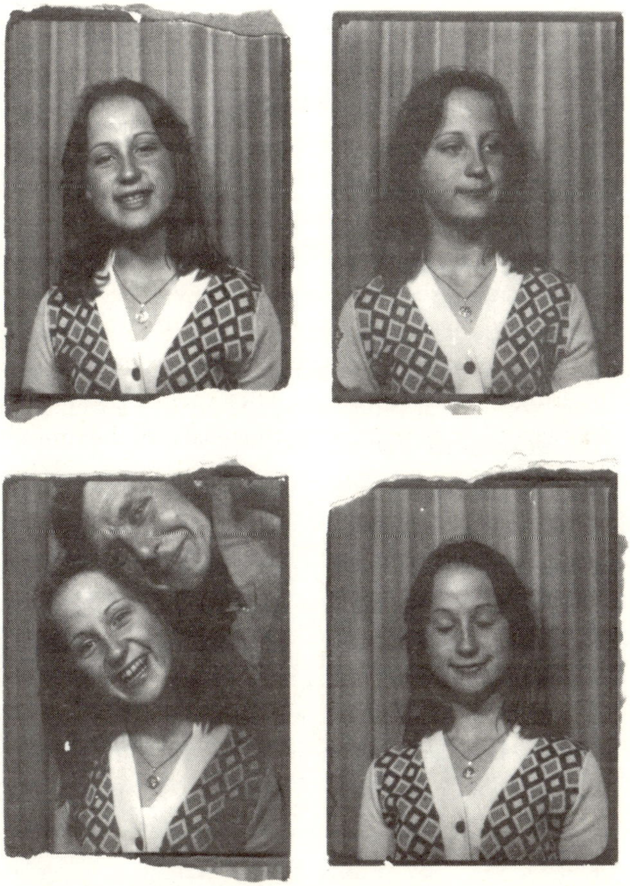

'dinner' (lunch) and the noise was unbelievable. Every time someone smashed or dropped anything, which seemed to be every other minute, the whole hall would erupt with cheers. Young, sweaty 'waiters' (blokes carrying giant trays of dirty dishes or food) strutted up and down the aisles replenishing the school-like trays at the 'buffet' table. God knows what was in that food; it was horrible. Nevertheless we couldn't wait for meal times because we'd see these two blokes that we needed to get off with.

'Mine' was called Pete and I instantly fell in love with him because he was the spitting image of my hero, David Bowie. He had the proper Aladdin-Sane look but without the make-up. He even had

Dave's snake hips and wore tight, high-waisted loon pants. He was Scottish and had a very heavy Glaswegian accent. I couldn't really understand what he was saying most of the time but that didn't matter, I wasn't interested in talking to him. 'Pauline's' was called Chris I think, but if not then it was something really 1970s like Keith or Trevor. He was a big bloke, tall and muscular and much more manly than Pete. They shared a 'chalet', although it was hardly a chalet, as all it had was a tiny room with two very narrow single beds in it, a small chest of drawers and a piece of material pinned on the wall for a curtain. There was no bathroom; you had to go round to a big communal block about 100 yards away. How they lived like that all summer I've no idea.

Anyway, we did manage to get off with them after picking them up at the disco and of course went straight back to their room where we all had sex in the same room at the same time, though not with each other. Looking back, it was a bit sordid, but that was what Jim McClaine did so it's what we did. Then we got up and went back to our own chalet. The next night Pauline was with Chris again but Pete just ignored me all night. I couldn't believe it, I'd been dumped after one night. I was so distraught and felt such a gooseberry I left Pauline and Chris to it and went and sat by the pool on my own. While I was sitting there 'What Becomes of the Broken Hearted' by Jimmy Ruffin started playing over the tannoy. It was almost too much to bear, and as I concentrated on the lyrics I broke into wracking sobs, screaming at the top of my voice, 'IT HURTS!' – referring to my poor little heart that I thought was so broken, it actually did.

Needless to say, the rest of the holiday was ruined and I spent it in a terrible teenage sulk. Pauline, being the good friend that she was, carried on seeing Chris the whole time. Cheers, mate! I didn't mind really – I probably would have done the same thing.

I had got it so bad that as soon as I got back, I acquired some Indian ink and I tattooed a 'P' on my wrist because I knew I could always wear my watch to cover it up and my mum would never know. And that's what I did. I even invested in a Swatch because they were waterproof and I'd never have to take it off. Then about 15 years later, while on a day out in Folkestone, I walked into a tattoo parlour where the artist tattooed a lovely little butterfly over the very rough and illegible 'P'. I'd finally moved on from the David Bowie lookalike.

At 15, I met and fell in love with the man I thought I was going to be with for the rest of my life. He was rugged and handsome and unfortunately much older than me, but I was a little minx then and I place no blame on anyone for anything. He had the biggest car I'd ever seen, a Ford Zephyr, or was it a Zodiac? We used to park it either on the cinder track or up the garages and have sex in the back because it had a giant big bench seat. He didn't seduce me, I absolutely and completely stalked him while lying about my age – I told him I was sixteen and used to lie about having jobs and going to work when I was still at school. This ruse was foiled one day when I saw him on the bus going down the Loose Road. I was in my uniform and socks with my satchel on my back, going to school. I cried the whole day, proper, loud, painful sobs. I was inconsolable. Really, the teacher thought someone had died. I was besotted, but all he ever did was try and get away from me. And who could blame him? This was dangerous territory for a twenty-two-year-old bloke. Poor guy, he always tried to let me down gently, but I would cry and tell him I loved him over and over. My school jotter is full of love letters and his initials are all over the cover. It all ended eventually when he went to prison – was that an extreme measure that he maybe engineered to get away from me?

My jotter is also full of fantasy letters that I wrote to him in prison. Quite disturbing when I read them now because I'm talking as though he's my husband and I'm taking care of things at home while he's 'away'. In my letters I'm not even at school, I've got a job working at the MoD!

Reading them now I can't believe I had such massive bunny-boiler potential. Scary stuff.

Anyway, when he came out he got married, so that was that.

I saw him again about ten years later when I was lying on a beach in Corfu and two blokes walked past. I thought I recognised them but no, it couldn't be. It was. It was him, my long-lost first love. I had a drink with him and even though he was still rugged and handsome I was quite glad I hadn't married him and had his babies.

I got over him fairly quickly and set my sights on Dave, my friend's brother. I was older then, nearly sixteen. A late developer, I was only just growing into my figure. I spent all the money I had on a bright red Gossard Wonderbra and I used to go round their house wearing it with what tits I had thrust up as far as they would go, and I'd literally stand about four inches away just looking at him, saying nothing. In my head I was saying, 'Come on, you know you wannit!' but it never actually came out. Eventually I got off with him at a party and we did it on the bathroom floor which was really romantic. Then we did it again behind the curtain at the Tudor House disco.

I really was a terrible little teenage minx for a time and believe it or not, writing about it now I'm a bit shocked at how blasé I was about sex. But (and I have really tried to think this through) although I was an impressionable youngster who'd fall in love if a boy so much as looked at me, I really did honestly love having sex. Whether it was in a car up the garages or behind the curtain, anywhere, anyhow, anyone. I simply couldn't resist it. It wasn't a power thing or a control thing, I didn't use it and it didn't use me. Luckily it was the 1970s. I'm glad I went through that age of discovery in that decade because HIV hadn't arrived and so sex hadn't yet become life threatening. It was just what everyone did and no one seemed to mind. I don't think I had anything more than a healthy obsession. It was the thing that we thought about the most and whenever there was a film out that was reputed to be a bit racy, we'd do our damnedest to get in, even if it was an 18 certificate. One such film was *Mandingo*. Never mind that it was about race and slavery, we'd heard that there was a full-on sex scene with a sexy black man so we simply had to see it. Slavering teenagers or what? We also tried to see *Last Tango in Paris* but we couldn't get into that one.

I never worried about getting pregnant because, as I've said, I was a late developer and didn't start my periods until just before my sixteenth birthday, at which point I rushed off to the family doctor and asked him to put me on the pill. It was good that I didn't really need it until I was 16 as then there was no obligation for him to tell my mum. I'm sure she knew, she wasn't daft, but at the same time I think she knew I wasn't daft enough to get myself up the spout.

She never stopped me going out, or seeing boys and I was careful not to parade my behaviour in front of her but sometimes I went too far. There was one time when I'd been out and I'd been given a lift home by another bloke from the pub. He had a van and we were sitting outside my house, just talking and it was getting quite late but I figured that because I was outside Mum knew where I was so it would be OK. Anyway, it wasn't OK. Mum came storming up the front garden path, opened the door to the van and dragged me out and into the house like a bag of dirty old laundry. In my diary I wrote:

---

15 Thursday (15-351)

Boring Day yet again. Went to Parkwood and Blue Door. Bit scared to go in becouse of Linda Ferguson but she didn't take no notice of me. Barry Parko took me home got outside my house and Brian Channer-Stevens came along so we took him home then went down Singhams. Got back outside my house and sat talking. Mum came out and showed me up.

She was only protecting me; this guy was, again, considerably older than me but at least I was 16 by then. Looking back, it might seem a bit worrying how many grown men were interested in teenage girls like me, but it didn't strike me as being at all odd at that time. And in any case, I preferred them older. Then.

CHAPTER 6

The First Time I: Fell over and cracked my tooth while wearing a tank top on my head

(The Independence Chapter)

I couldn't wait to get to work. That was a good thing, actually, considering I didn't really have a choice. If we wanted something, Mum usually couldn't buy it, so we had to pay for it ourselves or do without. Kim had been doing a paper round for a while. So as soon as I was old enough – well, before I was old enough, since I was 10 when I started and I think you were supposed to be 13 – I got one too. Mum knew Mick who ran the newsagent part of the shop on Willington Street, which was way too bloody far away from our house to be doing a paper round from, especially as we didn't have bikes. It meant getting the first bus at 5.45am to the shop, then the bus would wait at the top of Westmorland Road for exactly 10 minutes – just enough time to run down to the shop, pick up the papers in our paper bags and run back to the bus. Missing it meant walking an extra mile even before you could start delivering the papers. I had about 35 papers in my bag. It was 1971 so I was well clued-up on Nixon and Watergate. The most popular title then was the *Daily Mirror* by a long shot, but by the time I'd given it up for a proper job the *Sun* was well and truly in charge. This was the share: 22 x *Mirror*, 5 x *Sun*, 2 x *Express* (still a broadsheet then), 3 x *Mail*, 4 x *Sketch*. Funny isn't it, that I can't remember people's names that I met last week but I can remember all that? I did that round for about three years until I could get a Saturday job, seven days a week, 362 days a year (no papers on Christmas or Boxing Day and Good Friday) and I got 18s (90p) a week. That's how I know I was 10, because full decimalisation didn't kick in until 1971 and my pay started off at 18 shillings. I spent most of it on my school uniform or clothes from the Freemans or Grattan catalogues, paying them off at 4s (20p) a week.

Sundays were a nightmare. The papers were nowhere near as heavy as they are now, but they were still weighed-down with supplements. It was the weight of the newspapers that was responsible for me falling over in the tank-top hat that mum had made me. I'll never forget that hat. My grandma had sent down a bag of clothes and in it was a black and white crocheted tank top. It was the most awful tank top you ever saw and there wasn't a hope in hell that any of us were going to wear it. So Mum made it into a hat. For me. The winters were really cold then so I did need a hat, but *Mum*! I wore it, I had no choice. Even when I was old enough to do my paper round, I still wore the hat. I ditched it after I fell over in front of a bus load of people one morning. The bag was so heavy round my neck that as I got off the bus, I tripped on the kerb and despite trying to retain my balance the heavy bag got the better of me and my face hit the kerb, breaking my front tooth. I didn't care about the tooth, I was mortified because I was wearing THE HAT. As I said, nightmare.

Not only did I have to carry and deliver all the Sunday papers, but Sunday afternoons I had to go out again and collect all the money for the weekly bills. The only saving grace was that I got to know all of the customers and because of that, used to clean up at Christmas with the tips. On Monday morning we'd take all the money back up to the shop and hand it over to Mick. And we never got robbed, not even once.

In order to earn even more money I took up babysitting when I was 13 years old. A couple that Mum knew from the pub had asked her if she knew anyone that would be interested in looking after their two kids for a couple of nights a week. They were a young couple, probably approaching their thirties I would have thought. They were so 'seventies' and reminded me of the characters in the

Mike Leigh play *Abigail's Party*. He always wore 1970s checked jackets and roll necks and she always had long flowing dresses on with her long black hair parted in the middle. He had his own business and a nice car, a Mustang. I always saw them as swinging. Not in a wife-swapping sexual way, but in a 'swinging seventies' way. They were kind of cool. And rich. Kim took the job first but as her social life got busier I gradually took over. They lived in a big detached house, which I thought was really posh because it had two living rooms. One for best, where the cream leather three-piece suite was, and one for living in. I don't really know what the point was of the other one as they never used it. I used to go in there and just sit on the sofa wondering what it would be like to be rich like them. I was a terrible babysitter. I'm not really a coo-chi-coo sort of person and the little girl was just a baby when I first went to look after them. Quite what they were doing leaving me, a young teenager, in charge of a little two-year-old boy and a brand new baby always baffled me. Especially as there were no mobile phones then, so I had to wait for them to ring up half-way through the night if I thought anything was wrong. I wouldn't have known, I was too busy scaring myself half to death watching *Tales of the Unexpected* with its creepy music.

Then, as if it wasn't mad enough letting me babysit, they took me on holiday with them. Of course I was gagging to go, my first foreign holiday, I'd only ever been to holiday camps or chalet parks on the south coast. As we drove up from Maidstone to Luton Airport I'll never forget the M1 and its lights all the way up the middle. I thought, *this is it, I'm outta there*. I think it was that drive that planted the seed of adventure in my mind; at that point I knew I didn't want to live in Maidstone for the rest of my life.

Anyway, needless to say the holiday was a disaster. We went to Majorca (Magaluf, to be precise) and it was the beginning of the big British exodus to the beaches of the Med. Right from the start it was a nightmare. For them. On the plane I showed my true credentials as the worst babysitter in the world when the little girl, who was still only two years old, was howling because her ears had popped under the pressure. As her mum cradled her with beautiful maternal sympathy, all I could offer was a curt, 'Surely it doesn't hurt that much?' which didn't get a good response, to say the least. Then to my horror, I was designated a room with the two kids! *Noooooo!* I thought. But I was getting a free holiday so I shouldn't really have expected any different. I did though. I honestly thought I'd just have to babysit a couple of nights while they went out, not get the kids dressed in the morning and get their breakfast! Jesus! I wasn't the nanny, I was the babysitter! The kids would wake up at the crack of dawn and run around playing. When they finally managed to wake me up, which was difficult as I was a teenager after all, I would just shout at them to shut up until they sobbed off to their parents' room next door. I got a nice tan though.

I also worked as a waitress in the Rumpy Bar. I had to think long and hard about the Rumpy Bar while writing this because I wasn't sure if I'd made the name up. But it really existed on Week Street, long gone now, and although it was a burger bar the same as the Wimpy, it dressed itself up as a proper restaurant with a big model cow that was cheekily patting itself on the 'rump' outside. It was the sort of place that poor people went for a 'meal out' if they were feeling flush because upstairs it did differ from the Wimpy in that it had tablecloths and booze. Pauline and I both got jobs there and we were paid 20p an hour. We worked most evenings after school from 5pm until 8pm and at weekends from 9am until 8pm. That meant that if we worked three evenings a week and both weekend days we'd earn the grand sum of £6.20 each. It may not have been much, but it was still money, and I never had pocket money, just earnings. My stint there didn't last long because I got the sack for not filling up the plastic tomato-shaped ketchup dispensers quickly enough. It was my first sacking, but not my last. I left the Rumpy Bar and went straight down to the Golden Egg and got a job in there, but only lasted a day because I thought it was even worse than the Rumpy.

As soon as I was old enough I got myself a Saturday job in one of Maidstone's top boutiques, Snob. Helen – one of the gang from school, who I'd always looked up to and admired for her taste and fashion sense – was already working there and very kindly put me up for a position. I'd been in the shop thousands of times, lusting over the stuff and making mental lists of what I'd buy if I had the money. When I went in for the interview I couldn't believe I was actually going into the office at the back. It was painted red, just like the shop and had giant hanging rails everywhere with all the clothes that hadn't even been put in the shop yet. At 15, this really was a dream job. Snob was the trendiest, hottest boutique in town and I was up for a job there. When I got it I thought I was *it*. I bought an outfit that I wore every week – light grey, skin-tight, high-waisted, massive flares and a white cropped top that didn't actually reveal any midriff because the trousers were so high they met it at the bottom – I wore it with my grey corduroy coat with the big lapels and my black wedge-heel boots. I thought I looked great. I hadn't started putting on weight yet and was still quite teenage skinny. Not as skinny as Helen though, who I always thought looked much more at home there and had real style, a unique way of putting things together. She was my fashion mentor.

When I left school I went to work there full-time. I think my mum would have loved to have seen me go on to further education but it just wasn't an option for me. I'd gone to the wrong school for a start, where it was assumed that there were no aspirations to university – hence the lack of required exams. But the main problem was money, again. Although grants were widely available Mum simply couldn't afford to keep me at home while I went to college. There have been times when I've looked back and wondered what path I might have taken if things had been different. I've certainly met people who did go to university who talk about the valuable life lessons they learned there but I had that too, just in a non-academic way. The only part of it I lament is that it might have taught me to focus, to pay attention and to think clearly. I have the most un-methodical mind in the world, my thoughts are like Alphabetti Spaghetti. All the letters and words are there but nothing is in order. I'm a bit of a scatterbrain in that respect. But apart from that, I have no regrets.

And anyway, at the time, I just wanted to get to work. I'd virtually been supporting myself for some time with my various forays into the teen workplace but now I needed more money. There were clothes to buy, discos to go to, boys to meet and, most importantly, I needed to save up money for when I could learn to drive.

So I left school as soon as I could. Luckily, Snob were opening a new jewellery department and I was given the job of running it. I earned £25 a week which I thought was loads – what would I do with it all? Every Friday I received a little brown envelope with some writing on and the cash would be inside. For that I had to work eleven days a fortnight, taking only one day off every two weeks. I didn't care, I loved going to work; it was like shopping all day – almost my whole week was spent working out what my purchase of the week would be. I had to buy something every week because I was getting 25% discount. Also 1% commission on everything I sold! Considering I was only selling jewellery at 20p and 30p a go, I would have had to sell about 300 pieces to earn an extra £1, whereas in reality I probably only sold about fifty in a week. I spent all day lovingly dusting, re-arranging and making the stand look appealing and because it was new, I even had my picture in the *Kent Messenger*, the local paper. I spent all of that money on clothes and cakes and started saving a little bit for a car. I couldn't wait to hit driving age.

There was a much less formal atmosphere in the shop since the assistant manageress, Pat, was now the manager. Gill and Cherry were my favourite colleagues; I thought they were ancient but they were probably only in their late twenties at the time. Cherry was a right minx and used to make me laugh with her tales of naughtiness. She was obsessed with hand cream and would constantly be in and out of the toilet washing her hands and slavering on the hand cream, all the way up her arms. I wonder if it paid off? They were both so stylish too. I tried to emulate them but always felt like I wasn't quite getting it right. My favourite outfit was a denim boilersuit with giant flares or white or navy Inega jeans with cap-sleeved or vest tops. It was the summer of 1976 and the shop was stifling, you kind of had to wear as little as possible. I even resorted to floral cotton dresses at one point. Problem was, it was so hot that no one ever came in so there were no customers and no commission.

Delivery day was about the only time there was any work to do. We had to get all the new stock in and put it all out, move the stuff around. I was on my feet all day but I was never bored.

1976 was a great time musically and another thing that I loved about the job was that I was put in charge of the music most of the time because it was situated near my stand, which was right by the door. Music was an important part of the shop's ambience and was played via 8-track cartridges on a player that resembled the game Mousetrap, in the way it pushed the old cartridge out and round a clear plastic bridge to the back of the queue to play again later. 8-tracks were a good idea because they played on a loop and were in four (I think) sections. However, the tape always ended up getting stuck in the machine and they'd go really slowly, so eventually every single song sounded like Tom Waits. There were about 10 albums that played nearly all of the time and every time I hear any of them I'm wafted back to that shrine to fashion and all things 1970s: Steely Dan's *Pretzel Logic* and *The Royal Scam*; Santana's *Abraxas*; Elton John's *Goodbye Yellow Brick Road* and *Rock of the Westies*; Rod Stewart's *Never a Dull Moment* and *Atlantic Crossing*; David Bowie's *Ziggy Stardust*, *Aladdin Sane* and *Young Americans*.

I became so interested in music I left Snob to go and work in the record department of Boots. Music wasn't the only reason; it was more money and Kim worked there in the pharmacy. A single 45rpm vinyl record then cost nearly 50p which seems a lot now, considering you can get a single on iTunes for 79p. Buying records was a real event in 1976. They still had the listening booths, which were like big hair-drying canopies. They had holes in the wood and if you wanted to hear a record before you bought it the assistant would put it on and you'd 'pop over to booth number three' and have a listen. Often you'd get whole families craning their heads into one little booth and they'd all stand there clicking their fingers and tapping their feet in a real 1970s kind of way. I'm smiling at that thought, and it reminds me that my first single was 'Two Little Boys' by Rolf Harris. My dad bought it for me from Gooses Record Shop in the High Street which also had the booths, but I was only nine years old so too small to get my head inside one.

I was happy but really all I wanted was an office job. Didn't matter what it was as long as it was in an office. That was the extent of my career ambitions, to work in an office, because somehow it just seemed to have more of a future to it than just working in a shop.

Around this time Mum was working as a barmaid in The Fisherman's Arms, the smallest and oldest pub in Maidstone. I think it was built in the fourteenth century. It was so old that if you were over five foot you had to bend down to get in the door. I couldn't stand up in there. It was cosy though and the landlord and landlady, Griff and Eileen, were like two old, giant, walking, talking teddy bears. Anyway, one of the regular customers was a bloke called Haydn Jones (great name, reminds me of the song, 'Nathan Jones' by The Supremes) though it was HBJ to his friends. He was the boss in an office across the road from the pub. I think he had a soft spot for my mum, so when she asked him if there were any jobs going for me he said yes.

That's how I left Boots and got my office job as a key-punch operator for Cluttons, the upmarket estate agents and property managers who looked after huge chunks of the Crown Estate, Church Commissioners and Henry Smith's Charity property portfolio. Actually, until I moved to London I didn't realise what any of that meant, but basically they are three of the biggest and wealthiest landowners in the country and I was inputting their rental duties into a 'computer', which was a desk-sized keyboard with an eye-level screen with two compartments for standard-sized data cassettes, which were actually music cassettes with data on them. Each day there'd be a pile of forms to input and that was all you did. There were two of us doing that all day. The main computer was in the next room and it did actually take up a whole room, even though it probably didn't have even half of the power and capabilities of my current mobile phone.

I felt so important working in an office. I bought all the necessary gear – flannel trousers, knee-length skirts, houndstooth check hacking jacket, white shirts and low-heeled court shoes. Trouble was, at that time I was going through my punk phase and my smart clothes didn't really go with my hair, which was shaved really short (about ¼ of an inch all over) with ten long spikes for a fringe. There was nothing I could do to make it look 'normal' or respectable. In fact I looked ridiculous (see *The Style Chapter*).

I was also approaching 17, the age when I could start driving lessons. In fact, I applied for my licence to start on my seventeenth birthday so I could get cracking on my dearest ambition: to learn to drive and pass my test as soon as was humanly possible.

Stan was another of Mum's contacts from the pub, and he was a one-man driving school. His car was a little blue Mazda with dual controls and he was quite old but very patient. I was a good pupil though; I had spent many, many hours in my boyfriend Martyn's Morris Marina studying his driving and silently mimicking his foot and hand movements so I already had quite a good idea of what to do.

I was confident too. But it was a confidence that was born out of determination and resolve. Boredom also played a part. Living in Shepway I felt hemmed in, and the car was to be my passport to freedom and adventure, my ticket away from the trap that I could see Kim falling into – one that wasn't too dissimilar to my mum's. I knew from an early age I was never going down that road. Watching my mum struggle all I could see was drudgery, and when Kim came home one day, at the age of 24, and told her she was pregnant by the guy she would eventually marry I could see the disappointment on my mum's face, watching history repeat itself. I remember being horrified at the thought, which made me even more determined to get out there and live.

My driving lessons were £3 – a great indicator of the time and my age. I spent most of my money on the lessons, sometimes three a week, but I was still living at home and earning about £30 a week so I could easily afford it, even after paying my mum the bargain board rate of £5 a week.

Anyway, it paid off because just before my eighteenth birthday I passed my test. Not first time though. The first test I failed because of my crap three-point turn, which I thought was brilliant. I knew I hadn't passed as soon as we pulled back into the centre. The examiner's face said it all.

The tests were much easier then than they are now. You did the driving bit then they asked you a couple of questions about the Highway Code and that was it. Now, you have to virtually sit an exam. Sod that! Another good reason to be grateful for being old.

Stan was great, he said it was just nerves and told me to apply for another test straightaway. About a month later I took it again, but on the way to the centre Stan handed me a half of a little tablet and told me to take it. I had no idea what it was but he assured me it was harmless and would help with my nerves. Of course Valium wasn't really something that a driving instructor should be giving to his young pupil but I took it anyway. It did calm my nerves and I passed with flying colours.

I'd already bought a car in anticipation. It was a Mark I Ford Escort in brown. NKE 248F. 1968. It was only about 10 years old, but blimey, it was in a right state. The paintwork was metallic brown but previous owners had obviously tried so hard to shine it up with T-Cut that it was virtually stripped of its paint and looked like it had been set on fire. I'm surprised it even had pedals because from the outside it looked like it should have been powered, Flintstones-style, by your own feet, which could have gone through the floor at any minute it was so rusty. £350 I paid for that car. I can't believe that now because in 1978 £350 must have been the equivalent of about £3,000. I had a bit of money saved and borrowed the rest. All I know is that the car came from Tenterden and on the day I picked it up, I went out. And I mean *out*. I picked Helen up and drove up the A2, through the Dartford Tunnel and into deepest Essex. Fearless teens we were, in pursuit of disco. I think we went to Canvey Island to The Goldmine or it could have been the Lacy Lady in Ilford – both clubs we'd heard of but never been, and were dying to go to. How the hell did I know where I was going? There was no sat-nav and I know I didn't own a map. We must have just relied on signposts and rough ideas. But when you're young you don't care if you get lost, you just find your way out of it and it's a great way to learn how to not get lost again.

Mission accomplished.

That car facilitated so much adventure I should have kept it and put it in a box. I'm sad because I don't even have a photo of it.

I only gained total independence in 1980 when my mum remarried and left home to run a pub. We were happy for her because it was all she ever wanted to do, run her own pub. But we all had doubts about the new man in her life, mainly because we felt he didn't like us. We never expressed our disapproval, even when she went on to marry him, but he did indeed turn out to be another unsuitable husband and after they divorced she continued running the pub on her own, which was a dream for her.

So, at the grand old age of twenty, and for the first time, I finally had my own room. In fact, I was left with the whole house to myself because Mark and Tracy had gone to the pub with Mum, and Kim was ensconced in a tiny council flat elsewhere on the estate. Even though I had been dying to live on my own, I didn't really like it. It was too spooky at night and I couldn't sleep. Mum suggested swapping the house for a flat on the estate which, with hindsight, was madness. Council houses were like gold dust and if you had one, you hung on to it, even if you had to sub-let it illegally. It must have been all of about 30 seconds after we put the request in for a swap that a flat came up. So I moved and finally I had my own flat. Only problem was, I had to pay all the rent and all the bills.

I was still working for Cluttons and, relative to the time, it was quite well paid. Especially considering what I actually did – which, most of the time, was fall asleep at my terminal. You see, I had to take on other work because the money from one job just wasn't enough. I've still got my payslips and I was taking home £246 a month; I could just about do it when I was living at home (when all I had to pay out for was nominal board to Mum, my car, clothes and going out) but with all the expense of my new-found independence I simply had to have more. So I got myself a couple of evening jobs.

First, I got some shifts as a waitress in Dixie's Diner, an American joint in town where Helen and I used to spend our Saturdays, eating burgers and getting chatted up by the manager, Mister Cab, and his mate, the assistant manager, Dave. Dixie's was a cool place, the first of its kind in the area, and it became more of a destination than a regular restaurant. It had the red-and-white checked tablecloths, traditional Heinz ketchup bottles on the tables, a visible grill where various chefs cooked up the burgers, and it played fantastic soul music mixtapes the whole time – Marvin Gaye, Curtis Mayfield, The Isley Brothers, Maze. Best of all, it was open all day, every day, until midnight; and then even later when it got itself a late licence. The attached wine bar had old bus seats for chairs and one of the very first computer games, Asteroids, on a giant machine in the corner.

Mister Cab was pretty cool too and after I finally gave in to his advances I ended up sort of going out with him for a bit. Well, for quite a long time actually, but we were never officially 'going out'. It wasn't official because Mister Cab had a bit of a reputation at the time for being a sometime ladies' man, a lothario even. His famous chat-up line was 'Hey, you've lost weight!' Even if you hadn't, he knew it was a winner with the female of the species. He lived above the shop in a one-room apartment which had the vital playboy accessory, a swinging bed. It was a real bachelor shag-pad. The bed took up nearly the whole room and hung by hefty chains that were secured to the wooden beams overhead. He was a good laugh and great in the sack but I never really saw him as 'boyfriend material'. Despite this, he pursued me relentlessly. The way I saw it, I loved my single life, I had my own flat, several good jobs and a nice car; what did I need that aggro for?

So after the first big swing, I spelled it out, 'Right, don't get serious because I don't want to go out with you or anything,' which must have sounded like I was issuing him with a challenge. Turns out it was like waving a red rag at a bull. For the next couple of years he set about the task of making me take those words back by trying to get me to fall in love with him, while still pissing about with a load of other girls. He did manage to wind me up a few times but, because I had my own car and flat, I would just get up and go home. No drama, no tears. Well, there were tears once. I couldn't get home and he was with someone else so I cried outside the building so loud that he had to come out and take me home. Actually, I did kind of fall for him and he taught me a hell of a lot about music and about life. He took me to see Aretha Franklin at the Hammersmith Apollo, which was amazing because it was her last trip to the UK before she stopped travelling. He also made me a storage box for my LPs. He was a skilled carpenter and he made it from scratch out of an old wooden door. Thirty years on and I've still got it and it's still got my albums in it. He taught me about exercise too; he was an ex-army fitness instructor and although he went about it in a fairly over-the-top and strict way, I do have him to thank in part for me not getting very, very fat (See *The Food and Weight Chapter*).

I was fond of him. I must have been. Because when he lost his driving licence, I saved his bacon by taking the staff home for him. Now that doesn't sound like much of a task, but the restaurant didn't shut until midnight and by the time everyone had cleared up, it wasn't time to leave until about 1am. So, even if I wasn't working there that night, I would go home, go to sleep, get up, drive down to the restaurant, pick up the staff and drive them all home to various locations (never anywhere near each other) around Maidstone and the surrounding areas . . . in a Bedford van. I must have been mad! I don't even remember him paying me for it. The advantage for me, he said, was that I got to keep the Bedford van and drive around in it whenever I wanted. Great. Come on, let's all go up to the Lacy Lady in the van! He did have some front sometimes; I don't know how he got away with it.

Mister Cab only really showed me how he felt once when, for my birthday, he gave me a Bill Withers record. In it, there was a kind of love letter, which directed me to the lyrics of the songs on the album. I suppose it prevented him from actually having to say the words himself. I've still got that album but I can't find the love letter. I reckon he came round one day and destroyed it, fearing it would ruin his reputation and expose him as the soppy old romantic he really was. When I left for London he was quietly gutted, I think. But I told him, 'You had your chance, but you blew it.' He's now happily married with a couple of kids, still living in Maidstone and ageing well, it has to be said.

I loved working at Dixie's and as well as waitressing I assisted on the grill, worked on the door allocating tables and taking the money, and when Mister Cab went on holiday he left me in charge, even though I was only 20 years old. I felt so grown-up and important and it made me feel ambitious for the first time in my life. I loved being the boss and had no problem tackling the drunks and troublemakers who got rowdy in the bar from time to time.

I also got myself my first proper bar job in Maidstone's first and only nightclub, The Warehouse. There was a great feeling of anticipation preceding the opening of that club, a real buzz and excitement about it. As soon as I saw the advert for staff in the *Kent Messenger* I thought, *I want a bit of that.* I went for the mass interview but it was more like an audition or a model go-see. The two owners just lined up all the applicants, who were all female (I don't recall the ad saying they had to be, but how deliciously un-PC if it had) and literally pointed at you if you were through. It seemed so obviously all about what you looked like, as you didn't even have to speak.

Anyway, somehow I got the job and started work there on the opening night. It was bloody packed. You couldn't move. Everything sold out and they must have taken a fortune. I didn't stop from 8pm until 2am. Just me and one other girl ran the whole section of the club known as the 'Lounge Bar'. It also had a long bar which was by the riverside and a disco. After the opening night I was usually assigned to the long bar. I worked with two women most of the time who I also thought were both really ancient, Vivien and Mary. They were probably only about 30. Vivien gave me a bit of advice back then. I was talking to her one day about her beauty routine and she told me that after she'd had a shower or a bath she put moisturiser on, all over her body. Every time. I couldn't believe it; how could anyone be bothered? But she said, 'Do it and you'll thank me later.' So I did and I am eternally grateful to her for that, as people have said that I do have very soft skin. I mean, it's getting a bit old and wrinkly now but it's bloody soft.

Working there really opened my eyes to another world. This was a proper club where the moneyed people would come to socialise. I met a lot of new people there who I thought were acutely interesting, although I thought they were really old too.

One such gang was led by a bloke called Stuart. He was the best-looking bloke I'd ever seen but he was untouchable. And there was a girl called Ruth who I always aspired to be. She had a cottage up the Loose Road, a Volkswagen Scirocco and she dated a bloke who was almost as good looking as Stuart but not quite. I thought, 'God, how old do you have to be before you have all of that?' I couldn't wait to be her, have my own house, a flash car and a super-gorgeous boyfriend. One of the guys in the gang was called Roy. He was quite short, even in his stacked heels. He worked for the GPO (General Post Office) and used to drive around in one of their big yellow Commer vans. He was a really lovely bloke and the total antithesis of my type at the time but I went out with him: a) because he asked me, and b) because I thought it might make it easier to get to Stuart. In short (sorry Roy), I used him. It worked. I did get to Stuart . . . eventually.

Somehow, me and two of my friends, Helen and Anne, managed to get invited back to Stuart's place one night. We were just sitting on the sofa and he was being very entertaining as usual and was going on about how he was going to get this Calor Gas heater up the stairs to the bedroom. Anyway, I offered to help him carry it up there, and then, while I was up there, I had sex with him, just like that. I'm not sure who seduced who but I didn't care, he was too gorgeous not to.

When Roy found out he wasn't really upset or surprised. All he said to me was, 'Carol, you used me as a stepping stone, didn't you?' I couldn't deny it. But he did say it with a little smile on his face so I think I'd been rumbled way before that.

I didn't see Stuart again until I bumped into him 15 years later in 1994, in Zilli's Bar, Soho. I was sitting at a table with my friend Laura when this guy walks in. He was wearing a dogtooth checked suit, carrying a mac, and was talking to everyone because he seemed to know everyone. I turned to her and said, 'Ask that bloke what his name is.' I was too shy to ask myself. So she did, and it was Stuart. At which point I asked him, 'Do you remember me, we had sex in 1979?' He said, quite simply, 'No,' and walked off into the night. It was all too funny. Anyway, we were obviously destined to be friends because I bumped into him again a couple of years later when I was in a club with Zoë Ball who I'd been working with on the *Big Breakfast* (see *The Working Breakfasts Chapter*). He was all over Zoë because she was famous, buying her champagne and getting us in the VIP area, and I asked him again if he remembered me. This time he wasn't so rude and he pretended to. What was funnier was that night a friend of Stuart's gave me his phone number. He said he was a millionaire. He looked familiar; I had probably seen him in the Warehouse all those years ago. Anyway, I never called him but I kept in touch with Stuart and actually now he is one of my best friends. He came to my fortieth and my fiftieth birthday parties and I see him whenever he comes to London.

As for the other guy, the millionaire, (see *The Dating After Divorce Chapter*).

CHAPTER 7

The First Time I: Went out wearing a bin-bag, fishnet stockings and not much else

(The Style Chapter)

It took me a long, long time to find out what suited me. I was a style disaster until, I'd say, around my thirties. I always loved fashion though and loved reading the catalogues, needing and wanting the very latest stuff. I was usually the first to wear something, even though it probably didn't look right.

When I was very young I didn't have much of a choice about what I wore. It was hand-me-downs or nothing; Mum couldn't afford new clothes for all of us, so Kim got new stuff, I got it second and poor Tracy had it last. Some of the old photographs of us all together make that sad but simple fact so obvious. Now when I look at them I think we look cute, but whenever my mum looked at those pictures it would break her heart. She'd get genuinely upset because we all looked so mismatched and badly fitted, even though I actually thought she did a very good job of making us look presentable. In fact, one of my favourite photographs of all time is of my brother and me getting into my dad's car. I can only gauge how old I was because it was the Ford Anglia that I remembered the registration plate of – BKE 873B – so it was a 1967 model. Therefore I must have been seven or eight, my brother Mark nearly two years younger. We look like we should be on the cover of a retro style mag – flip-flops and socks for me and shorts, a nifty shirt and seriously cool Wayfarer shades for Mark. We both look pretty pleased with ourselves so I'm sure I wasn't unhappy with my attire. But there was never any point in objecting, anyway, because Mum would just say, 'Put it on, you're wearing it,' and that would be that.

I was aware of what I was wearing from quite an early age, but my first real style memory was a desperate need for some flowery loon pants from the catalogue. On reflection, perhaps it was a good thing that I never got them.

In my tomboy years (until I was about 10) my uniform was Levi 501s with the Red Tab and the big 'E' in Levi. They had the red inner stitching and we bought them in Millets or the army surplus shop on Stone Street. Non-school footwear consisted of nothing but old-style black-and-white bumper boots. Levi's jeans weren't pre-shrunk, so the trend was to buy them a size bigger and then sit in a scalding hot bath while they shrank to fit. Madness. Putting them in the washing machine had exactly the same effect but it wasn't anywhere near as dramatic. They had a different quality too; the denim was heavier and kind of fluffy. I loved them. They washed and wore really well, fading and ageing with you. Jeans just don't fade like that anymore. Or maybe it's because I have so many pairs now that I don't wear any one pair often enough to wash them enough to fade them. But I would pay good money to get my hands on a pair of those jeans, original, unworn and unwashed. The other thing was how tight they had to be. Jeans couldn't be even slightly baggy anywhere. If you didn't have to lie down on the floor while your sister zipped them up with a wire coat-hanger then they were just too big.

The tomboy thing was the cause of my first fit of angst. Because I had short hair, I would often be referred to by strangers as 'sonny' or 'son' and things came to a head when I was coming out of a phone box and the lady going in said, 'Thanks Lad,' as I held the door open for her. I was so upset by it that I wrote a letter to a comic problem page, *Bunty* or something like that, and, unbelievably, it was published. It went along the lines of, 'Dear Bunty, I have short hair and I wear jeans and bumper boots all the time and people keep thinking I'm a boy. What can I do?' The advice was simple, if not a little obvious: grow your hair and wear dresses more often. *Twats*, I thought, *what did they know?* and carried on exactly as before.

The tomboy look was OK for weekends but going to school was a different matter. With us, practicality came first at all times in terms of shoes, coats and things. In the late 1960s/early 1970s all the other girls at school had candy-striped capes and matching caps whereas I wore a navy-blue duffle coat from Gordon Higgins for about five years. My friend Gaynor never minded swapping with me and I would wear her checked smock coat with the bow at the back while she wore my old duffle. I thought that was really kind.

When I started my paper round, I spent all the money on clothes. On 90p a week I couldn't afford much even paying over twenty weeks with the catalogues. But there was always Martyn Fords, where Pauline's mum Nelly worked. It was like the Primark of its time, with the cheapest clothes in town. But Martyn Fords clothes weren't so nice and people would laugh if they knew you got stuff from there. Funny how that's changed; people are proud to boast about getting a dress for £1 now. But back then, choosing the one, single, exact-right thing was paramount and there was something lovely in only being able to afford one thing. It was so much less confusing, because whatever you chose, that was what you wore all the time. I'll never forget that long grey corduroy coat and the wedge-heeled boots. I loved them so much I didn't mind wearing them every day, which was a good job because that was all I had.

I wish I were a bit more like that now; after all, you can only wear one thing at a time and choice confuses me. I have some beautiful things in my wardrobe that I've only worn a few times but can't wear now because they're just out of date. Of course I do have things that I wear all the time but they're practical things – I'm talking about fashionable things, the sort of stuff I used to dream about as a kid.

Some years ago, still searching for my style, I discovered designer sales. They were twice-yearly warehouse sales of end-of-lines and over-produced, unsold designer stock. I bought so much stuff, simply because it was cheap, but most of it I never wore. I took great piles of it to a resale shop in West London and when I tallied up what it had all cost and, moreover, what it would have been worth had I paid the full price for it, it made me feel quite sick. Especially as they gave me about £300 for the lot. Urgh, I still can't think about it. But at least it stopped me buying things I don't need – up to a point! I have a rule now: every time I buy something, something else has to go. That way I can keep my wardrobe under control. However, the same can't yet be said for shoes – but therein lies a huge psychological problem which probably does stem from a childhood of shoe rationing.

I *loved* the 1970s. The fashion was immense. And as a teenager I was right there in the thick of it, working in Snob. I wasn't quite old enough for hot pants but I just made it for massive flares and crop-tops. Jeans were just becoming fashionable and whereas before you could only get Levi's, Lee and Wrangler, now there were fashion brands emerging. Brutus, Inega and Fiorucci were the must-haves. I've still got my first pair of Fioruccis in what I call my 'dressing-up box'. It's not a big box and there's not a lot in it, but what gets selected to go in there has to be really special. My first pair of cowboy boots are in there because, quite simply, they are works of art. I bought them in R. Soles on the King's Road and they were about £60, which was a lot at the time. They've got huge, stacked, Cuban heels and are fairly pointy. I loved them and will never throw them away. Ditto my first pair of leather trousers that I bought from Joanna's Tent, also on the King's Road. They're a plum colour and so 1980s they're painful – peg style with pleats and very high and tight on the waist. I can still get into them though. Just.

In the early 1970s when I was first allowed to go out to the youth club I got quite precious about my clothes and any that I did buy I treasured. Often, however, Tracy would borrow things without asking and I'd go ballistic because she wasn't as clean as me (a truth that she admits to herself!) and she ruined them with her pungent body odour. (I would like to point out that it was a pubertal phase she was going through at the time and she doesn't now pong, thankfully.)

Going out for the first time was such a big thing. I can completely remember what I wore. I went to the Howard de Walden youth club in Maidstone, on my own for some reason, and I had on a navy-blue swing skirt with a white circle pattern on it, white plimsolls, a white, 'granddad vest' T-shirt and my navy-blue school cardigan. As I've said, doing something for the first time is always exciting but that night was exhilarating. That's probably why I went on my own; I was just determined to go out. I didn't realise it at the time, but that night was the beginning of a life of going out and having fun, laughing, drinking, dancing and loving and as I walked down that road towards the building (a church, by the way) I absolutely knew that that was what I wanted to do. Sounds shallow doesn't it, when some people want to change the world and have lofty ambitions to eliminate poverty? But it's never too late and I can always do that later. When I've stopped having fun.

By far and away my biggest style disaster era was in 1976 when the punk scene hit Maidstone. Being the style icon I thought I was, I couldn't ignore it, so I became a part-time punk rocker. Part-time, because during the week I had to do my dead-straight office job at Cluttons. This meant that on weekdays I'd be in my flannel trousers, smart blouses, shiny shoes and hacking jacket, then from Friday night I'd don something completely ridiculous like a big, black, oversized man's jacket from a charity shop, shiny leggings, silver shoes and a T-shirt that I'd ripped and then safety pinned back together after defacing it with a big felt-tipped pen. It was my take on one that I wanted from the boutique on the King's Road called SEX, which was owned by the King and Queen of punk, Malcolm McLaren and Vivien Westwood. On special occasions, like when we went to the Marquee in London to see The Damned, I wore: the big black jacket; a black plastic bin-bag with holes cut for arms and head which I emblazoned with safety pins; a pair of vintage gold stilettos; ripped fishnet stockings, and er . . . that's it. On top of that, I'd spend hours piling Vaseline in my hair, followed by tons of talcum powder, so it would stiffen and stick up in the air. Then I would stand at the bus stop on the corner, get on the bus into town, walk from the bus to the train station, buy a ticket, get on a train and sit there all the way to London where I would then get on a tube train to Oxford Circus before walking again down to Wardour Street. Dressed like that. No wonder my mum's face was a picture. She never tried to stop me, she just rolled her eyes and said, 'You look bloody ridiculous.' Ha! What did she know? I thought I looked wild and no one at that gig would have known I was only a part-timer. It was a great gig, X-Ray Spex supported and I wanted to be Poly Styrene up there belting out 'OH BONDAGE, UP YOURS!' while getting gobbed on from all angles. Everyone gobbed at everyone and everyone pogoed – a dance where you simply jumped up and down, the higher the better, and if you craned your neck and arched your back it was even more authentic because it was named after the popular 1970s toy craze the Pogo Stick, which allowed you to do exactly that, but with the aid of a sprung pole that was impossible to balance on. After about five minutes (unless you were on serious drugs) you were pooped, but with the room being so packed you could just lift up your feet and carry on, because there would be so many people in there. Being a punk was so exhausting. Not to mention a fire hazard.

However, the most amazing thing about all this behaviour was not that I would go out dressed like that in the first place, not that I was happy to have people gob their snot all over me, not that I travelled for two hours for the privilege then travelled another two hours home afterwards, but that I would do all that walking, travelling, pogoing IN HIGH HEELS. And I mean REALLY high heels. Really high GOLD heels. It's amazing, because now I can't even get down my own stairs and into the taxi without walking like Dick Emery. *Ooh, you are awful!*

At weekends, we'd all traipse up to London again and literally walk up and down the King's Road all day. One time, we were peacefully strolling, posing, checking out the other punks when suddenly a fight broke out and there were police everywhere. I can't be sure but I think some Hell's Angels had decided to walk in the opposite direction, or something equally meaningless. We had to get out of the way so this random punk turned to us and said, 'Quick, come with us, we'll go to the dentist's.' I thought I was hearing things but followed him anyway up one of the side streets where he unlocked a basement door and we all took shelter for the rest of the afternoon in a room with a big dentist's chair and all the paraphernalia, until the coast was clear. It was the most surreal day and when I told people afterwards I'm certain they thought I was on drugs or something.

If we didn't go to London, we'd hang out in a shoe shop. Platform 9 was at the bottom of Gabriel's Hill in Maidstone and the only three punks who lived in the town would congregate there and intimidate the customers. The girl who ran it had orange hair, great make-up and real piercings. The shop wasn't selling punk regalia though; it was selling proper 1970s platform shoes which were so huge and high they should have come with a health warning. I loved the 1970s for being such a fashion melting-pot like that.

I bought all the right music too. I had albums by The Clash, The Vibrators, The Sex Pistols, The Damned, Generation X, Siouxsie and the Banshees, The Buzzcocks, Eddie and the Hotrods, The Ramones, The Slits, X-Ray Spex and Sham 69. I got rid of them all though after I grew out of that phase and realised what a hideous noise it all was – apart from The Clash and The Stranglers, who weren't even that punky anyway.

Despite my haircut and record collection I was still a rubbish punk and after about six months, much to Mum's relief, I concluded she was right and went back to the soul scene. It was just too difficult being a punk. It took too long to get ready and it really wasn't very nice getting home and having to wash dried snot out of your hair or your clothes. But the main reason was because I'd met a bloke called Martyn that I liked so much I dumped punk for him. I was very grateful to him for dragging me out of that style delusion but he was also very handy as he was the bloke who helped me learn to drive. But it didn't last because he was too posh for me and would never let me meet his parents or tell anyone we were seeing each other. One night, coming back from a disco, I told him I'd lost my house keys so I could go back to his, but instead he drove us down to Dover and we sat in the car on top of the White Cliffs until I could go home.

Quite cute for a number two

Mum on the 'best day of her life'. .. well, it was at the time

Mum and my Auntie Eileen (my Godmother at my Christening. My Mum looks so beautiful in this photo.

Here's Dad behind the counter at David Greig's

Here's Kim the protector doing her bit. The matching t-shirts mean we are still rich kids here

We look like urchins in this photo. I hated that dress, it was SO itchy

Kim, Mark and me with my little buckle (belly)

On the killer trike, pre-death defying descent

My favourite photo ever – very 1967 – Mark even has the obligatory toilet chain accessory, so of the time

Is that a paparazzi I see in the distance? Good job I've got me shades on

Get the chimp off me or I'm calling social services!

I can tell it's the first day because my uniform still fits

Not so sweet sixteen. The shorts could be a bit tighter, don't you think?

Mum in her Elsie Tanner guise. 'Come on Ena, let's get down the snug!'

In the kitchen of 195 (believe it or not, that kitchen was white once!)

Here's Mum at her happiest, in her slippers sitting outside her bungalow

Grandma and Grandad's Golden wedding anniversary with all the grandchildren – April, Sharon, Mark, me, Tracy and Kim at the front

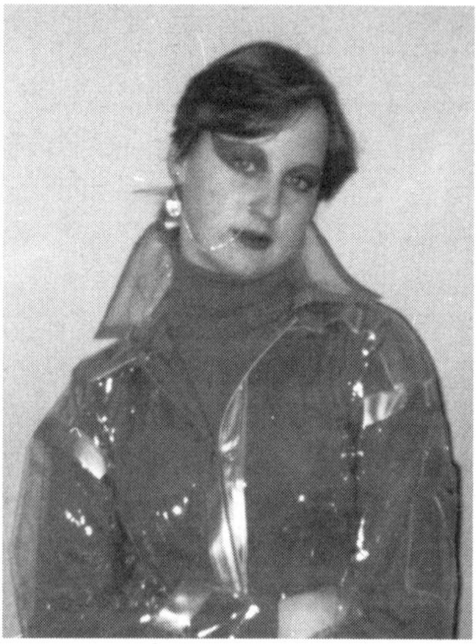

A punk in a rust polo neck?

My first full time job in Snob flogging plastic jewels, fans and straw bags

Went to Crete, got the t-shirt and my first TV job!

An excellent example of bad, 1980s style. And dancing

Posing for 'Playboy' in Jamaica, 1991

Steve and Simon's wedding party – they're not holding me up, honest

Five go mad at Pontin's in 2008 – Emma, Kim, Tracy, me and Holly

Perhaps it was because, post-punk, I didn't look much better. Peg-leg trousers and high Cuban-heeled cowboy boots with a tweed jacket and a patent satchel? And of course I still had the ridiculous punk hair. Not a good look.

Growing the punk hair out took ages but then when it had I made my biggest hair mistake ever when I had a perm in 1978/9. I remember going round to 'The Bizarre' (a house where everyone went to smoke dope, see *The Turning 40 Chapter*) and my friend Bill looking at me with absolute incredulity and saying, 'What have you done to your hair?' Being thick-skinned, undamaged and overly confident (as you are at 18) it didn't even register; I simply replied, 'I've had a perm, don't you like it?' It did look shocking – I looked like a cross between Brian May and Thora Hird – and it took literally years to grow out.

In the 1980s I looked ridiculous too because I thought I was Princess Diana. Honestly, I modelled myself on the late princess with her bow-tie blouses and nice A-line skirts.

But then came the thing that completely changed my sartorial life: the *Next Directory*.

OK, so it was really nothing more than a catalogue, but it was a *posh* catalogue. I went mad, bought everything and even got into debt trying to find my style. But despite my best efforts, I still looked wrong. So I gave up looking for it (my personal style, that is) and waited until my thirties when I was happier, thinner and I'd met someone that I thought I'd be with for the rest of my life.

CHAPTER 8

The First Time I: Ate a whole catering-size cheesecake in one go

(The Food and Weight Chapter)

I used to be a right pig. Seriously, it was touch and go that one day I would be grossly overweight. It started with something my mum said when I was probably about eight or nine.

I was tucking into a mountainous plate of mashed potatoes with something or other (probably sausages), peas and gravy and she said, in a manner laced with approval, 'Ooh, Carol's going to need a bigger plate soon!' Well, to my little ears that was a signal that the more I ate, the more praise I would get. Don't get me wrong, it wasn't that I was craving attention or love (well, it might have been my middle-child syndrome kicking in again), it was just that I always wanted to please my mum and if eating loads would do it then that's what I would do. After that I set about having second helpings of everything, all of the time. It wasn't a conscious decision but overnight I'd acquired a habit of over-eating to such an extent that unless I felt so full that I had to be horizontal, I hadn't had enough.

Food has always been a bit of an issue for me, but never so much that it's caused any kind of real eating disorder. Mum was good enough not to hand one of those down to any of us. She always maintained a healthy weight, never went on about it or counted calories, and she ate the same things all the time, had three meals a day and fried everything in lard.

OK, I'm not fat. I'm not skinny either. I'm fairly 'normal' I think – or normal for me, let's say. Genetically I'm quite lucky, I suppose, because I'm tall – 5'9" to be precise – and I weigh 9st 12lbs at the time of writing, but that changes, and I can be anywhere between that and 10st 4lbs without anyone really noticing. Height is very useful when disguising excess weight as there's more area to cover, but I am not a superhuman being with a jet-propelled metabolism that means I can eat all day and not get fat. Of course if I did, I would, so I don't, because I know it would make me unhappy. But let me tell you, I do eat as much as I want, which these days is as much as I need because thankfully, I've left my greedy days behind me.

And I'm sorry, but staying a healthy weight IS that simple. The reason people think it isn't is because the dieting industry complicates it all by feeding us all sorts of myths, miracles and secret formulas. Which is why I don't believe in diets or anything the industry tells me.

The business of dieting is worth tens of billions of pounds a year. Food companies, drug companies, private surgery clinics, publishing, magazines, advertising, miracle diets, slimming clubs: the list of people who make money out of the misery of weight gain is endless. And of course they don't want it to stop. There is so much money to be made in keeping people away from the simple and inexpensive truth of how not to be fat. How many diet books have you read or have you got? I've got one. It's not a diet book per se, just a little calorie bible that I bought in the early 1980s when I was trying to educate myself. It did but it also meant I wouldn't eat anything without consulting it. My theory is, the more you think about or obsess about something, the more of a problem it becomes. So, if all the women's magazines were to remove the words 'weight loss' and 'diet' from their covers, perhaps people wouldn't be constantly made to feel inadequate, insecure or, worse still, desperate. Buying into it all is like falling in love with your captor, it simply perpetuates the problem.

I think we all know this. But it doesn't stop us buying the book/DVD/exercise machine that never gets read/watched/used because we think it will just make all our wobbly bits go away.

Of course it won't. The only thing that works is accepting the fact that, if you don't use up the energy (calories) that you consume, it will make you fat and being fat will make you unhappy, which will probably make you eat more, which will make you even fatter. That horrible symptomatic cycle of behaviour is, I know, very hard to break.

How do I know this? Well, because it almost happened to me.

It wasn't just my childhood mission to keep clearing my plate that gave me problems; I'm sure I was always predisposed to weight gain. I was chubby compared to Kim and when you look at pictures of us together when we were little, Kim was long and lean, skinny even, whereas I had the fat cheeks, the little buckle (a buckle is a tummy that might be flabby or just sticky-outy but gets its name from the legendary entertainer Fatty Arbuckle, whose name says it all) and the porky little legs.

So the all-you-can-eat mentality from the mashed potato day was fine all the time my metabolism was in fast-forward child/teenager mode. The problem came at 16, when I started earning proper money and could afford as many cakes and biscuits as I wanted – all the stuff that had been seriously rationed all through my childhood. I really went for it. Fresh cream apple turnovers were my favourite and handily there was a Bowketts the Bakers right by the bus stop on the High Street in Maidstone. After finishing work at Snob, the boutique I worked at, I would pop in to Bowketts and buy not one, but two fresh cream apple turnovers and sometimes a chocolate éclair or vanilla slice to have as a starter. Then I would eat them all on the bus on the way home before having my tea. I considered this three thousand calorie feast a snack, nothing to be concerned about. And I didn't have to worry, not until I stopped being a developing teenager and became an adult. However, when my metabolism slowed down, inevitably I put on weight – loads of it. Funnily enough, it didn't bother me at first; I just bought bigger trousers.

It got worse when I started frequenting restaurants in Maidstone like Dixie's Diner and Trotters. I discovered that there was more to life than egg and chips, bone pie, beans or spaghetti-from-a-tin on toast, Birds Eye frozen beefburgers, fish fingers and rice pudding –

the cheap and cheerful regulation 1960s grub that I'd been brought up on. I tasted proper burgers with relishes, pizzas, lasagne, cheesecake and black forest gateau all for the first time and my taste buds were raging.

We'd go to Dixie's nearly every Saturday and have a 'Number 7' (quarter-pound burger in a bun with salad, chips and coleslaw) for lunch then hang around all day and eat another one for dinner. The burgers were good ones, proper meat, not cheap rubbish full of bollocks and brains – though they served those too. They were called 'Number 5s' and they were popular because they were only £1 with chips, but you didn't get any salad or coleslaw. They also served the 'Cab Burger' named after Mister Cab, the manager and that was a whopping 1lb! I only ate one of those once; I was greedy but not that greedy. The chips were hand cut on the premises, blanched and cooked to perfection. They were simply the best chips and there was no limit to the amount I could eat. Then I found out how good they were with mayonnaise. Aside from that there were the home-made pizzas, spaghetti bolognese, steaks, chocolate fudge cake, brownies and, oh my God, the cheesecake.

I think, actually, the cheesecake was the beginning of the end. I simply couldn't stop eating it. The black cherry one was my favourite. I remember one Christmas I bought a whole one and took it home. A whole one was approximately 20 restaurant-sized portions, so about 20,000 calories, probably more. I was having Christmas with Mum at her pub, but I hadn't taken the cheesecake up there to share with everyone because I wanted to eat it all by myself. I was tetchy all day and I couldn't wait to get back to my flat. When I did, still stuffed from all the turkey and sausage rolls, sweets, pies and God knows what else, I got into bed with a bottle of Liebfraumilch and the cheesecake and I ate the whole thing. Afterwards I felt disgusting – so disgusting, in fact, that I cried. That might have been partly due to the bottle of wine I'd washed it down with, but nevertheless, it was horrible. I almost wished, for a fleeting moment, that I could suddenly develop bulimia but being sick is anathema for me. The next day I woke up and something clicked. I was gross, getting really fat and, worst of all, I was guilty of one of the most foul deadly sins, pure gluttony. I have never eaten cheesecake since. The thought of it still repulses me.

I was clearly making up for lost time but my metabolism was grinding to a halt and in my brand new red Fiorucci jeans my legs looked like big red balloons. I was in danger of turning into Gwyneth Paltrow in *Shallow Hal*. I had hit my twenties but I hadn't yet made the link between eating loads of food and getting really fat.

It was worse because Mum had left to go and run the pub and left me on my own. I had no idea how to look after myself and lived off Kentucky Fried Chicken or fish and chips most of the time. I had never had to fend for myself before, my tea had always been on the table when I'd got home.

As a result I was tired and malnourished. Haydn and Esme (the bosses at Cluttons) took me to one side, like concerned parents, and asked if I was feeding myself properly; of course I wasn't, but I said yes. I didn't tell my mum because she would have made me move back in with her instantly. Also, she was the most unsympathetic mother when it came to illness because she swore it made us worse if she was (probably true). Even when Kim broke her coccyx she simply said, 'Have a bath, you'll be fine.' Anyway, Haydn and Esme persuaded me to go to the doctor's. He prescribed me vitamins, which I thought was outrageous. Here I was, dying of exhaustion and all he's giving me are a few vitamins! But bloody hell, they worked and within weeks, even though I was still doing three jobs, I was radiant and bright as a button. That set me on the path to health because it made me realise how important what you put into your body is. That was helpful, to say the least, but after that horrible episode I decided I needed to start doing some maintenance.

At around the same time I'd started working at Dixie's as a waitress and sort-of-dating Mister Cab, who, with his penchant for very thin girls, was dead set on giving me an eating disorder. He'd be openly flirtatious with skinny women and make comments about my huge (!) 28" waist. I tried not to take him too seriously but clearly something had to be done. However, there was no way I was going to stop eating all that lovely food so I took up exercise. Well Mister Cab, who just happened to be an ex-army fitness instructor, took it upon himself to give me and some of his other fat friends and employees some friendly exercise classes. In fact, what he did was take us to the local army barracks and put us through a virtual assault course. It was horrible; I nearly died. I think he genuinely liked watching us suffer so I ditched that idea and joined a gym.

Gyms, in the kind of 'health club' sense, didn't really exist in Maidstone in 1980. All you had were sports centres or YMCAs, boxing or specialised sports facilities where people went to exercise. The upmarket type of health club (targeted at people who didn't want to go to a public centre that reminded them of school) was a new thing. I'd read about one opening in the local paper. I think it was the first private gym in the whole of Kent and was called the Bob Prowse Health Club. In fact, it's still there; what's more, the owner, Bob – who is Dave Prowse's (Darth Vadar's) brother – is also still there, looking exactly the same as he did when I joined 30 years ago! I joined as soon as it opened and went every night I could after work, before I went off to do my other jobs.

I did get quite obsessed, possibly a little bit addicted, but it's easy when you can clearly see the results of your hard work. And it was hard work. My stomach was like a washboard, solid as a rock and as flat as a pancake. I loved going to the gym and would get really stressed if I had to miss a night. After Christmas I'd be in there the first day it was open, on the sit-up bench, reciting what I'd eaten over and over to motivate me into doing another 20. Mince pie, one, two, three, four . . . Cake, one, two, three, four . . . It was madness.

Another reason I loved it was because it brought another sort of pleasure during a certain, special exercise – and this was not an easy exercise, trust me. You had to lie down on a bench with your legs hanging off the end, then you lift your legs up to right angles with the rest of your body. Three lots of 20 was my quota, but I couldn't stop then, because after about 750 of them, whoosh! I wasn't quite sure what was happening but I knew I liked it. I think the best way to describe it would be to say that some girls like to go horse riding for the same reason, while some sit on washing machines. It was a familiar feeling but one that I'd never had solo before, even though

I'd reached the grand old age of 20. Anyway, I don't think anyone noticed because I didn't vocalise my enjoyment or anything, but as I got up I always looked around to see if anyone was looking before I did it all again. No wonder I had a concrete stomach! It was a welcome bit of pleasure, I thought, while doing something totally bloody tedious. After all, these were the days before iPods and TVs to amuse you while sweated your arse off.

In the end, I think I began to take exercising too seriously. I even posted off a photo entry to a local competition – 'Miss Southampton', or something like that – but it was one of those competitions where everyone won, so it wasn't a big deal. Bodybuilding wasn't my thing; the idea of bulking up and looking like an orange, shiny bloke with wiry hair and a tiny waist never appealed. I was into body conditioning which meant lots (hundreds) of repetitions of exercises with fairly light weights. This toned the muscle as opposed to tearing it, as heavy weights would. Do you know, even though I say it myself, I looked quite good; but of course I didn't capitalise on it or appreciate it then. You never do when you're young, do you? I don't even have any decent photos of myself looking like that. I also spent a lot of time on the sunbed so I was really brown (probably a bit too brown) and not an ounce of flesh moved when I walked or ran. I admit, I loved being like that – so much so that I started to get quite obsessed with food too.

I started buying slimming magazines and became overly interested in the calorific value of everything. Still, to this day, I know roughly the calorie content of everything and anything, although I don't think about it as much and I'm no longer doing mental calculations as I eat my dinner. Back then though I did start to bore myself with it, and while the book did teach me a bit about healthy eating, what I was doing wasn't really healthy because I was overdoing the gym work and eating next to nothing. I also kept a very detailed and meticulous food diary, writing down every single thing that passed my lips, even down to the number of lettuce leaves in my salad. Basically, I'd have nothing for breakfast, cottage cheese and salad with no dressing for lunch and more salad with a couple of beef or ham slices for my dinner. In between I'd drink very weak black coffee and if I went out I'd drink Diet Pepsi or slimline tonic water. My thighs became the barometer of my weight. I'd measure them every day and if they changed by even a millimetre I'd stay in the gym even longer.

I was all muscle and about 9st 5lbs, so if I hadn't have worked out I would have been about 9st 2lbs, which is a bit too light for a woman of my height. I must have been underweight because my periods stopped for about nine months. I finally snapped out of it after a bout of very serious flu where I couldn't get up, move my head or talk, let alone eat or drink for nearly two weeks. I lost another stone and when I put on my 'skinny' Gloria Vanderbilt jeans (which were always a bit snug) I looked a bit like a walking x-ray. It was quite frightening, so after that I started eating normally again.

I kept up the gym until I moved to London in 1982 where I couldn't afford to join one. After that my body returned to its normal wobbly self and I got bigger; not much bigger – about two stone heavier would have been the peak – which for my height still isn't that heavy and certainly not outside the so-called 'healthy BMI'. But being that weight just wasn't natural for me, it didn't look good and when I was, I'd always want to be smaller.

Despite my massive calorific knowledge I was still eating too much crap and in the late 1980s when I joined a gym again, I overcompensated. Did an hour on the stairclimber? Ah, that means I can eat a GIANT bowl of pasta with creamy carbonara sauce. I also still had a taste for cakes then and would down a whole pack of Mr Kipling Bakewell Slices in one sitting. Doughnuts? Gimme gimme gimme! I drank pints too, lots and lots of pints of lager on account of my Canadian lodger and his mates who treated my flat like a hostel, filling it with cases and cases of Oranjeboom cans.

So I bought another book called *Fit For Life . . . Looking Good and Feeling Great*.

Looking at it now, it's very dated and obvious. However, at the time it was a bible and when cost has prevailed over nutrition for a good chunk of your life, basic nutrition needs to be learnt. That book is still on my shelf; it's like an aide mémoire to me but, moreover, it's also a reminder of how things might have been.

I'm relatively happy with myself now, even at this age. Of course I can see things deteriorating, but it's not bothering me that much yet. I would love not to have bingo wings and I have a pair of 2.5kg dumbbells sitting on the kitchen top that I will one day pick up while making my morning coffee as planned, but for now they just sit there screaming silently at my flabby biceps. I would like to have my young skin, arms and un-saggy arse and tits back, but it's not going to happen unless I spend Madonna-style amounts of time in the gym and stay out of the sun – neither of which I'm prepared to do – so I'll stick to my little routines and hope for the best.

Looking back, I think I benefited long term from my mad exercise phase. My muscles were probably still developing, and shaping and toning them then probably didn't do me any harm. People still think I work out all the time but I don't. I'm a member of a gym that I go to regularly but I only use the sauna and the showers. The real reason I go there is because it's just over a mile from where I live and I walk there and back. That's my workout and it seems to do the trick. For now, anyway; I'm fifty after all and we all know what that means. My theory is that you don't really need to do much but you do need to do something and also be realistic about what you eat.

No one is born fat. Some people are naturally heavier, bigger, but not fat. Fat is what we make ourselves and if you don't want to be fat then you have a choice not to be.

Here's a typical schedule of what I eat and how I exercise:

Breakfast: Two pints of warm fresh orange juice/water mixed (three parts water, one part orange juice), half an apple (save the other half for tomorrow), one prune Activia yoghurt (I don't eat the prune bit, it's too sweet but the yoghurt is creamier and less sour than the natural ones), two pieces of dried fruit, black coffee.

Lunch: Either a jacket potato with cottage cheese, no butter, tomato ketchup and black pepper, or a ham sandwich, or soup with extra vegetables (steam fresh), and toast and butter if there's any bread.

Dinner: Uncle Ben's two minute brown rice, steamed vegetables, fresh chillis and chilli oil, chicken breast.
Snacks: Babybel Light cheese, wasabi peas, Twiglets.

That's presuming I'm not hungover, but if I am:

Breakfast: Entire contents of fridge, leftover anything from last night, bacon or sausage sandwiches, toast and peanut butter, fried eggs.
Lunch: Crisps, chocolate and chips.
Dinner: Pizza Express pizza with hot pepperoni and a hair-of-the-dog glass of chianti.

If I go out to dinner:
Everything and anything but never puddings; cheese, but no biscuits.

Tips:

- Eat from a small plate and with small cutlery. It's called the in-flight illusion. You see, when you eat on an aeroplane, it looks like a lot of food because it's crammed into a very small space (just like everything else on the jet). Then because you use small knives, forks and spoons it takes ages to eat so again you think it's a lot and your brain tricks your blown-up, bloated tummy into thinking it's had enough.
- Never eat frozen, processed meals.
- Get to like chilli. It's good for the metabolism and it makes even the dullest, blandest food tasty. Better than salt any day.
- Instant mashed potato is not as bad as you think.
- Pot noodles are; they're worse.
- Make vegetable soup with bought stock or Marigold bouillon and frozen vegetables. Eat loads of it; it'll fill you right up and it's good for you, with hardly any calories.
- Invest in a hand blender, it will change your life.
- Shut the bloody fridge and go for a walk instead.
- Don't eat desserts. Yes, I know it's easier said than done but

just don't eat them and then you won't hate yourself for being a greedy arse.

- Eat proper butter. Low-fat spreads are a false economy because you just use more and what's the point of that when they taste like shit and are made from recycled sump oil?
- Stop buying exercise DVDs and diet books; they will only make you fat.
- Take a good look in the mirror and think really, really hard about how much you don't want to be fat and how easy it would be not to be.

And if all that fails then stalk Gillian McKeith and get her to sort you out.

CHAPTER 9

The First Time I: Went to London to marry Simon le Bon

(The Back to London Chapter)

In 1982, after 18 years away – having been moved to Kent at the tender age of four – the bright lights of London were beckoning me to come home. It was time. I'd served my sentence in Maidstone and I'd been working in the same office for nearly five years which, if I'd stayed another, would probably have meant that I'd have stayed there forever with no hope of escape. Helen was already in London working at *Cosmopolitan* magazine (although she was still living in Maidstone) and I was quite envious of her exciting, glamorous life. Every night when I got home from work at 5.15pm and I was sat in my council flat, with my car parked outside, I'd phone her up. 'What can you see?' She'd verbally paint a picture of her office and the view of Victoria outside the window beyond because, excitingly, she'd still be at work, even though she had a long train journey home. I felt so trapped, so staid, so set in my ways, so bored. I had no boyfriend – well, I did, but he was pissing me right off – and I'd been out with all the blokes I was interested in, worked in all the clubs, bars, pubs and restaurants I wanted to work in, spent enough time in the gym and, moreover, my brother was living at home with me in the flat and his feet stunk so bad I had to get out.

I'd always dreamed of going back to my roots. I've no memory at all of living there the first time but although it's often assumed that I'm from Maidstone because I was brought up there, I was actually born in London. St Mary's Wing, Whittington Hospital, N19.

Every time I went there, whether it was with my dad to visit my nan in the East End or my auntie in Chelsea, or a school trip to the Natural History Museum, I was always in awe of London. Isn't it strange how four children can be brought up in exactly the same house, in exactly the same way, and yet turn out so differently? I don't think it ever occurred to Kim or Tracy that they might not live in Maidstone for the rest of their lives, that they might not marry the boy up the road and have kids. To them, it just seemed like the most natural and normal thing in the world to do. To Mark and I though, it was anathema. A few years after I upped sticks, Mark, by then a qualified civil engineer, got a job constructing the new runway in the Falkland Islands after the war and scarpered off there for a few years; much to my mum's distress, I might add.

Helen and I plotted and planned my big move for weeks on the phone because if I moved up there then she could too, as we could share a flat. Only problem was I didn't have a job yet and I had no idea how to get one, as every job I'd ever had I'd got because of who I knew. Snob – Helen. Boots – Kim. Cluttons – Mum. Now it was up to me, but I was scared.

Helen came up trumps again. She told me that her boss's wife, June, had a vacancy in an office place she was managing in the Victoria area and I should give her a call. I remember when Helen told me this, it was like, *oh no, this is real, I'm actually going to do it*, but I couldn't, I was too nervous. It was such a big step. After a lot of faffing, I drew on my motto that I invented for myself when the junior school bullies weren't going to let me get second helpings of school dinners and I said to myself over and over, 'There are some things in life you just have to face,' and about an hour later I picked up the phone. I don't know what I was worrying about. June was lovely; she seemed very pleased to hear from me and invited me in for an interview. *Oh my God*.

On the day of the interview I dressed in a typical 1980s sand-coloured, wool, pinstripe suit with big old shoulder pads. I met with June and the guy behind the project, Paul de Savary. Paul was part of the de Savary brothers dynasty – Peter is the one you've probably heard of, the very rich landowner who usually ends up in the paper because he claims he's leaving none of his fortune to his kids. Anyway, Paul's sitting there with June and they're telling me what the business is and although I look like I'm listening, it's going right over my head. All they really want to know is: Can I type? Yes. Can I operate a switchboard? No, but I say yes. Paul says something about my accent but that can apparently be 'sorted out' and so off I go. Already feeling like a local, I went off to the Chicago Rib Shack to meet Rupert my on-off boyfriend for dinner. He was living in Vauxhall at the time and that night I stayed with him and got the train home early the next morning. I already felt like I didn't want to leave; this was my town now and I wanted to rule it. Well, not rule it, but paint it a little bit red.

Thankfully I got the job, so I handed in my notice at Cluttons and moved into a flat in Highgate on 18 September 1982. It was about half a mile away from where I was born. Talk about going back to where you came from. I didn't really feel an affinity with it though, just wild, ecstatic excitement mixed with mild trepidation at what was in store.

Especially as I was convinced that if I moved up to London I would meet Simon le Bon and marry him. Duran Duran had just come on the scene and I was wildly in love with him; he was perfect for me. So I was delighted when I found out one of the girls I'd be working with, Cathy, was from Birmingham and that she had met Simon. She even said she thought he would like me . . . of course he hadn't yet spotted Yasmin on the cover of *Elle* so there was still a chance, I convinced myself, in a slightly delusional way.

Rupert helped me move. We hired a van and took my bed and a couple of bits from the flat, and my clothes. It was sweet of him really; he helped me a lot with the move up to London. He was very handsome was Rupert, almost too good-looking, and very, very posh. I first met him when he was working behind a bar in Maidstone. I couldn't believe it when he started making it very obvious that he thought I was a bit of alright, coming over all Leslie Phillips with his twinkly eyes and 'Hellllloooo's. After our first date he came back to my flat and stayed the night. The sex was pretty unremarkable, which wasn't surprising – I'd always assumed that really good-looking blokes never really had to try too hard so weren't ever really that outstanding in the sack. Anyway, in the morning we went out for breakfast (two boiled eggs) before I took him home. My car at that time was a Mark II Ford Capri, OVE 581M (what is it with me and number plates?) and when I took him home it emerged he lived somewhere right out in the sticks. When he asked me to turn left down this tiny little turning I said, 'Blimey, this is a funny little road'.

He replied, 'Er, it's my driveway.'

I knew then it wasn't really going anywhere. I realised just how different we were when he wouldn't introduce me to his parents (another one), and when we were utilising his giant house one weekend when they were supposedly away, he was totally on edge in case they came back. Somehow, I don't think he'd have been so worried if it had been Henrietta from down the road that was staying the weekend, but it wasn't – it was his little bit o' rough, common Carol from the council estate. Anyway, he dumped me, which was no big deal. We could never have been serious because although he was really nice, he was a bit too vain, just a tad too full of himself in those days. His mates were always taking the piss out of him for it. I bore absolutely no grudge against him and we stayed friends but one Valentine's Day I decided to play a little trick on him. I bought about 30 Valentine's cards, got various people around the office to write soppy messages in them, then sent them round to our regional offices for them to post them back to him both at his home address and at his work. Consequently, he was the recipient of 30 Valentines cards that year, much to the absolute and total astonishment of his mates. It was a costly exercise but, bloody hell, was it worth it. I bumped into him a few years ago and took great pleasure in telling him that it was me and he didn't really have 30 admirers scattered all over the UK. He so did not want to believe it. With hindsight it was a pretty elaborate trick to play on someone, but at the time I thought it was such a good idea and would really amuse everyone, which it did. After I told him though, it felt a bit cruel because he was a little bit crestfallen.

Anyway, my new flat in Highgate had two bedrooms, but I was sharing it with Helen and a girl called Debbie so they had the bedrooms and I had the living room. The only communal rooms were the bathroom and kitchen; not very sociable, but at least it meant we could afford to pay the rent.

After we'd finished unloading and putting my bed together Rupert took me out for a drink. We went to The Holly Bush in Hampstead, a really old historic pub that's a bit like a warren, with loads of rooms, stairs and alcoves. As thrilled as I was to be going out to a pub in London, when I got there I just wanted to leave because I felt so awkward and out of place. Everyone was dressed very casually in jeans whereas I had donned my best 1980s fancy dress. I wore my plum leather trousers, white court shoes (WHITE COURT SHOES!) and a white batwing top with a really big off-the-shoulder thing going on. It sounds hideous now, and I suppose it was, but it was standard 1980s clubbing gear and not really suitable for a quick drink in the local. It was my first London lesson after coming from a provincial market town where everyone always dressed up to go out whatever night it was and wherever they were going. I made a mental note to dress down to go to the pub in future.

My job was at a place called Executrade. Just typing that word evokes such fond, funny memories. It was in the business of temporary office accommodation and office services and I was the new receptionist. I had to work a Plessey switchboard, which was a problem because (despite what I'd said at the interview) I didn't have a clue how to start. There were also newfangled IBM word processors running WordStar and WordPerfect all over the place too. Again, not a clue. However, I wasn't daft and picked it all up quite quickly. At least I could type; I didn't lie about that at least. I was paid £6,500 a year, which I thought was heaps, and – considering how much prices have gone up and wages haven't – I suppose it was. I had to wear a uniform. All the front desk and office staff had to. It was a replica of the BA kit at the time, a navy-blue pinstripe skirt suit with a waistcoat and white shirt which had to be fitted and it was actually made by BA. I had to go all the way to Hatton Cross near Heathrow for a fitting, but until that was done I had to wear someone's cast-offs which were often way too big or way too small for me. I felt like a right chump, especially when I was selected as the house model and I had to pose for pictures for the promotional brochure and an ad for Telex services in *The Sunday Times*.

NOW EVERYBODY CAN BE ON TELEX IN THEIR HOME OR OFFICE.

From only £29-50 per month!

Datalex is the telex you need — but thought you couldn't afford.

It's the telex system that gives you 24 hour control over your telex traffic — at a fraction of the traditional cost.

Join the telex revolution!

Who wins? Datalex users.

Who loses? The conventional telex user sending less than 100 telexes a month, and the company who still thinks it can't afford telex.

Join the telex revolution! T21/10

Please send me details of Datalex

Name: ....

Address: ....

.... Tel: ....

Datalex
Asphalte House, Palace Street,
London SW1E 5HS
Telephone: 01-828 7981
Telex: 913001

DATALEX

Executrade operated like a hotel but with offices instead of rooms. It was a funny old business and all sorts of people would come and go, paying by the hour, no strings, no questions asked, no commitment. Mailing addresses, typists at your disposal, send your telexes. In those days some people were so dodgy June used to demand cash deposits.

The dodgy types never fooled me. There was one old guy who was there way too long and always had an excuse for not paying the bills. It was just him but he had a variety of young assistants come and go. He was always dropping names of various minor celebrities he'd met who he'd claim were his friends, most of them dead. In an effort to try to fool everyone he'd often phone down to reception and say, 'Yes, it's Mr Conor Tist here, Suite 7b. Could you do something for me?'

To which I would always reply in a bored and irritated manner, 'Yes, what?'

Unfazed, he'd go on: 'Yes, could you tell me what seventeen million multiplied by thirty-nine thousand is?'

I'd roll my eyes and say, 'Sorry, but we don't have a calculator with enough numbers on to do that for you,' and put the phone down. Then he would appear in the reception in person and insist that everyone run around trying to do his dumb calculation for him. Of course it meant nothing, it was just his pathetic way of trying to make out he was doing millions of pounds worth of business. Everyone else humoured him but I couldn't; I thought he was an idiot and he knew I'd rumbled his little ruse. Anyway, I told everyone my theory that he was a con man but they didn't listen and carried on believing he was a very wealthy man and a valuable customer who was good for the business. Needless to say, one morning we turned up and his office had been cleaned out, including some of the furniture owned by Executrade. They should have listened to me.

Talking of frauds . . . The question of my accent (which Paul had mentioned in my initial interview) came up again a few weeks after I'd started there. I didn't think it was that bad, but apparently it wasn't even London, Cockney or plain old East End. It was Kentish. Estuary, I think they call it. In any case, I was deemed 'not acceptable' for dealing with clients face-to-face from a front desk so I was sent for elocution lessons. I had to go and see an old man in Maida Vale in his very big, very old house that was full of books and when you walked on the rugs the dust flew up in your face. In the teaching room there was nothing but a lectern in the middle of the room, one chair and a blackboard.

He made me read poetry by Tennyson and taught me how to prrrrrronounce my vooooowwwwels in such an exaggerated way I would often, rather rudely, collapse in a fit of exaggerated breathless laughter. He taught me how to PRRRRRRRO-JECT MY VOICCCE so people at the back of the room could hear me. What room? I was a receptionist not an evangelist. I began to sound like Hyacinth Bucket. It seemed so fraudulent, this common Kent girl trying to sound posh. After a few weeks, though, I really started getting into it and because it was 1983 and I was living in Chelsea I started to model myself on the ultimate Sloane Ranger herself, Princess Diana, and started wearing pie-crust collar or bow-tie blouses which, had I not been 22, would have made me look more like the Queen Mother. By the time he'd finished with me I was actually speaking like the Queen, saying things like, 'One doesn't feel like eating lunch today.' What a twat I must have sounded like. No one said anything though and after a few months it all wore off, although I do still slip into it now and again when I'm on the phone, apparently.

I'm not sure where it came from but I had a spurt of ambition while working at Executrade and before long I was running the show. After June left, a girl called Gill was in charge and when she left I took over. I was in my element because I wasn't on the front desk anymore and so didn't have to wear the BA strip. I invested in a black trouser suit which I wore almost every day. I had to hire and fire people too, which was a massive responsibility; I didn't enjoy firing people, but then you'd have to be pretty bloody sadistic to enjoy doing that. My age did cause a problem with some of the service staff and a couple of the older ones left because they didn't want to be bossed around by a 23-year-old cocky little upstart.

I met some real characters while working there. Malcolm was a godsend. He was a Chinese guy who seemed to know everyone. He became a good friend and, as he owned property all over the city, when our tenancy in Highgate came to an end he stepped in and let me stay in his flat in the King's Road. It was so cool living in Argyll Mansions, which was right opposite the old fire station (now Sir Terence Conran's Bluebird restaurant emporium). I was so lucky. I had the place all to myself. I never paid him rent, although I did try many times. I didn't even have to sleep with him but I'm sure everyone thought I did. One of the other great things Malcolm did for me was to introduce me to proper Chinese food. He would take me to all the best restaurants in Chinatown, where he knew everyone, and we'd have dim sum until it was coming out of our ears. I still love it to this day and go nearly every Sunday to a little place near where I live in Camden.

Then there was another Paul. He was possibly the funniest man I'd ever met. I'm even smiling as I write that. He rented an office at Executrade for a while. He used to have this car, I think it was a Porsche, and it had a small loudspeaker tannoy thing fitted to the bonnet, which was connected to a microphone inside the car. That meant that if he stopped at a crossing, he could (and would) verbally abuse the pedestrians crossing the road. He'd say something like, 'Oi, you. You with the red coat and the black boots. Hurry up will ya, can't you walk a bit faster?' People would be totally confused as to where the voice was coming from, while we were all squeezed into the car literally rocking with mirth. He would have made a brilliant producer of *Candid Camera*. One day he turned up at the office with a remote-control car, which he placed in the road outside the office on Palace Street. It was like it was parked up. Then, from high up in the building, he'd operate it like it was a real car, holding up traffic with it, doing wheelies in the road, and if anyone got out of their car to try and pick it up he'd make it whizz off or use a real tannoy from the top of the building to say, 'Leave the car alone. Don't touch the car.' People's faces were so funny as they tried to work out where it was coming from. God knows how he ever made any money; he was always pissing about having a laugh. He was so funny that one night when everyone came back to mine for a bit of a party, I allowed him to drag me into my bedroom and have sex with me while everyone was just the other side of the door partying. It was really sexy and very fast and furious and I really wanted to do it again but it never happened and I wasn't going to chase after him.

Victor was funny too, but for all the wrong reasons. He was a friend of another of the characters that worked at Executrade, Nigel. Victor had the most unbelievable apartment right opposite the office in a big, typical 1970s block. It was like walking onto the set of *Austin Powers*, with its beige 6-inch thick shag pile carpet, circular bed, hanging Perspex chairs and brown velvet sofa and chaise longue. It matched him perfectly. He looked a bit like Jason King from *Department S* but with long hair as opposed to big. He always wore flares and a checked jacket that looked too small and had patch pockets and rounded lapels. He wore shiny beige boots, walked with a bit of a cool stoop and usually had a fag on the go. There were a lot of gatherings round Victor's and occasionally they'd descend into sex parties where people would take their clothes off and sometimes go off into the bedrooms and have it off. It seemed like a perfectly normal thing to do at the time, like going for tea.

When we weren't at Victor's or my flat, the local drinking hole was Carriages Wine Bar. The 'wine bar' was one of the defining characteristics of the 1980s. They sprung up everywhere and suddenly people stopped going to pubs and went to wine bars instead. Carriages was so called because it was right opposite the Royal Mews on Buckingham Palace Road where all the horses were and the royal carriages were stored. It was a small bar with a glass front, little wooden tables and a long bar with stools the length of it. Graeme, another character who became a friend, was its most regular customer and he took great pleasure in introducing me to the joys of fine wine and teaching me all about it. He did know his stuff and was a bit of an expert and we'd sit there for hours and hours 'tasting' different wines and always going home somewhat paralytic having had no dinner but for a giant bowl of smelly peanuts. My favourite was Alsatian Pinot Noir and if I ever see it today I always buy it because it's so evocative of that time . . . very fond memories.

After two very exciting years in London working for Executrade I left to go and marry a Greek boy I'd had a holiday romance with three years earlier.

CHAPTER 10

The First Time I: Nearly ended up dressed in black cleaning the step

(The Greek Chapter)

Everyone should have at least one holiday romance in their life. My first one had some completely unpronouncable Greek name, so I'm just going to call him Bob. I met him on my first holiday to Greece. I was 21 and on my first all-girl foreign holiday to Corfu with my friend Helen.

Booking a holiday before the internet was such a palaver. Having to go to a travel agent's, look in the window at probably non-existent cheap holidays, go inside, wait to be served by a nonchalant assistant who would invariably come up with something completely unsuitable because the one you picked in the window isn't available that week, was all par for the course. But we'd never been abroad together before so we wouldn't have minded if it had taken all day. We'd spotted a card in the window: £99 for fourteen nights in Corfu. That can't be right, we thought. It was. So we booked it. The total price was £112 with tax. We were so excited and it was so cheap, or at least we thought so. Actually, £99 in 1981 was quite a lot considering I was taking home £249 a month for my main job, especially as you can still get deals like that now and this was nearly 30 years ago.

Anyway, we packed our bags, went off to Gatwick and headed for Greece. When we got there we went in search of the rep to take us to the accommodation. On the booking form, it said the name of a hotel. But what we didn't know (and more importantly, what the travel agent didn't tell us) was that it was just a ruse and sorry, but there was no hotel. This was because, in those days, the airlines weren't allowed to sell flights without accommodation because the Greek authorities didn't want people sleeping on the beach – you had to have somewhere to stay. So agents would put a spurious name of a hotel on the booking form so that you and they could get away with it. Suddenly it didn't seem like so much of a bargain. We were a bit scared because here we were, in a strange country, at the airport, with no one to look after us and no idea what to do. Embarrassed, we trundled off down the road on foot without a clue as to where we were going. It was blisteringly hot and, since it was in the days before anyone had bothered to invent the wheelie case, people had to actually carry their suitcases. I had a giant-sized beige PVC case that I could hardly lift, yet alone carry, but I think the need to get away from a slightly humiliating situation caused by our own naiveté and a dumb travel agent gave me the inner strength to march off with it in hand. After walking for about 20 minutes we happened upon a hotel. We could still see the airport but noise didn't even come into it, we needed somewhere to stay. We walked in gingerly and asked if they had a room; luckily they did so we checked in for the duration. It was a cost we hadn't budgeted for that almost wiped us out so we had to be careful with our money from then on.

It turned out we weren't that far from Corfu Town; or so we thought. We got directions from the reception and information about buses and stuff. God, we were so clever! As we walked into town that night, stopping on the way to overfeed our greedy faces with all this new and exciting food, we realised we weren't so clever after all, because it was much further than we thought and what we thought was the main town wasn't, it was a little place outside called Garitsa. No wonder we were both looking at each other thinking, *is this it?* The restaurant wasn't shit though. I'll never forget that little place; it was a typical Greek taverna with a few tables and chairs outside and no menu. To order food you had to go into the kitchen and have a look at what was cooking. We couldn't believe it. My diary reveals that the first night there I had macaroni pie, green beans in tomato sauce, a kind of vegetable stew (like ratatouille) in loads of olive oil and greasy Greek chips. I couldn't get enough of it. And as money was tight we ate there every night, even when we found our way into town and all the nightclubs.

The second day we travelled to a beach away from the town. We walked all the way into the proper town and caught the bus. But it was worth it because on our second time there we were approached by some disco touts.

31 May 1981
Got chatted up on beach by Bob, he told us to go to Tropicana Disco. He said I was very white but he liked me. Got chatted up again on way home by goons. Went to Tropicana in evening.

That night we went to the Tropicana Disco and danced our socks off. There were so many boys there – too much choice. Bob turned up and made a beeline for me and at the end of the night. Helen went off on a scooter with some bloke and I went off with Bob in a car to a strange café in a square somewhere that turned out not to be open. Somehow we both got home safely in the early hours but looking back I can't believe we did that.

That first night I refused to kiss him, so on the second night we went to the Tropicana again but he went off with someone else.

1 June 1981
Tropicana. Went home. Bob went off with a dog and caught VD. What a wally.

Wally? What kind of language was that? It's not even really an insult!

Here was a bloke who'd gone off with a 'dog' and probably caught some horrible disease and all I was calling him was a wally?

2 June 1981
Tropicana. Stayed with Bob.

Who's the wally now?

The language in my diaries is such a sign of the times. Wally? Goons? VD?

Bob lived in town in a very, very small apartment that he shared with Marcel, a very, very small Belgian DJ who repeatedly introduced himself as, 'Marcel, the best DJ in the world'. In fact he was the DJ at the Tropicana Disco and that was about it, but we humoured him. The others didn't. There were a group of about six of them, all different nationalities who'd argue for hours over who was the 'best DJ in the world' but somehow they never knew any of their names. The arguments always went like this.

Marcel: I am the best DJ in the world.

Bob: No, the best DJ in the world is Greek.

José: No, he is Spanish.

Gino: You are all wrong! He is Italian!

And so on. Helen and I would be in fits.

It was basically a one-room flat and Marcel slept under the window in front of the kitchen on a wooden camp bed that had a sheet for a mattress and a plastic carrier bag for a pillow while Bob's bed was in the main space on the other side. There were no curtains so whatever we did in there was probably viewed by most of the residents in the buildings opposite. No one seemed to care.

On the third Tropicana night I stayed at Bob's and we had sex (with a condom, just in case). He was a really horrible kisser. Janice Dickinson once described kissing Mick Jagger as 'like making out with a seabass'. Well, it was like that. In fact, Bob was a bit like an animal; his face was kind of contorted when he was doing it. It put me right off. I don't know what sort of signals I was giving off but at one point he disappeared to the kitchen area and when I turned around I saw him carving a giant cucumber to the shape of a penis, all the time looking at me with his contorted face as if to say, 'I bet you can't wait for this!' I wasn't alarmed but I did indeed discover that the cucumber was definitely not meant for a salad. Not that I entertained it; good God no. I couldn't have anyway because I was laughing hysterically, which I think must have hurt Bob's macho Greek pride since he took hideous offence and disappeared into the night leaving me in his apartment.

When I got up the next morning Bob was nowhere to be seen and I had absolutely no idea where I was. Worse still, I only had my disco clothes with me.

Somehow I found my way back through the little winding streets to the hotel and Helen and I swapped adventures. Apparently she'd been introduced to a guy who called himself 'the biggest man in Corfu'. The mind boggles doesn't it? Anyway, we carried on going to the Tropicana every night until the end of the holiday while spending days on the beach with Bob (who eventually stopped sulking) and Marcel.

On the last night of the holiday, having had enough, Helen stayed in at the hotel and I went out for a final time with Bob. He was getting very clingy and upset but I'm not sure I completely believed he was. Then when it was time to say goodbye he had tears in his eyes and begged me not to go. When I said I had to, he begged me to come back as soon as possible. I thought it was a bit over the top and to shut him up I said I would but then he didn't believe me so I gave him a gold signet ring that I wore – no idea where it came from but if it was one of my other exes and you're reading this, sorry! – to try and convince him I would. It didn't have any particular special meaning so I wasn't really bothered if I ever saw him again. I also gave him my phone number and address. Then, believe it or not, for the following three years we kept in touch by letter and through mutual acquaintances who worked out there. I did speak to him occasionally but the conversations were quite stilted and we'd always get cut off. All he would ever say was, 'Come back to Corfu, we will be together.' I'd say yeah, hang up and then it would happen all over again a couple of months later.

One letter was particularly sweet and it did actually make me really want to see him again. Especially as he said he'd pay for my ticket.

So, in the summer of 1984, three years after I met Bob, I went back to Corfu. He was no longer working at the Tropicana and was living back on the mainland, where he was from. I went with some friends who were planning on staying out there for three months. I only went for two weeks and on the ninth day I was there I went over on the ferry from Corfu Town to see Bob and stayed for three days in a house. I asked him whose house it was and he told me it was his. It was somewhere to stay, so I didn't question it.

For those few days I had a great time. We went to bars and restaurants, sat out in the square, went out on a speedboat waterskiing around some of the most beautiful bays I'd ever seen – I got really good at it, even if I say so myself. I was feeling that I could get used to the life there. Bob took me out in his car; he even let me drive it around the coastline, which was, I have to say, pretty stunning. He told me he was a footballer, that he spent his summers in Corfu and in the winter he travelled the world playing football and visiting his family who lived in various exotic locations. I swallowed it all, believed every word, and when I left I promised him once again that I'd be back to see him again.

But this time he wanted me to go back to marry him. Mmmmmm, now there was a proposition. I wasn't in love with him or anything, I didn't even like kissing him. The sex was OK, as long as I didn't look at his face. I was surprised at myself but I was thinking about it.

I went back to work; I was still working at Executrade but by now I was the boss, running the show. I canvassed everyone from staff to clients to friends and family. Most people said 'go for it' but there were a few doubters who thought I'd gone completely mad and I probably had, because even after much discussion and consternation from work colleagues and family, I did it. I packed in my job, bought a ticket and moved all my stuff down to Mum's to store. I wrote that in a letter to a friend at the time. Notice I didn't say 'ready to ship over to Greece', like I knew it would only be temporary.

I set the date to leave for 29 August but I told Bob I was coming a week later than that. My friends who'd gone out there for three months were around until the middle of September so I planned to spend a week with them before I went off to be a Greek wife.

They were staying in Kavos on the southern tip of the island and after I'd had my hen-style week of fun with the girls, Bob came over from the mainland in a speedboat to pick me up to take me to my destiny. I didn't really know what I was doing but I thought it would be an adventure so I went along with it. I even ran up the jetty in slow motion with my arms outstretched, dropping all my stuff like they do in the movies. I didn't even think about what might happen. I didn't consider the possibility of being a Greek wife and that within months I'd be swathed in black and cleaning the step while he sat out in the square with all the men drinking hideously strong cups of Greek coffee and smoking rotten fags all day. I'd like to say I was just being a carefree youngster, and to a degree I was, but I was also pretty deluded. My mum thought I'd gone stark raving bonkers (again) but still she didn't try and stop me – she just said, 'Oh well, if you don't like it you can always come home.' Which was true; it wasn't like I was fleeing to the moon or anything.

I said my emotional goodbyes to all my friends who I'm sure couldn't believe he'd turned up. After they'd met him, they just sat on the beach while I went off to my new life with my little bag and my future husband.

We made it back there in the little speedboat, but only just. You could see the land but it took ages to reach because the sea was so rough and there were four of us in the boat bouncing all over the place. Everything, including me and my bag, was soaked. Writing that now I'm thinking, *why wasn't I scared?* Being young and having no fear was such fun – I didn't really appreciate it.

As soon as we got there we went straight to his house. Funny thing was, his mum was suddenly living there. Or she was back from her holiday, more like. I didn't think it looked like a footballer's house the first time I went there, even if it was in Greece. He introduced me to his mother and we had one of those nodding conversations that you have when there isn't a mutual language, where you just smile at each other and laugh. She made me a revolting cup of coffee and sat me down inside on a kind of mattress bed thing in a cave-like room I hadn't seen before. At this point Bob disappeared (again) and left me with her. I kept looking round, thinking *where's he gone?* He didn't even say he was going off! He was gone for ages and there wasn't even a telly I could put on or a magazine I could read; nothing to do but just sit there. All the time his mother was outside, cleaning the step, while I was confined to the cave. I wondered if this was some kind of weird engagement ritual. Eventually my fiancé came back and told me he'd had to book a hotel as we couldn't stay with his mother until we were married, it wasn't allowed. Oh great, it was his mum's house so he didn't even have his own place. He's a footballer and he doesn't have his own house? We're going to LIVE in a hotel? This time I questioned it and my incredulity led him to tell me his house was being built and we got in the car and drove up to a remote place in the hills where he pointed to a half-built house. This wasn't an unusual sight in Greece then; apparently there were advantages to not finishing houses because if you did, then you had to pay tax on them. I was beginning to smell a great, big, giant rat but still I went along with everything.

After driving around we went for dinner in a remote fish restaurant. What followed was just too awful for words, but I'll do my best. I ate baby squid. They were delicious, loaded with garlic and olive oil, but he was eating them too so I didn't think he'd mind a bit of garlic breath. However, although they tasted alright, one of mine was obviously rotten because within about forty-five minutes of eating it I had the most diabolical shits I've ever experienced. I told Bob about this but I don't think he quite understood. I must have been in the restaurant toilet for about 20 minutes. We had to get back to the hotel. He didn't seem concerned at all that all the way back I was in agony and at one point made him stop the car while I rushed into the bushes.

When we got to the hotel the first thing I thought was: *he's left the 's' out of 'hotel'*. It was like a youth hostel and, once again, I felt like I was in a movie. There was an old guy behind the counter, motionless, staring down at a paper, obligatory coffee and super-strong stinking fag on the go. He was so shrouded in smoke you could hardly see him. There should have been a bulb, with a moth flying round it, swinging in the wind above his head but there wasn't; instead the whole place was flooded with vile fluorescent light. I didn't care, I just needed the toilet.

The room was awful. It was the height of summer and there was no air-conditioning, just a fan in the middle of the room. The windows were all open so the air was like mosquito soup and the toilet was right behind the bed with a curtain for a door. I know we were getting married but I really didn't know him well enough to have him listen to me expelling water from my bum with great force and farting all night. Nightmare. Especially when the toilet wouldn't flush properly even though I was abiding by the Greek rule of putting all the paper in the bin and not down the loo. The bin was soon full and it wasn't a nice smell, to say the least. I was on and off the pot until about 3am and when I finally felt like I'd exorcised the rotten squid completely I tried to get to sleep. I was miserable with dehydration and mozzie bites, so what did he do? He started trying to have sex with me! With the face! I couldn't believe it. I was dying, for Christ's sake; he had no chance. He wasn't happy (not a very good sign at all) so once again he got the hump and pissed off into the night. I had no idea where to and I cared less.

I lay there for a bit, exhausted. The mozzies were driving me mad sssssing past my ears, biting every spare bit of flesh. There was no bottled water and I was dehydrating fast. It was hot, I was sweating from the poisonous fish, and just to cap it all, where the squid had been cooked in so much garlic it felt like someone had planted a bulb of it in my mouth but wrapped it in cotton wool first. I felt completely and utterly wretched.

At that point I looked around and a little light went on in my head. It took a while, I know, but at least the bulb hadn't gone – I just needed to put a shilling in the meter. Finding strength I got dressed, gathered up my things and legged it, ran away as fast as I could, without looking back, hoping and praying that Bob wouldn't be driving past me on his way back to the hotel. I knew the port wasn't that far, and I had a rough idea that the first ferry back to Corfu was at about 5am. So I ran and ran and ran. Like Forrest Gump.

I got on the ferry and headed back to my friends, sleeping on the deck all the way back to Corfu.

A couple of hours later I was back in Corfu Town; all I needed to do was get the bus back down to Kavos. Luckily I knew the place well so it wasn't a problem.

They were already on the beach when I got back and as I strolled up towards them I expected them to be at least a bit shocked that I was back, but they just laughed. They all knew I'd be back, they just didn't expect it to be the next day – but then neither did I. Luckily I had a return ticket (you couldn't buy singles on charter flights then) so I had another week with the girls, most of which I spent dodging and hiding from Bob who kept coming over to look for me. The rest of the time I spent with a young, blond boy from Kent called Steve. Well, I was on the rebound, wasn't I?

Needless to say when I got back to the UK the phone was taken off the hook. No one was surprised. Executrade were so convinced it wouldn't last they hadn't even filled my job, so I went back to work there just as though I'd been on holiday.

CHAPTER 11

The First Time I: Stalked a popstar and became a groupie

(The First TV Job Chapter)

I never had a plan and apart from a few bursts in my early twenties, I've never been ambitious. I'm not, however, without aspiration, but mostly I have just flitted from job to job, generally enjoying what I do and being happy just as long as I was working and earning money. And although I never shied away from hard work or getting my hands dirty, I always had my eye on the easy option. How lovely it would be if I could do something that was fun, relatively easy and cool? I was thinking this the whole time I was watching a television channel that I had become hooked on while living back with Mum at the pub in Maidstone.

In 1985, I was still working in London (as a temp) but I'd got myself into a bit of debt and no longer had a place to live up there. That meant I used to have to get up at 5am and get the coach to Victoria to go to work. I wasn't exactly unhappy, because I'd been doing a long-term temp job for CSC (Computer Sciences Corporation) in Savile Row and I'd made a lot of good friends there. That said, the travelling was killing me. By the time I'd got home and watched a bit of telly it was time to go to bed in preparation to do it all again the next day. But the telly I was watching then literally changed my life. Once again, I was dead lucky. I didn't do anything really to achieve my dream or even to help it along – I just ended up being in the right place at the right time.

Back then, cable TV was just starting up and Maidstone, having been wired up for it since the early Rediffusion days, was one of the trial areas. You didn't have to pay for it, it was just there when you turned the little A, B, C switch on the wall. I didn't have much spare time but any that I had was sat in front of the telly watching this new cable channel called Music Box. I couldn't believe it: music videos back to back, 24 hours a day and nothing else except a presenter, sat on a box in what looked like a very small room, telling you what the last video was and what was coming next. I was an addict. I'd always listened to radio but this was radio with pictures. The rise of the music video was happening around this time. Before this medium a lot of artists didn't bother with promos, but now there was no getting away from it, you had to or you'd get left behind. Music Box was the proper precursor to MTV. It paved the way, and all but disappeared when MTV launched in the UK in 1987. It was fairly revolutionary. I loved music and was enthralled by the pictures that went with all those classic 1980s songs that they played over and over again. Whenever I watched I dreamed of what it might be like to work there, but I never thought in a million years I'd ever get the chance and, lacking in drive as I was, I certainly wasn't going to try to do anything about it.

That year I went on holiday to Agios Nikolaos in Crete with Helen. It wasn't the first time I'd been; I'd gone out there to work a year earlier but my time there was curtailed on account of the fact I'd got fired from my job as a holiday rep and couldn't afford to stay. It was a harsh sacking since I'd done so much to get that job. It was well dodgy; I had to go for an interview in a hallway in a weird office block. I'm sure they weren't supposed to be there. I knew it wasn't right because the ad had said that there were no languages necessary and you had to pay for your own uniform, flight and accommodation once you got there. Who in their right mind would apply for a job where effectively you were paying them to employ you? Yep, me. No wonder I got the job – no other mug would have applied for it. So I went and booked a flight; £150 it was, expensive given it was 1984, and I'd only be using it one way! Before I left I had to go back to the dodgy hallway and try my uniform on for size. I gave them the £60 (sixty quid!) for it and tried it on. It.

Was. Hideous. Pale blue polyester with an A-line skirt just below the knee, except mine was so big it was more like just above the ankle. The jacket was even bigger. I looked like a junior school pupil who'd borrowed her sixth form sister's jacket. And I was paying for it! How wrong could they get it; I'd been measured up when I went for the interview.

I went out there in March on a flight to Athens, followed by a ferry from Piraeus (the main harbour) that took 14 hours, so we had to sleep in a bunk overnight. There were three of us mugs altogether: me, Cathy and Nick. The other shocking thing about it was, because it was out of season, the ferries were few and far between so we had to wait about 11 hours for one once we got to Pireaus. For the first six weeks our jobs were to clean the villas. They'd been empty all winter and they were cold, damp and filthy. This might sound strange, but I loved it. It was real manual work, something I hadn't done for years, so by the end of the day, I really felt like I deserved my dinner – which was great because I loved Greek food, and even though I ate loads, I still lost weight. I was good at cleaning. I did it really thoroughly and took pride in it.

But I was a shit rep. When the holidaymakers came and I had to collect them from the airport and do that speech thing on the coach I was useless. I dreaded it and would get Cathy to do it whenever she was around. I just felt like such a jerk, because I didn't believe what I was saying. The whole exercise from start to finish was about selling excursions. So the speech on the coach (which would go a double-long way so you had longer to sell to the punters) was sell, sell, sell. The problem was the excursions were shit. Overpriced, overcrowded and shit. I wanted to tell them, *if you just go and sort it out yourself or hire a car, you can get it for half the price!* The damned excursions were to be my downfall. I was sent out one day to flog them on the beach but instead I just ended up sitting around talking to my mates. The boss caught me and ordered me back to the office. The boss was horrible. I think he fancied his chances with me but he was revolting so I made it plain he didn't have a hope in hell. Anyway, he gave me a list of passenger names who were flying back that Friday and as he handed me the list he said, 'Here, and put your name on it.' Well at least they were paying for me to go home, I suppose I should have been grateful for small mercies. Trouble was I didn't want to go home, I was enjoying myself. But I had no money and no job and nowhere to stay.

That's why I was dying to go back. Helen and I weren't on an 18-30 holiday, just a cheap one, but we behaved like we were. The first night we arrived we were walking into town and passed a place called the Aquarius Pub. There were the usual touts (blokes who were employed by the bars to get customers in) outside, beckoning everyone (especially girls) to come in, and on that first night we did, and for the rest of the holiday we never went anywhere else. Which was exactly their plan. The guys at the bars had a system whereby they'd lure in the new arrivals, find out which songs they liked and then play them over and over until the next group came in and your songs would be ditched in favour of the new lot. We didn't mind, it was a fun bar and there were even some tasty boys working there that we could get off with.

One of the songs they played for us was 'New York, New York' by Frank Sinatra and every time they played it I took my clothes off. Not sure why, it just seemed like a funny thing to do at the time.

One evening while we were waiting for the night-time shenanigans to begin, we were sitting outside the Aquarius Pub, enjoying the last of the day's sun, when I spotted two girls – one of whom was wearing a T-shirt with the Music Box logo on it. Of course I had to talk to her, find out where she got it. When I went over I discovered that she actually worked for them, as did her friend. Nicola and Denise were their names. Nicola was amazed. Despite having worked there for ages, she'd never actually met anyone who'd ever seen it. I must have bored her stupid with my thoughts on how brilliant it was. In the end she gave me the T-shirt (I think to shut me up) and I didn't take it off for the rest of the holiday. How bloody exciting! I wanted to know everything. What was Simon Potter like? Was Suni really tall or short? Is Gaz Topp really crazy mad? And Martin Buchanan, shouldn't he really be reading the local news in Norwich? They were all the presenters at the time and

Nicola and Denise actually knew them! Suddenly they were our new best friends for the holiday and somehow I knew I was going to stay in touch with them.

After we got back I did stay in touch and met up with them a couple of times, going to the offices to meet them for lunch. I'd walk through their offices with them trying my absolute best not to be impressed or starstruck, but even though there weren't any real stars there – they were all stars to me. Then one day Nicola phoned me and said they were looking for a new presenter, would I be interested? She thought I'd be 'brilliant' at it. It hadn't even crossed my mind that I might be considered as a presenter (I would have worked there emptying the bins) but I said I'd give it a go. I applied to the Head of Production, a woman called Jane Kelly (someone who became a mentor) and duly went along for the audition. I wasn't very good, just too self-conscious and nervous. It wasn't really what I wanted to do but after the audition, even though I was shit, I couldn't help fantasising about how brilliant my life would be if I were to get that job. I mean it must have been at least £20,000 a year! In the end I didn't get it – Lulu's little sister got it. I was like, 'Oh well,' and duly phoned up Jane (how very forward) to tell her that I didn't mind not getting the job but if anything else came up, even doing the post or anything, could I please, please, please be considered?

A couple of weeks later, she called. She was looking for an assistant. I went in to meet her and she told me that it wasn't a load of money and it was a lot of work – it wouldn't be the easy life of a presenter. I told her I didn't care, I just wanted the job, but she kept going on about it not being a presenter's job. I tried to explain that actually, I really didn't want to be a presenter, I just went for it because it was a job at Music Box. I don't think she believed me but she gave me the job anyway. I was in.

My leaving party at CSC was a riot. I got a Tarzan-o-gram complete with banana in the pants and everything. It was probably the last normal job I ever did.

Jane was a hard taskmaster. She didn't suffer fools and she expected everyone to work as hard as she did. She was razor-sharp, focused, super efficient, methodical and didn't miss a trick. I enjoyed working for her because I learnt a lot and I worked hard. But I soon got into the general malaise that was common to most people who work in TV (except Jane of course). I mean, I'd always been a bit of a skiver, doing the bare minimum if it was boring, but I'd still get the work done. There it seemed everyone just sat around chatting, drinking coffee or reading the paper after getting into the office at 10.30am, doing half an hour's work from 11.30 to 12, then going for lunch until 3 then doing another hour's work (in between gossiping) before going to the pub at 5pm! I liked that bit and I think that for the whole time I worked there, I went to the pub after work every night. Most nights didn't end at the pub either because we'd end up in some club (usually The Wag Club in Wardour Street) or at a party until the early hours. I don't know how I did it because I'd always get up and go into work, but then I was only 26. My party partner in crime was Jane's sister Ruth, who worked there as a PA (not the secretarial type, the production type). She was much younger than me and knew all the best clubs to go to. I also made friends with a girl called Alex Jackson whose job it was to do the post. She is now a very important woman in TV and I have a lot to thank her for, but more of that later.

Jane's title was 'Head of Production' so she was overseeing all the shows Music Box was producing. There were about 30 hours a week – a lot of original TV for any channel, let alone one without any money, so it was all done as cheaply as possible. The presenters would record all the links then a director and a PA would sit in a room compiling 60-minute shows, as live. That meant that they'd act as though it was being broadcast as it was all being fitted together. The PA would work out all the timings of the videos and the links and the director would call the shots to the tape operators. It had to be done that way to save time and, most importantly, money. My job was to assist Jane in the checking and double-checking of all the job sheets and purchase orders to make sure they were billed correctly. It was quite boring, but I was just happy to be there.

Funnily enough, even though it was still only 1986, I got to use email for the first time. Every week the chart would come through, and it was my job to circulate it to everyone in the company so they'd all know what they should be programming. The way it worked was a right rigmarole. There was a dedicated landline phone, with a dial (a dial!) by the computer and you'd have to dial into a computer and as soon as you heard a high-pitched 'beep' you had to shove the handset into a rubber receiver that was attached to the computer. It always took about 15 attempts to get a connection, and when it did connect it would take about 45 minutes to send a single file. Quite often it would drop out just before it finished and you'd have to go through the whole process again. In these days of permanently connected, high-speed broadband it just seems hilarious what you had to go through.

Musically and (more importantly) music video-wise, it was a golden era. Classic songs and classic videos every single one of them: A-ha's 'Take on Me'; Bon Jovi's 'Living on a Prayer'; Duran Duran's 'Rio'; and the one I literally could not take my eyes off, The Blow Monkeys' 'Digging Your Scene'.

He was the lead singer and as soon as I saw him in that video I felt like I already knew him. His face was so familiar, but of course I didn't know him at all. Maybe I had in a past life, but in this one he was a pop star singing this amazingly catchy tune on my telly. His name was Dr Robert. I had to meet him, but how? I'd never been a groupie before. I had no idea where to start; what did you do, who did you need to know? I developed quite a serious crush, a mild obsession, like a teenage infatuation. I put pictures of him up on my wall and wrote him a letter which I gave to my friend Mabel who knew a guy called Hector, who just happened to be Dr Robert's flatmate. I don't know if he ever got it.

I looked up his tour dates and dragged my sister Tracy down to Folkestone where we checked into a B&B and trotted off to see them do a gig at the Leascliff Halls. I've no idea how but afterwards we got backstage and before I knew it I was in a room talking to Dr Robert himself. I definitely turned into a stupid girl. I said, 'I wrote you a letter, did you get it?' Total confusion took over his face. I persisted. 'Yeah, I wrote you a letter and gave it to Mabel, you know Hector's Mabel?' Nothing. He offered me some chocolate from a giant bar of Cadbury's Dairy Milk. I nearly fainted. The next bit is all a bit of a blur because about five minutes later, Tracy and I found ourselves back at the hotel where the band were staying. Which would have been fine, had I not been dressed like a minstrel. Well, I wasn't exactly dressed in the full garb but I had a red jumper on under a black tabard and my hair looked like it had been modelled on a lop-sided Friar Tuck. Honestly, it was like someone had put a basin over my head and cut round it, crookedly.

Even more unbelievably, I ended up in his hotel room. We were getting on quite well but as soon as I said, 'Ooooh, I can't believe it's you,' he lost interest and threw me out. I wasn't upset or put out or anything – as far as I was concerned it was mission accomplished. I got up, grabbed my sister who was entertaining the bass player and we tried to run back to our B&B. Unfortunately we didn't know where we were, so even though we left their place at about 4am, we didn't get back until around 7am. By that point we were starving so went straight into breakfast and ate two boiled eggs each between bouts of such hysterical laughter that everything we ate got spat straight out again. It has to be up there in the top 10 funniest nights of my life ever.

I ended up doing Jane's job at Music Box after she left and I stayed there for a couple of years working under the new boss, Mike Hollingsworth (or Mr Anne Diamond, as he was better known then) where I became embroiled in an alleged scandal that involved him, me, a newspaper and was front page news (see *The Winning Chapter*). Then one day I was made redundant, which was marginally better than just getting the sack. If you were made redundant at least you got a few quid rather than just a 'see ya!' Even though I worried about money when it happened, I was always fairly sure that something better would come out of it and it usually did.

CHAPTER 12

The First Time I: Passed out on a car bonnet in St Lucia

(The Winning Chapter)

The reason I don't do the lottery is because I know I won't win. Yes, I know you have to be 'in it to win it' otherwise you've got no chance. But one in 14 million is, effectively, no chance. There's another reason. I don't want to live with false hope. I'm quite happy with my lot and even if I didn't have such a lot, I guarantee I would still be happy. Life isn't always about stuff. Or money. It's about enjoying what you have and loving and being loved.

Then again, it is nice to win something occasionally, isn't it?

I swear, until 1987 I had never won anything in my life. Well, not that I could remember anyway. There's a vague recollection somewhere in my addled brain that I won Miss Something-or-other during one of the Maidstone carnivals when I was dressed up on a float, but I'm sure it's been cast aside because everyone won something so it didn't count.

OK, so I did come first in the long jump on school sports day once. However, my childish and filthy teenage mind ruined that moment, as you will have already read.

So that's my sad catalogue of wins until my finest hour in 1987 when I won a dancing competition in St Lucia. I'd been sent there by my boss at Music Box, Rob Jones. God knows why he sent me though; they needed a reporter/presenter and I'd never done it before in my life, apart from loads of auditions that I was always totally crap at. I couldn't believe my luck. From what I know, the St Lucia

Tourist Board had agreed to run a competition whereby two Music Box viewers would win a free holiday there and we would make a promo film of it all and run it on the channel. The crew was assembled: regular cameraman, John, and his soundman partner, Tony, a director, Rod, and me. Brilliant, I thought. It couldn't have been more perfect because I quite fancied Rod.

Only problem was, because I'd never really presented before, I was totally shit. I wasn't prepared – but in my defence I didn't really know what I was supposed to be doing. And I was huge! I don't mean, big in the world of TV presenting, I was just much bigger than I am now and way, way too big to be on TV in a swimsuit. I did an interview with the manager of the Marigot Bay Resort who was miniature, tiny and really brown, and next to her I looked like a giant beached white whale that was about to take up wrestling. I wasn't prepared wardrobe-wise either, and all I had was a black shiny swimsuit which had long thin straps and looked like a bodybuilder's kit. Over that I had a green sarong roughly hitched around my very wide midriff and a pair of thick, black, rubber sandals. I had no make-up on, my hair wasn't done. It was just hilarious. No, it was a disaster.

Anyway, while I was there, we had to do all the tourist things with the winners – a couple of very young girls from Turku, Finland. Just my luck; there was no chance of getting off with Rod, not with these two young things around. He couldn't take his eyes off the little dark-haired one. Anyway, one night we attended the famous street party at Gros Islet where I managed to get a little bit tipsy, which obviously made me think I could dance. We were in a dancehall and I was doing wild reggae dancing convinced I was an islander who was once married to Bob Marley. So as soon as they announced that we had to clear the floor for the Reggae Dancing Championship of St Lucia 1987 competition I was in. I didn't have a partner but there was one stray Rastafarian guy who was also dancing alone. I grabbed him and we duly entered ourselves.

I can barely think about what happened next, it was so fantastically, awfully embarrassing. There were about six other couples who'd obviously been practising for ages and had been looking forward to this moment for months. They were all specially dressed up in their best reggae-dancing outfits and some serious booty was being shaken. Their make-up and hair was immaculate. I think we went on last. The others were good. I wish I could remember the song we had to dance to. I can't because I think I've wiped the whole episode from my hard drive. Well, not all of it, because I remember doing our thing and I was shakin' my booty like I never had before. I was quite pissed and just followed him really, but even though we didn't know each other I seem to recall it got quite sexy. I wasn't wearing any 'dance hall' gear at all; I had white trousers and a white denim jacket on. As the music stopped everyone we knew was cheering. The Fins, the crew, Rod. No one else. Despite this mild disapproval, bordering on hostility, we won. The Rastaman and I hugged and kissed and danced some more but that was it. There was no prize-giving ceremony, no prize. We just won. So we went outside and smoked one of his 'pure Jamaican ganja' spliffs in celebration and after one puff I turned into a rag doll and passed out on a car bonnet. The Fins thought this was hilarious. It was lucky they were there because they held me up on the way to the taxi. Next thing I knew we were in the little ferry boat from the main reception to the bungalows at Marigot Bay and I couldn't stop laughing. In fact, I think I laughed myself to sleep despite the fact that there was a moth the size of a B52 bomber in my room.

Then, later that year, something even more ridiculous happened.

I was living in Fulham, West London, and my landlord was Malcolm, the lovely Chinese guy who was an endless source of help to me when I had moved back to London from Kent. I was back working at Music Box but temping as the boss's assistant. The boss was one Mike Hollingsworth, whom I'd worked for briefly before I was made redundant the first time. I got on well with Mike. We talked, but it was always professional and work related and I'm sure he saw it that way too.

From where I lived it was quite a long bus ride into work. I used to wait on the Fulham Road, just down from Earl's Court, and occasionally Mike, because he lived in Putney, used to drive by, see me, and give me a lift. Someone took this as something more than it was and sold it as a 'story' to one of the tabloids who duly printed it, clearly implying that I was having an affair with Anne Diamond's husband – which was of course completely untrue, but became big news at the time because Anne was the star of the early morning sofa over on TV-am.

The story ended up getting way out of control (I was even labelled a 'scarlet woman') and for the first time in my life I was chased up Charlotte Street by the paparazzi. I'd done everything to avoid them that day but got caught sneaking out of a side window of the building. It was only funny because I wasn't famous and I hadn't done anything remotely scandalous.

Well, of course I wasn't a scarlet woman but no one believed me. Even my friends gave me funny looks as though it were true. Was it damaging? It could have been, I suppose. I might not have got another job on account of the bad publicity and people thinking I was a marriage-wrecker, but then again, it might have given me all sorts of openings. I didn't really think about it that much. I just laughed it off and did nothing. Mike, being married, was understandably furious. He look legal action and sued them for libel.

I simply couldn't afford to do the same. However, I kept getting harassed by various papers who were offering me 'substantial sums of money' to tell my side of the story, as if there was one. They would be at my flat with their fingers on the door buzzer constantly. They drove me mad, and for a couple of weekends I couldn't go out.

I was horrified and a little freaked out, so I phoned a guy I was working with at the time, Richard, an experienced ex-tabloid journalist who'd worked on Fleet Street proper. He'd even door-stepped a few people. However, like a lot of hacks, he wanted to get into TV and he was working as a researcher on the same show as me, *Jameson Tonight*, a new nightly chat show on Sky One. I was the guest booker. I liked Richard and we got on really well, and although I didn't fancy him at first (his trousers were too small and they were those polyester Crimplene ones by Farah that everyone wore in the 1970s, but they weren't only too snug, they were too short too) there was something sexy about him and the more I hung around with him the more attractive he got. He later became my boyfriend, but more of that later. I knew he'd know what to do and he referred me to an equally experienced lawyer called Henri Brandman. I made an appointment with him straight away and went to see him as soon as I could. He advised me to wait and see the outcome of Mike's case. Then, if he won, I should go for it too. I didn't want to but I had confidence in Henri who certainly knew what he was doing, having done it many times before. I knew that if there had been no chance of winning he wouldn't have let me go for it. It was an open-and-shut case, wasn't it?

It wasn't.

It was the most stressful time of my whole life.

'No win no fee' didn't exist in the UK at the time, so libel trials had to be paid for up front, the whole lot. Even though Henri knew I would win, I still had to pay him as he did the work. The other fatal anomaly was that if you took the action and you lost, you were liable for the paper's costs. And we're talking horrific sums of money here. The prospect was frightening and because the paper decided to call my bluff, thinking I could never afford to take it all the way, they took it to the wire. I had a bit of money saved which I put in myself, but as the case went on and I had to get opinions from counsel, or whatever it is, the costs soared.

I borrowed money from my brother, from work; I even tried my dad. I had been in touch with him on a semi-regular basis during the 1980s. I went to his son's wedding in the West Country and had seen him a few times in London. He'd even come to stay at my flat with me, although I have zero recollection of this but for the entry in my diary:

Wednesday 16 May 1990
Dad stayed tonight. We went to the pub, then got a pizza and came back to the flat. He was looking through the photos, and was feeling very guilty. He said he'd love to meet Mum and talk to her, but he couldn't because he'd break down. Quite right. I don't even know if I like him, but the scary thing is I can see a lot of him in me. We stayed up talking, drank a bottle of red wine, and that was it.

I had no compunction asking him because I kind of thought he owed me something and always assumed he was doing OK; after all he was a successful businessman, wasn't he? Well no, he wasn't (well not at that time anyway) because he told me he'd gone bankrupt and he had nothing. Strangely, although I was pissed off that he couldn't, or wouldn't, lend me the money, the news pleased me. Was that wrong? I still don't know, but that's how I felt. I stopped seeing him after that – not because of the money but because I felt disloyal to my mum, even though she said she didn't mind I think it still upset her.

With no help from Dad, the cost of the case was getting to me. But also I became obsessed with them catching me out in some way, even though I hadn't done anything wrong. I felt guilty because they made me feel guilty for fighting the case. I gathered witnesses, checked with everyone what they thought had happened, trawled the newspaper archives at Colindale (by hand as you did then, there was no microfiche or internet records) and generally bored everyone to death about it – myself included.

There was a chance, too, that if it did go to court they could quite easily have set about destroying my character. I had visions of them descending on my home town, making lucrative offers to all the boys I'd ever slept with in order to make sure I was portrayed as a slut who would have had an affair with a married man. So even though Mike was victorious they might have thought they'd have a better chance with me, having been a proper loose woman for most of my life.

Richard (the sexy journalist I'd sought advice from) ended up being my boyfriend, but not before I put an end to his bad wardrobe. All his too-small trousers went to the charity shop and we went shopping. He ended up looking like a TV producer instead of a hack – much better! He was really quite handsome with piercing eyes and such an impressive air of confidence. He was a bit weird the way he saved old newspapers, but that was the only dodgy thing about him. We had a good time, going out almost every night for dinner and he never let me pay, he was a bit of an old-fashioned gent like that. But it wasn't a good time to be with me. I was a nightmare. In fact, reading back through my diaries at the time, I can't believe he put up with me for as long as he did. He was with me throughout the case and when it made me short-tempered, obsessive and grumpy, who did I take it out on? Yes, Richard. To make matters worse, I'd gone and got myself pregnant, had an abortion that didn't work and had to be done again, took too much time off sick and got the sack from *Jameson Tonight*.

So I had no job, was deep in debt, up the spout and was doing my best to piss off my adorable, kind and patient boyfriend. I definitely had my finger on the self-destruct button. It was a dreadful time and without Richard I couldn't have got through it. He was so supportive and, frankly, I treated him like shit.

It was difficult to work out which was the most awful: the libel suit, getting the sack or being pregnant. It was close, but even the horror and stress of the case couldn't have beaten the nightmare of an abortion that didn't work. I don't really know how I got pregnant. Well, of course I do, but I was on the pill and as far as I knew I hadn't forgotten to take any. It makes me think that as women approach 30 the body knows its time is running out and really goes for it as if to say, *this is your last chance love, you better take it*. It took me a long time to realise I was pregnant though. For about four weeks I was back and forth to the doctors with debilitating tiredness and nausea and they kept giving me tablets for IBS. The only things I could eat were porridge, pea soup and banana custard. Smoke and booze became like poison to me. How many clues did I need? As soon as I found out I set about arranging the termination, which might sound callous but I was never planning to have children, plus it couldn't have been at a worse time. It was impossible. Richard was very understanding and didn't try to change my mind. So I had the abortion, a wholly unpleasant experience that I hated myself for having to go through, but it didn't work. My body was obviously trying to tell me something – it wasn't giving up that easily. So for four weeks I was in chronic, excruciating pain while my body tried to cling on to the little life I had tried to destroy. The doctor had said it would work itself out but in the end it got so bad I was taken in for an emergency D&C on the NHS.

★

I knew about a week before that they were going to settle out of court but it was still touch and go because, if I'd refused the sum they'd put into court on the grounds that it wasn't enough and then it had gone to court and the jury had offered me less than the sum they'd put in, then I still would have ended up paying their costs. Suddenly it seemed like I couldn't win.

I did think about pulling out but I couldn't do that because I'd have lost all the money I'd already paid and wouldn't have been able to pay everyone back. Also, I was convinced that that was what the paper was hoping I would do.

I got the letter of confirmation from Henri on the Saturday morning. Saturday mornings were radio days by then. As you will read in the next chapter, Chris Evans was already a friend and he'd asked me to do a slot on his show. He came to pick me up as usual and I opened my post as we drove down Haverstock Hill to the studios. I knew that one was from Henri and was a bit nervous about opening it. I didn't say anything to Chris or Andy, the producer, who was also in the car, but they were with me on the case and knew the stress I'd been having with it. Suddenly I let out a scream. The car was full of nervous excitement as I read the contents of Henri's letter.

Chris stopped the car in the middle of the road. It was relatively early so it didn't exactly cause a jam. He got out first, followed by Andy and me as we jumped and danced around the car in the middle of the road, me waving the letter around. I was so elated but I couldn't relax completely until the money was in my account so I asked everyone to say nothing, especially on the show. Unfortunately Chris did, and I was so cross I walked out because he'd done it, for whatever reason, on purpose.

Anyway, I was determined not to let him spoil my day and as soon as I got out of there, I called Richard who just happened to be around the corner. He came and picked me up and we went shopping. My little present to myself for getting through it all and winning a great prize was a pair of shoes from Stephane Kélian in Sloane Street. And those shoes, although 20 years old, are still in my dressing-up box. As I've said, not much makes it in there, but those shoes did.

On 31 May 1990, almost exactly a year after I instructed him, I went to Henri's office to pick up the cheque, took a photocopy of it and express cashed it through my bank account.

CHAPTER 13

The First Time I: Found ginger hair attractive

(The Meeting and Dating Chris Evans Chapter)

Before I say a word about the mad years that were my relationship with Chris Evans, let me make a few things clear. I don't do regrets because everything I've done in the past plays a part in making me who I am now, but those years certainly left their mark on me. I'm not sure what effect they had on him – if you read his autobiography you'd hardly know we ever were married. We've both moved on and have each consigned our relationship to where it suits us for it to be, but reading my diaries from that time brought me face to face with the person that being with him had turned me into, and it's not a pretty sight. It was an insane and difficult time for both of us but I can only tell you what it was like from my point of view. He probably has a very different story but it's not one he seems likely to tell so history will have to make do with just my side of it!

In 1988 I was still working at Music Box but I was now a producer on a show called *Formula One*, presented by a new young talent from Scotland, John Leslie. My desk was opposite the spiral staircase. One day I was standing there, back to the window, on the phone and a bloke came down the spiral staircase, all legs and bright orange ginger hair. It wasn't that that struck me first though, it was the height, the jeans and the oh-so-confident swagger that got my attention. I stared at him like I would have done had a live dinosaur walked through the office. It felt like I imagine it would if a ghost walked through your house – a kind of presence as opposed to an actual person. Weird. As he turned and walked away I couldn't take my eyes off of his bum. It just looked great in his jeans. I thought, *why didn't mine look like that in Levi 501s*? He was carrying a recording machine and heading for Andy, who at the time was reading the news live to camera. I noticed he had thick-rimmed glasses, like Ray-Ban Wayfarers with faded lenses. And his mass of thick ginger hair was all quiffed, Proclaimers style, in its dazzling orangeness. What I didn't realise was that right up until that moment, I had always, rather unfairly, had a negative view of ginger hair. I'd dismiss it instantly because my brain automatically responded with disgust, so I would normally feel repulsed. This time there was none of that.

His name was Chris Evans and I'd been warned that he was coming by our mutual friend, Andy Bird, the head of Music Box News (who now happens to be the head of Walt Disney International!) to do a report on us for his radio show in Manchester. Andy kept telling me how brilliant he was and I just thought, *yeah, so what?* I never was easily impressed.

But I was intrigued as he swanned around with his antique tape machine, giant headphones and microphone, sticking it in the faces of various members of staff while he questioned them on what they were doing – all the time wondering, 'Why doesn't he want to interview me?' He couldn't have been there for more than 20 minutes but he left a trail of something and I kept trying not to wonder when I would eventually get to hear this report.

It was a few weeks later and Andy came in with a tape and told me to listen to what was on it. By this time I'd completely forgotten all about Chris and when Andy was telling me what I was listening to I had no idea what he was talking about. When I finally remembered I suddenly got all interested. The piece he'd edited together about our little TV station was a feature called 'File-o-Flea' and I thought it was absolutely brilliant. It was him with his voice speeded up Pinky-and-Perky style to make it sound like he was a flea doing a report for Chris's show. Now I was impressed.

I didn't see him again until he strolled into another place I was working, Radio Radio, nearly a year later. He'd been fired from his job at Piccadilly Radio for telling a bad-taste cat joke and literally couldn't get arrested, let alone another job in the business. He'd applied to everyone who was anyone in the business and strangely he'd kept all the rejection letters, which he showed me one day. Even more strange, he seemed rather proud of them, which I couldn't quite work out. So Andy, being a good friend, brought him down to London, put him up and gave him a job for £30 a day but as well as being his friend, Andy knew Chris had something and I think he always knew he was going to be famous. Mind you, I'm sure Chris did too.

Radio Radio was owned by Richard Branson. It was an overnight syndicated service for independent local radio stations. The idea was to get very high-profile presenters – Johnnie Walker, Tommy Vance and Bob Harris – then broadcast it through the night and sell it to them so they wouldn't have to run their own stations or pay any presenters directly. Jonathan Ross and Ruby Wax were the really high-profile names and Chris and I both ended up working on what were Jonathan's first radio shows. I was originally employed as the 'traffic manager' which meant I dealt with the scheduling of all the advertising on the station. Trouble was, there was only one ad for most of the time the station was on air, so I didn't have a whole lot of work to do. Spending all day deciding where to put one advert meant that all I did was mess about and laugh and with Chris working there, that wasn't difficult. It was a riotous time.

Chris's girlfriend at the time was called Sara. She was small, pretty and blonde and really clever. She spoke about 10 languages. This was when I started to think about him differently. Before, he was just an oddly attractive, weird-looking clown but if this impressive woman was smitten then he must have something. Obviously I didn't do anything about it but I was surprised at myself, shamefully, for the ginger reason again.

We spent a lot of time together then, Chris, Andy and me, going to the pub and doing Jonathan's show. We all used to traipse over to the studios with tons of booze and everyone including the guests would have a few drinks and sometimes end up half sloshed. I still have cassette recordings of those shows and believe me, Jonathan sounds exactly the same.

Chris was a brilliant producer. He always had an idea and even if it looked bad on paper, he'd force it through and make it work. I think he might have peaked when he forced us all to do karaoke with Frank Sidebottom, or did I imagine that?

Sometimes, I thought I detected that Jonathan wasn't always completely happy to go along with it but in the end he was persuaded. We also worked on Steve Davis's show – he did a soul hour and had the best record collection I've ever heard. I've still got some of the 12-inch singles he gave me from his own label. It was funny going over to the local pub afterwards for a pint and playing a game of snooker with Steve. People would walk in and literally stand there aghast. Or they'd look suspicious, like they were expecting to be on *Candid Camera*. This was 1988 and he was world champion then and had been for about five years. In fact he'd won everything.

Radio Radio didn't last long in its original form – hardly surprising given the lack of advertising revenue and the disproportionate costs of presenters and booze – and morphed into The Superstation with unknown DJs and a skeleton staff. As a result, I was 'let go'.

I went off to work as a guest booker for Michael Hurll Television on a nightly Sky One chat show called *Jameson Tonight* presented by Derek Jameson, the ex-Fleet Street editor – the show where I met Richard. I'd never done it before but had observed Chris booking guests for Jonathan's show at Radio Radio. He'd never done it either but he had a fantastic ability to just get on with the job, however daunting. I admired his tenacity and his ability to focus exactly on the task at hand. He was fearless and confident on the phone and even though I wasn't, it made me believe I could do it. I did it but I wasn't very good, mainly because I hated having to do all that grovelling to demanding agents and record companies.

Chris and I stayed friends and one day he called me at work to tell me he'd finally got his own on-air show on GLR on a Saturday afternoon and would I like to come in and do a 'What's On' guide? I wouldn't say I jumped at the idea; I didn't even know if I could do it but I figured it would be a laugh to piss about in a radio studio on a Saturday afternoon with Chris, and so I said yes.

I had never spoken on the radio before then and I was dead nervous.

I bought *Time Out* and cobbled together a list of things Londoners might want to do over the weekend. I only had about three minutes to get it all in and I did it once an hour. There wasn't a name for the slot so it was first known simply as the 'What's On Guide', then I was called the Time Out Totty. Then when the show moved to the morning 10-1pm slot, I would often come with a hangover, so we called it, 'Carol's Out Of It'. And I ended up doing that for nearly the whole of the five years that I was with him. I didn't get paid at first, and even Chris was only getting something like £50 a show, but I didn't mind. It was funny having my friends listen in and hearing me 'on the radio'.

I had become a regular feature but every week Chris would still phone up and check if I was 'doing the show'. During one of these calls, where I always said yes, he mentioned that he and Andy (Bird) were going to Paris afterwards on a record company jolly. 'Paris? How? Who with? Why aren't I invited? Can I come?' I blurted out. Chris said he would phone the promoter who was organising it, a Scouser and all-round lovely bloke called Tony Byrne, to see if he could get me on it. He called back five minutes later – we were on. We were all going to Paris after the show to see Imagination play live! How exciting. So we finished the show at exactly 1pm and drove at breakneck speed to Charing Cross station where we got the train to . . . Ramsgate. Why were we going to Ramsgate if we were going to Paris? Because we were going to Dunkirk, that's why! Chris had only said it was Paris because he was trying to make it sound more glamorous than it was and also he didn't think I would have wanted to go if he'd told the truth. Probably true. When we got to Ramsgate we had to hotfoot it to the port in another car at even more of a breakneck speed to get the ferry. We seriously only got it with seconds to spare. It was typical of being with Chris – everything happened but only just. All the way down I was saying, we're not going to get the ferry, we're going to miss it. He would just say, 'Yes we will.'

In fact we were going to watch Imagination perform on the beaches at Dunkirk. On the ferry we had a few drinks (a bottle of red wine each, if I remember correctly) and when we got there we had a few drinks, but mostly we were just laughing all day. Luckily I'd taken my camera and the pics from that day still make me howl with laughter. We were on the beach with wet shoes, it was freezing cold, I'm sure it even rained at one point, but it was still one of the best times I can remember. Except I don't remember seeing much of Imagination although you could hear them for miles:'Body talk . . . doo doo doo . . . ' Brilliant. Well the booze and hilarity must have had an effect on us because towards the end of the evening Chris and I got a bit drunkenly amorous and were going on about how much we liked each other. As you do. It was only drunken affection but it was nice and I remember thinking, 'We shouldn't *really* be doing this.' It didn't go anywhere but when we got back to London the next morning, after travelling all night with Chris having a major sick attack on the ferry, he tried to persuade me to go to Manchester for a friend's birthday party. He was going straight from Charing Cross to Euston to get on another train to go up there. I felt completely abominable having sobered up on the ferry and subsequent train and couldn't think of anything I wanted to do less. I needed my bed and no amount of good-time party talk was going to change my mind. It had been a brilliant 24 hours but it was over.

Chris eventually moved out of Andy's place and into mine, but only as a lodger. He was still with Sara who was living in Manchester. I had a two-bedroom flat and he took the small room for a while. Although we clearly fancied each other, nothing ever happened except a bit of heavy flirting and suggestion, which always ended when the phone rang and Sara was on the other end. I used to think how disloyal he was and I should probably have been less complicit but I squared it with myself because it was him who had the girlfriend, I was single. And it wasn't as if she was a friend, I hardly knew her. In fact, she never liked me, but I never really knew why.

Chris went to live with Sara when she moved down to London but it all went tits up with them and when they split up he got his own place, a mews house in Belsize Park with Andy Davies, the producer of the GLR radio show. And that's when we got it together properly. I was 30, he was just 24.

He was working with Andy Bird again, doing a morning show

called *Power Up* for BSB (the square satellite dish lot) and they were looking for a female co-host and Chris and Andy asked if I'd like to audition for it. Course I would! What a laugh that would be. Be on telly for an hour a day, earn a bit of money; it was a dream job. Trouble was, I'd never really been on telly before either and whereas I could get away with the radio because no one could see me, on TV I was always way too self-conscious. I'd already discovered this during numerous screen tests and try-outs when I was at Music Box, so I had no illusions of being brilliant. Anyway, I gave it a go. It was a bit unfair though because Andy and Chris wouldn't tell me any stuff that was going to happen so I couldn't prepare anything. I did OK-ish, I thought, but I knew I wouldn't get the gig and I wasn't too bothered. After the test we all went to the pub (of course) and as it was a nice day, we stayed there and inevitably got a bit drunk. I remember that day well because Chris was being so funny that I had that laughing thing where you literally can't get your breath and you think you're going to keel over and die. We were quite pissed but not totally, more relaxed, and later when Chris and I went back to his house we had sex for the first time. For quite a long time. All over the house. It was good. Fairly adventurous, quite energetic and good.

So good in fact that we were still doing it 30 minutes before he was due to go on air for his evening radio show on GLR, *The Greenhouse*, which he was still doing as well as his TV job and the weekend show. As he rushed out of the house half dressed I hung about there, waiting to see if he'd make it. He did. Of course he did. He always did.

The next day I felt a bit guilty, though I wasn't quite sure why. Maybe it wasn't guilt; I think I was a bit worried that I might have ruined our friendship by having sex with him. Especially as I didn't hear from him for a few days. However, that turned out to be because I didn't get the job and he just didn't want to tell me. But Andy told me anyway.

So after that we kind of did it again and became embroiled in a relationship of sorts. There was never any official 'boyfriend/girlfriend' conversation that I remember. But we did do almost everything together and we laughed so much.

We went to football to see Spurs play, we went on holiday to Portugal with Andy the producer, to Sicily on our own; we went to balls, parties, the pub (a lot) and weddings . . .

There were many fine examples of Chris's brilliant timekeeping and his ability to always just make it but one classic occasion was when we were invited to Andy (Davies's) best friend's wedding. At the time, Chris had a Saab, a big black one. In fact, I think he had two. He'd decided he was going to get celebrities to sign one of the cars and then auction it off for charity. So all the guests he had coming into *The Greenhouse* at the time were on there. The problem was, he hadn't given them a delicate paint pen to sign it with, but a big paintbrush and normal household paint. The result was a car that looked like it'd been vandalised by a team of three-year-old decorators. And this was his car that he was driving around in! Certain friends of his refused to be seen in it and would hide if they thought anyone would see them. I thought it was hilarious, the looks that people would give you, like 'Oh my God! What's happened to that car!' So the day of the wedding we had to finish the show and leg it down to West London in this car. The wedding was in a beautiful stately home with a long gravel drive all the way up to it. We were late, of course, and arrived just as the congregation were perfectly posed for photographs on the lawn outside in the sunshine. There was no hiding the fact that we were late but it had to be one of the best entrances I've ever experienced. We didn't know they were going to be outside on the lawn so Chris drove up the driveway at quite a speed and as we pulled up outside the house he stopped with such a force that we skidded and the car turned in a bit of a circle. He didn't do it on purpose, we just didn't want to be late. Then we saw them. Staring at the daubed car. I think they thought some gangsters had come to shoot them all out. Then Chris and I literally fell out of the car. Looking back, it was rude, really rude. We hardly knew the couple. But I couldn't help it, I honestly couldn't get my breath and I couldn't stop laughing. Luckily they did see the funny side of it too.

The radio show really was our lynchpin. It was the one thing that really bound us together; it was like tying up the whole week with thousands of friends. People were still coming down to sit in the studio. Security-wise it was amazing that that was ever allowed because there were no checks and anyone was welcome. It was done on a kind of first come, first served basis but we just packed them in until we really couldn't take any more. They would bring in either booze or biscuits, which all contributed to the Saturday morning ambience. After the show we'd all go to the pub.

If we didn't go to the pub we'd end up back at Andy and Chris's house, or at my flat where we'd play 'I Want You' by Bob Dylan really loud while dancing round the living room and drinking red wine until it was coming out of our ears. On the way home we'd play 'Billy', a game that consisted of someone leaning out of the car window and shouting 'Billy!' to random pedestrians as if you knew them. The idea was to do it so convincingly that they'd wave back or look at you like you were mental. I never laughed so much as when we were playing that game. We had such a good time it wasn't funny. Well, it was, it was very funny indeed.

We started to go to football after we'd put out an appeal on the radio for someone with a spare ticket (Chris had obtained one somehow) to the first game of the Tottenham Hotspur 1990 season against Manchester City and a guy called Jack, who was a Spurs supporter, came up with the goods. It ended up becoming a two-year, season-ticket-holding habit and Jack became a good friend. I wasn't really a football fan though. I'd been with Richard a few times and I liked the excitement and the atmosphere but all the rigmarole of getting there and getting home and the traffic and the parking and the police and not being allowed to go in the pub afterwards was all too stressful. Still, like a bloke I carried on going. We even went to the second game of that season, an away game. Jack had heard of an opportunity to get on the team plane up to Sunderland and asked if we'd like to go. We jumped at the chance and sure enough there we were at Luton Airport surrounded by almost the whole Spurs team including Gary Lineker. It was another brilliant day out but even though we didn't win (we didn't lose either, it was 0-0) it was an experience. Chris and Jack kept plotting to try and get me to sit next to Gary on the plane because they wanted an excuse to go and talk to him, but I was having none of it.

It was a good time to be a Spurs fan and I'm glad I was because I got to see them win the FA Cup in 1991 at Wembley, the infamous game starring Gazza's overzealous tackle that kick-started the beginning of the end for him. I can't remember who they beat in the final because in the semi-final they beat Arsenal and that was way more important. Apparently. I was never really blokey enough to get into all that North London rivalry and here's a surprise, I still couldn't tell you what the offside rule is. Ha! What a prize girl pretending to like football I was! I was a top-class football fraud! But I really did like going. The routine of it was somewhat reassuring and it was quite nice to wrap up warm and take a flask of tea in the winter. What used to piss me off the most about it though was the way the 'fans' used to rail *against* their own team. The abuse was incredible. Even though I was in the relatively safe, posh East Stand of White Hart Lane I sometimes thought I was actually in the away end. Going to football provided a very interesting insight into male mentality though, so I'm glad I did it. I carried on going after Chris and I split up but in the end I resented the constant disappointment because Spurs were just not very good that last season I went. Jack summed it up when he said, 'God, the only thing I look forward to coming here is a bagel and I don't even want one of those.' Then we won, and he said, 'Oh, what do we do now we've won?' It had been so long.

One of the best days we ever had nearly didn't happen. Chris had said early on that he had to go straight after the show, so I went straight home. Almost as soon as I walked in the door, the phone rang.

It was Chris, 'What ya doing?'

'Nothing much, I was just going to watch a film.'

'Shall I come round?'

Five minutes later he was ringing the doorbell and I went down to let him in. He was standing there wearing a pair of dark blue, shiny, cycling shorts, some dodgy plimsolls and not much else. He was carrying half a bottle of red wine and he had a big smile on his face. I was pleased to see him but evidently not as pleased as he was to see me. Well. He was no Errol Flynn but in his tight little shorts he was no Wee Willy Winkie either. He even turned around and showed it off to Andy who'd just dropped him off and was still sitting there in the car. Andy rolled his eyes and drove off. He'd seen it all before. We spent the afternoon in bed, drinking wine and just passing the time. It was hot outside. In the evening we had a ball to go to. It was Andy's college ball down in Kingston. I'd never really been to an all-night ball before; I always thought they were only for posh people and had no idea what to wear. It took ages to get ready because every time I put something on, Chris took it off again – we literally couldn't keep our hands off each other. I thought, *this is what it's like to have a proper boyfriend*, and I remember feeling very happy about the whole situation. Chris drove that night. He had a red Triumph Spitfire so, because it was a warm day, he put the roof down and we sped off to West London. The ball was full of very young things who all eventually ended up scattered around on the grass outside snogging or in some cases doing more than snogging. Exactly as you imagine a college ball to be.

We stayed until about 4am before getting back in the car to drive home. On the way back, the sun was coming up and as we were speeding down the A40 still with the roof down, enjoying the warm morning air, Chris suddenly stopped the car and we both got out to observe the most amazing sight. There were dozens of hot air balloons floating randomly as the sun came up. We stood there for what seemed like hours but was in reality about 10 minutes. It was so quiet, there was hardly any traffic. It was a Sunday morning and I had my peach satin dress on and Chris looked dapper in his smart pants and white shirt with his tie undone and I thought, *this is it*. This is one of those great moments in life that you must never forget. It was just beautiful. The perfect end to the perfect day. I knew I was falling in love with him right at that moment.

We had the 'love' conversation a few days later but we didn't actually say the word.

Wednesday 27 June 1990
Had to call Chris. Don't know why, just had to. I always think he's having such a good time all the time but he was asleep this afternoon and I just had to speak to him. My excuse was the money he owes me. But he knew that was an excuse. I told him I was missing him. And I am. But I am scared because if I go out with him, and he fucks me off, then we may fall out, and I really really don't want that. And he will fuck me about. I know it. He is young and he has loads of things to do. But I do love everything about him.
As he drove off tonight, he leant out of the car and said, 'I do ya know.'
I said, 'You don't really.'
'I do.'
'You don't, do you really?'
'Yes.'
'So do I.'
'I know.'
'How do you know?'
'I just do.'
'Bye.'
'Bye.'
Talk about insecure, but me or him?

Eventually he moved back into my flat and for a while, we carried on having a good time drinking in the local bars, Bar Beso and Blakes, going up to Warrington to see Minnie, his mum and of course we had the radio show and football. It was all lovely and we were just like a real boyfriend and girlfriend. But I started to get the feeling he was trying to make me jealous. It started with little things like, he'd stay out late, make sure I knew if he was out with a woman, flirt openly on the phone with other girls and hang out a lot with ex-girlfriends. One weekend he went off to Warrington to see his mum. Trouble was, he forgot to tell his mum but when I spoke to her on the phone she had no idea where he was. I never found out where he went. I would get so wound up that I'd often just tell him to piss off and we'd 'split up'. But then I would miss him and he'd convince me that there was nothing going on and we could make it work so we'd get back together. We were forever having 'make or break' conversations and all we ever seemed to talk about was us and 'the relationship'.

We had one of those conversations, a heavy one, in early January 1991 and because things had been getting really difficult between us, we decided to make some rules and give it a proper go. That meant no playing games, no going out alone with exes and being honest, more respectful and affectionate with each other, that type of thing.

I'd put all the confusion and stress behind me and I was happy. Especially as I'd also just got a new job, as European programme manager for The Walt Disney Company in Soho Square. My job was to manage and co-ordinate all the European regional Disney Clubs (the children's shows) and I also had to so something on the construction and building of Disneyland Paris, or Eurodisney, as it was called then. I didn't know anything about construction but, I thought, if they think I can do it, then I can (it turned out all I ever had to do on it was visit whilst wearing wellington boots). It really was a fantastic job and such an unbelievable opportunity – I'd get to travel, have my own office, £30,000 a year salary. I was over the moon. So over the moon in fact that when I walked out of the building after they'd told me I'd got it, I punched the air and screamed at the top of my voice, 'YES!' Never mind that people were staring at me like I was nuts, I didn't care. I couldn't wait to tell everyone, especially Chris, so I rushed home to tell him. I was still a bit shocked myself but nothing could have prepared me for his reaction. He didn't seem to be pleased for me at all; in fact, all he said was, 'Why did they give it to you?' Talk about pissing on my fireworks. It actually made me question myself. Did I deserve it? Could I do it? I still wasn't exactly clear what the job was; all I knew was that soon after I was to start, I had to go to Florida and visit the Disney parks (to be 'sprinkled with Tinkerbell's dust' is how the boss described it). It was his way of saying that once you've been there, you'll be so enamoured that you'll never leave the company. I doubted that was true but I was willing to give it a go, in fact I couldn't wait to get started. Of course I could do it; it was my job and I jolly well deserved it.

The fact that Chris wasn't so happy for me rang a little alarm bell, but I just put it on snooze and went and booked a holiday for myself and Helen to Jamaica for two weeks. I was to start the job as soon as I got back. He wasn't thrilled about that either, but why the hell shouldn't I go on holiday with my best friend? He couldn't go, he was working.

The week before I was due to go he announced he was going to Manchester. He had to go up there to help a mate who was in a band get his gear down to London for a gig, so he was borrowing a Volvo estate because he needed it for all the gear. Too much information, I thought, but I let it pass and off he went.

He came back on the Friday and as soon as he walked into the flat I knew something was amiss. But still, I ignored it. I was going on holiday the next day and I couldn't be bothered with him right at that moment. He had a look on his face that spelled out a thousand words and I could read every single one of them. I just didn't want to hear them come out of his mouth. I could see he was dying to tell me something so I asked him where he'd been. He carried on for a bit with the Manchester story but by then it was so obvious he wasn't telling the truth because he started to get a bit upset. So then he went down to the gym and when he got back, he sat down at the table and said, 'You're not going to like me after I tell you what I'm going to tell you.'

No, I'm sure I'm not, I thought.

'I didn't go to Manchester,' he said.

'I know,' I replied. 'Surprise me,' I continued.

'I went to Norwich,' he said, staring me right in the eyes. I knew one of his exes was working in Norwich at the time.

'Oh really, and what did you do there?' This time he didn't lie, so I got up from the table and as I did, I said, 'Don't be here when I get back,' and stormed out. He followed me, telling me not to go, but I ignored him. So much for giving the relationship a real go, eh? I just couldn't help thinking how he'd nearly ruined my holiday and I hadn't even left yet. And asking me not to go! Anyway, he was there when I got back. So was Kew Gardens; I'd never seen so many flowers.

While I was away in Jamaica I had a massage and a chat with the masseuse and I told her what had happened. She said, 'Everybody's allowed to make one mistake; you can't give up on the first time.' I doubted very much that it was the first time but I allowed him to stay when I got back anyway.

For a while Chris couldn't have been nicer, but it didn't last long. It never did. After the Norfolk/Manchester episode he decided to buy his own flat. He found one down the road from mine – it was nice, a studio house which was basically one room with a galleried bedroom and a little garden. I went to see it with him. He was well pleased with himself.

But all the time he was still staying with me we argued even though we were trying to go back to being just friends. Our rows were pathetic. We had one one night about a can of deodorant. It was so ridiculous I recorded it in a letter to a friend:

> *Anyway, the niceties ended again last night because he bought a can of deodorant. He's been living here for seven or eight months and in all that time this is only the second can of deodorant he's bought. And he uses it more than me. So, yes, I've always bought it. But you don't mind those things when you're shagging someone do you, so I never thought about it before. Anyway, we're not shagging now, and I haven't bought any deodorant for a long time. He's been asking me every day, 'bought any deodorant yet?' Fucking cheek!!! Well, I haven't and it isn't because I don't want him to use it, it's because I don't need it anymore because my mum bought me some Nina Ricci deodorant for my birthday (which I keep hidden by the way). Now, not only has he never bought any deodorant but he's never bought any soap powder, soap, toothpaste, shampoo, tea (maybe once), coffee (never), toilet rolls (I think he did once actually), and he doesn't even know what bleach or ajax is, but I've never said anything because I know it's pathetic and he's got a small room. But last night, he was in a bit of a mood because I'd been out and I was a bit squiff, well, he started waving this can of deodorant at me with a bitter and*

twisted look on his face, like fucking hell wasn't he the hero buying a can of deodorant two days before he's moving out and he's bound to take it with him anyway I thought. So I calmly suggested that he might have bought some of the other things that he uses all the time too, toothpaste – which had almost run out, squash – which had run out two days ago, but he'd forgotten them. I told him I thought that he should make more effort (I don't know why I bothered actually seeing as he will be moving into his own place in a few days but it made me so angry). And he went mad, told me to stop shouting (I wasn't) and then came into my room, said it was all a joke (OH YEAH?) and the punchline was that he'd bought two cans of deodorant and one was in my room, well very funny. So he threw the can across the room and it smashed four cassette cases that were on the receiving end just by my bed. Clever. And so this morning, he squeezed the rest of the toothpaste that was left down the toilet, and took all the bananas to work with him. Path-etic. So I left him a note this morning, saying, 'Sorry I didn't get the joke about the deodorant, but I got the one about the toothpaste down the toilet. By the way, I've emptied both cans of deodorant. Only joking. Signed, Bad Breath.' And now, I'm not looking forward to going home because he's sure to have done something else equally hilarious.

Soon after, he moved out. I got up just in time to see him going down the stairs, with his plants and that was it. It looked like the plants were walking all by themselves, like the plants were leaving me, not my on-off boyfriend. I said 'bye' but he ignored me.

Now, the reason I've included that little excerpt is just to illustrate just how mad it was, how much we didn't get on and how ridiculous we both were. It was typical of what it was like at the time, and had been for, well, ever since it started really. I can tell from that piece that I was on the verge of near madness, I must have been otherwise I wouldn't have bothered to write it all down in such detail. In fact, everything I've read from that period in my life, that part of the relationship, is like reading about someone else and it's hard to believe I allowed myself to indulge in such damaging and destructive drama. But I did because I hankered after the good times, that I knew we could have again if only I could be a better girlfriend.

Shortly afterwards I bought my own flat too, a one-bedroom directly below the one I'd rented for the past five years in the same house.

So we were living apart but were still winding each other up constantly. It was like a game and however much we talked about it, discussed it, looked for solutions, we just couldn't seem to get on. I started to blame myself for all the problems and was forever writing him apologetic notes, trying, even though I didn't really want to, to end it. I did want to be with him but not with all the drama and stress but couldn't seem to tear myself away and every time I tried to, he would pull me back in. He was like a Class A drug and I was well and truly addicted.

So much so that when he suggested marriage for the third time, I said yes.

CHAPTER 14

The First Time I: Was showered with second-hand confetti

(The Marriage Chapter)

It was never on my list of things to do, get married. Even as a kid in the 1960s when, despite the onset of free love and women's lib, marriage was still de rigueur, the society norm. I, however, never dreamed of the meringue dress and the handsome, rich husband like most little girls did then but, saying that, I hadn't consciously ruled it out either. People often think that I'd been put off by my mum's experience but it wasn't that complicated; it was simply that the idea wasn't there in the first place. I think I was always having too much fun to entertain it. I had other plans. Of course I'd had boyfriends but I never looked at any one of them and thought, 'Mmmmmm, marriage material.' I think I was much, much shallower than that.

So why then, at the age of 31, on 17 September 1991 did I marry Chris Evans (he was 25)? It's a very good question and one that I struggle to answer even now. I could just say, 'I don't know,' but that's a bit lazy isn't it? But I honestly don't. And while I don't regret it, I also don't like to admit that for a while back there, I turned into a crazy, dependent, fucked-up, idiotic human being who bears absolutely no resemblance to the person that I was when I met him.

This is especially clear after reading the very detailed accounts I wrote in journals at the time. I knew I needed to read those diaries but, in a way, I wish I hadn't, filled as they are with page after page, thousands and thousands of words of tortuous, delusional, self-justification and desperate attempts to try to make sense of our troubled liaison. Questioning myself, reassuring him, making promises and apologies, trying to work out why it was so difficult.

I've been trying to understand how that came about and why I allowed it to happen. Part of the problem, I think, was that being aware of his volatility, I always kept him slightly at arm's length, and as a result it gradually became a real competition of control. He was seeking some real commitment, maybe for the wrong reasons, and because I wasn't a willing partner – I wouldn't move in with him, work for him, sell my flat, give up my job or marry him despite numerous requests – he set about making all of that happen with a series of confusing and somewhat manipulative exercises. And the more I wouldn't comply, the worse he got.

He'd blow hot and cold, where he'd want everything and I was the love of his life then just disappear off with ex-girlfriends while saying he was doing other things. It did, actually, make me mad. He was so brilliant at being duplicitous that I was forever saying sorry and berating myself for not trusting him. It was insane and possibly the most difficult, traumatic and troublesome time we'd had for as long as I'd known him. Did he love me? I have some very convincing evidence that says he did. One thing's for sure though: I was madly in love with him, 'madly' being the operative word here for more than one reason.

Because here I was, a strong, independent, free-thinking woman with a great job and my own flat. I had just turned 31. These were supposed to be the best years of my life. In fact they turned out to be some of the worst. But I don't blame him, it was my fault for allowing it to happen. I just went along with it, believing that he really did love me and he really did want to marry me and then after we married, I persevered to try and keep it going despite indisputable evidence that I should have let it go and written it off as a big bad mistake.

It was beyond madness to get married but given the stress of the previous months, I honestly thought it would make everything all right. Back to how it was the year before that when all we did was laugh, have sex, get drunk and mess about on the radio. It had to because I had become so crackers, I genuinely thought I couldn't live without him. I didn't realise how soon I'd have to learn to.

It was a Sunday morning and he wasn't supposed to be in. He'd been out the night before and I'd stayed in, ruining another night convinced he was doing something untoward (he probably was) and trying to explain to him in writing why we had to seriously call it a day. Again.

Sunday 8 September 1991
He does care. I am going mad. Mad and neurotic. Why do I always think he's lying? I do not know the answer to this. Anyway, I spent most of last night writing him a note and each time I read it through, I saw me getting madder and madder and in the end, I just wrote a couple of paragraphs that weren't exactly neurotic and this morning I took it round. He was in, alone, much to my surprise. And all I thought was, why am I being such a bitch? What am I thinking? Why is this such a problem? I just don't know. Anyway, I gave him the note and he read it, laughing at my 'catsbum' comment. I think. Luckily he gave me a hug and even though I was determined to go to Maidstone, I didn't. Decided to get married instead and spent the day having sex even though Chris was half dead having been go-karting and partying at the health club until 4.30am while I was sulking over nothing at home. What a stupid cow. We went for lunch at the Haverstock and then went to my house. Told Mum I was getting married and she didn't believe me. Helped Chris with his washing, picked his car up, and then went for some scoff at the Chinese on Haverstock Hill. Then he went on holiday to Malta with Andy and Clare.*

Over nothing? It was hardly nothing and it was hardly a note. I've still got every attempt at that hand-written confusion and they're more like novels than notes. The first attempt was a three-page tirade

**Catsbum = what your mouth looks like if you're sulking or cross and you can't smile.*

made up of insults and personal attacks. They always started off like that and almost always ended up a soppy apology, blaming myself. But that's how nuts it was.

When he read my note, apart from laughing, he asked me if that was what I really wanted. No, it wasn't. (It was what I wanted last night but suddenly when he's asking, it wasn't.) He then posed the question, 'So what shall we do? We could get married.' It wasn't the first time he'd suggested it; he'd done it twice before (just three days before) but I'd always said no because I didn't believe he really wanted to be married to me. I thought he was only doing it to either wind someone else up or to see if he could get me to say yes. This time, completely against my better judgement, I gave him the answer he wanted.

He decreed before he left that we had to do it on the Tuesday after he got back from Malta and no one must know. I didn't question this last diktat but I probably should have.

I called Camden Registry Office but there were no free slots. A sign, surely? Probably, but I ignored it and asked if we could just come in and wait all day in case there was a no-show. It was Chris's idea and I thought it was bonkers but apparently it happens a lot where people don't bother to call to say they're not coming.

I was sitting at work when the phone rang, 'Hello, it's the Superintendent Registrar here . . .' *Christ, what have I done*? I thought, only listening to the first bit and thinking it was the police. The lovely man on the end said that he thought it was a bit sad (wasn't this whole thing?) to wait all day for a space so he was going to squeeze us in with a 15-minute slot on Tuesday at 3.15pm. That afternoon I went down to the office to pay the £15 fee for the licence. All I needed was proof that we both lived in the borough of Camden, which we did.

I went to the register office this afternoon. I have never been in such a dump in my entire life. It's a complete nightmare. I couldn't possibly have my mum there, she'd cry her eyes out, and not because she's happy but because the place is so awful. Felt really weird asking to make an appointment for a 'wedding'. The woman blurted out,

'What, you want to get married?' Do I? I thought. Yes I do, I concluded. So that was that, paid my £15 and left feeling really depressed because we have to wait a week now.

Eh?

When Chris called later from Malta I told him the news. He had told me to tell no one but he'd told Andy and Clare who also didn't believe it – and who could blame them, it was unbelievable.

I still told no one but I set about inviting people to the party that night. This was the reason it had to be Tuesday because it was the night of the launch party for a new TV show. So our wedding reception was to be a paid-for party in aid of something completely unconnected. Writing this now I still can't believe I went along with it.

I set about inviting a few of my good friends but I stuck to the rules and didn't tell them I was getting married; if I had done then I'm sure a lot more of them would have come. Most people couldn't though because of the short notice. I told my mum again and managed to convince her I was telling the truth. She pretended not to be upset but I think she was although she was happy for me to marry Chris because she loved him. When Chris told his mum, Minnie, her reply was classic. She asked, 'Who to?' Another sign.

There were so many signs.

We had a kind of joint stag/hen night, in the Holiday Inn Swiss Cottage Hotel bar with our friend, John Revell – we drank Molsen Dry beer and ate peanuts.

On the morning of the wedding we woke up together in a room at the hotel. I suddenly remembered I was supposed to go to work. I was still working at Disney. I rang my boss, 'Oh, sorry I can't come in today because I've got to go to a wedding.'

He said, 'Ah that's nice, whose wedding is it?' in an unsure tone.

I replied, 'Er, mine.'

'Seriously?'

'Yep, I'll be in on Thursday, is that OK?'

He still wasn't sure if I was taking the piss or not but said anyway, 'Sure, OK, see you then. Er, congratulations?'

For the occasion, I dressed in a black pencil skirt and a pink linen short jacket, my black lucky shoes (the ones I bought with my libel money) and a little black bag. It was a boiling hot day and I had tights on so my feet were swelling up and my armpits were beginning to sweat. Lovely.

There were no 'invited' guests except for my best friend, Helen, who met me outside the grim building with some dreadful flowers. They were deliberately, ironically dreadful, she'd bought them from a garage. They were funny at the time but thinking back they were a perfect metaphor for the whole event. Last minute, cheap and dead within hours. I remember we were laughing really hard at the whole debacle, especially when we were discussing how funny it would be if he just didn't turn up and I'd be jilted. On reflection I was laughing because I think I was quite wishing that would happen. Either that or it was a nervous laughter because I thought it might.

But then I saw him heading for the entrance of Camden Register Office, a horrible, ugly and imposing building that you just know is a government establishment. He'd literally come straight from work and brought his team with him under the pretence that they were shooting a feature for his show, *TV Mayhem*. So the wedding party consisted of Andy Bird, Andy Davies (Best Man), Gary, Clare, Martin and a couple of others I can't remember, all dressed in summer beach gear – shorts and sweaty T-shirts, flip-flops, that sort of thing. Chris had thankfully had the decency to change from his regulation short shorts and snotty T-shirt into a pair of long trousers and a nice shirt.

The whole thing was like some very big, bad joke.

As they all stood there, open-mouthed having realised what was going on, we ventured up the stairs and were put in a queue after checking in for our slot. Each couple got 15 minutes each. It felt like a production line. The whole place was like an old school with worn, dirty linoleum floors and crappy modern furniture. The room was hideous. Andy B was videoing everything.

The gang laughed all the way through the 'ceremony'. Everyone laughed when the registrar produced a pink, synthetic satin cushion for the rings. There were no rings, officially, but me being a traditionalist I'd brought my great-grandmother's band with me. Chris pretended to be disgusted but went along with it anyway. Within 15 minutes we were done. Man and wife.

Helen had her disc camera with her and took one shot. Unfortunately she left the film in the camera so long that when she took it to be developed, it didn't come out. Perhaps it's just as well; I could hardly bear the tragic evidence. Lucky too that the video Andy shot was accidentally(?) erased after we watched it, just the once, in silent horror.

Of course no one had any confetti so as we walked out of the building and down the stairs, Helen, rather thoughtfully, picked up some that had been thrown over the last couple from the stairs and threw it over us. It was quite possibly the most comically tragic moment of my entire life but as she did it I thought, it's another sign. How many did we need?

There was more. After the 'wedding' we walked along the Euston Road and went into an Irish bar where we drank some champagne with everyone. We didn't realise at the time but we'd dropped the marriage certificate on the floor and left it there. Luckily, Martin had picked it up and it remains to this day, the only real evidence that we did actually marry.

Later, Helen said to me, 'You know, at weddings I can usually guess how long it will last but this time I thought, I'm just not sure.'

Together, we all went to the 'reception'. It was awful. Right at the beginning, Chris got up on the stage and said, 'Ladies and gentlemen, thank you for coming. Today I married Carol McGiffin' and then walked off the stage. No one even cheered or clapped. Everyone just carried on drinking and partying. Of course they did, it was a party for a TV show launch, not a fucking wedding reception. Talk about confused.

I went over to talk to my four friends who'd heard the announcement. They just sat there, mouths open, staring at me. For ages. They simply couldn't believe it. Who could blame them? They'd sat and listened to me go on about the trauma and drama I'd had with Chris over the past year or so; they simply couldn't believe I'd married him. They clearly didn't like him. Not many of my friends did.

When my dad came up that time when I was trying to borrow money off him, he met Chris then and even he didn't like him! The only person I knew who approved was my mum, bless her.

We spent our wedding night in the Britannia Hotel in Belsize Park. The next day, which I suppose was our honeymoon, we went for fish and chips at Maxwell's of Hampstead on Haverstock Hill and then got in the Jag and drove around Essex looking for more cars to buy.

The following Saturday on GLR we played a mocked-up recording of the ceremony from a dictaphone and renamed the show, *Round At Chris's With His Missus* and the show got more and more popular.

Two of the things we decided to do straight away were: 1) to combine our bank accounts into one joint account. I was fine with this, even though, at the time, because I'd won the libel action against the newspaper, I actually had more money in the bank than him. And 2) live together, which had to be at my tiny flat as his house was being used as an office for Big & Good Productions, Chris's and Andy Bird's company that was making a new morning show, *TV Mayhem*, for TV-am. I don't know how we managed in that tiny space. It was on the middle floor of a Victorian conversion with barely any sound-proofing and every time we had sex the woman downstairs, who was an insomniac anyway, used to bang on the ceiling with her broom while screaming, 'Horrible noise! Horrible noise!' It was frightening.

I felt that both of these things were right. What's the point of getting married if you're going to keep separate money and not live together?

But first he had to tell his ex, Sara. This was a really big deal. I was exiled to the wine bar near his house while he made the call. Two hours it took. Why would you need two hours to tell your ex that you were married. Didn't she know? Apparently not.

Just two weeks after the wedding I had to go to Orlando for a Disney 25th Anniversary celebration. I wasn't away long, only about five days. Chris didn't want me to go and he questioned my loyalty to the marriage because I was willing to 'desert' him after just a couple of weeks. We'd discussed me working for him a few times but now he'd decided it wasn't a good idea, otherwise I might have blown out the Disney trip and resigned. The trip had been booked for months, almost since I started working there in February, but he still couldn't understand it. He also seemed to have forgotten that the whole proposal/wedding thing had happened in just over a week, just a couple of weeks before I was due to go off! So I went. He gave me a note before I left; it was in a Noel Gay envelope and it was a scrap of paper that had written on it, *'When you come back, come back and love me.'*

That note blew all my doubts away. I suddenly felt elated and confident that we'd done the right thing. I felt so happy on the plane; I kept reading the note and smiling. I couldn't wait to get back to him. But all that euphoria dissolved when I spoke to him from Florida one day – he was weird. Lying on the sofa, looking at all the photos of us on the wall he said, 'We've only been married a couple of weeks and you're in America and I'm lying here looking at the photos on the wall. What's all that about?' I had no idea what he was talking about. When I got home the first thing I did was call him. 'Wifey!' he shouted down the phone with another weird tone. He was at the office, the production team were still in pre-production for *TV Mayhem* but they'd moved out of his flat and into a place in St John's Wood. I was supposed to go over there but he swerved it and we arranged to meet in a café in Camden Town. When we did, he didn't even kiss me and as we were crossing the road, he blurted out, apropos of nothing, 'I don't think we should have a joint bank account.' Eh? Where had all this come from? I felt very uncomfortable. He didn't even ask me about my trip.

Christ knows what happened while I was away but it was a nightmare for weeks afterwards. We argued all the time, and I mean *really* argued. He didn't sleep and would get up in the middle of the night and go for a drive. We more or less stopped having sex (unheard of for us; we always did it, even when we hated each other), and we were definitely drinking too much. I tried to ignore it and hoped that he was just having trouble getting used to the idea of being married.

Chris did calm down and eventually I started working part-time for Big & Good Productions, as production manager on *TV Mayhem*. I was also still working for Disney part time.

There was a slight conflict of interest though because Disney were part of a consortium called GMTV that were in the running to take over the breakfast television franchise then owned by TV-am. When it was announced that TV-am had lost their franchise to GMTV there were cheers at Disney, where I happened to be, but obviously there were tears down at TV-am and Big & Good. Obviously my loyalties lay with Chris and Andy but I worked for Disney so I had to be seen to join in the celebrations. Chris wasn't happy about that at all and it was another little tack in the coffin of our very short marriage.

Luckily I'd made sure that the contract had been signed by TV-am execs before the announcement. Previously, this hadn't been thought of, but having been a production manager I noticed it and got it sorted. This meant that when TV-am cancelled the show, which they were going to have to, they'd still have to pay for most of their commitment to Big & Good. If the contract hadn't been signed they could have just said 'See ya!' with no financial compensation whatsoever. Chris and Andy and everyone who worked for them were going to do more than alright out of it. This still didn't win me any brownie points with Chris, as he continued to take it personally that TV-am had lost its franchise and he was going to lose his prized show.

By the middle of October he'd gone – moved back to his own house – and even though we were still doing the radio show together, at the end of it I'd get up and go, 'Bye,' even to him. It really was the beginning of the end and we'd only been married a month.

Pre-marriage I would have just told him to get lost, but now we were married I felt a responsibility to make it work and so I persevered even though every time we had a row he'd mention divorce, or he'd say, 'Well don't put up with it, then.' I probably should have got the hint there and then but I was convinced he didn't mean any of it.

After a couple of weeks we patched things up again and I moved into his house but before long it had all gone pear-shaped again.

27 February 1992
He's just told me he wants to end it. End the marriage because he doesn't like me. I admit I did do a horrible thing last night – I snatched the video controller out of his hand. Why did I do that? I don't really know actually but it's really pissed him off in a big way. I know I'm a moody cow I can't help it but he knew that. Maybe there's something else? But what for fuck's sake? I know he's got stress with Radio 1, no wonder. Perhaps he just doesn't fancy me anymore. Anyway – he can't put up with me! Well I can't put up with his fucking tantrums. This really isn't that bad.
Judge: 'So what are your grounds for divorce?'
Me: 'Well, your honour I snatched the remote control out of his hand the other night'.

It wasn't just the remote control that pissed him off. When I moved in I moved the furniture round a bit in an effort to stop it looking like a student den; I tried to make it homely but that just made him cross. In fact almost everything I did made him cross.

Me not being able to play golf. I really tried. I even had lessons. We went to Southport once in the rain and he made me finish the course even though I was so crap. My favourite shoes got ruined that day.

Me not having a hobby. After a row about Terry Wogan we had a row about me not having a hobby. I think he was still cross about the golf.

Me shrinking his hat. Actually it was the launderette that shrunk the hat but it was his favourite and it was my fault for letting the launderette wash it.

Me being a crap celebrity wife. I didn't blame him for this one. I was crap. At a celebrity football thing we were at, I inadvertently got locked out of the VIP area and because I couldn't say, 'I'm with Chris Evans, I'm his wife' to the goon on the door I waited outside for him until it had finished. About three hours later he came out and was so cross I cried.

Cross Chris peaked one St. Patrick's Day. We'd gone to drink green Guinness in a pub in London and there were loads of music people there, pluggers and record company types. We were both quite pissed and I'd flashed my tits (as I had a habit of doing when I'd had a few) so Chris started an argument (as he had a habit of doing when he'd had a few). It was a nightmare combination.

I hated rowing in front of people we knew so I left, got in a cab and went home. We were living in his Studio House at the time in Belsize Park and I'd not been in more than a few minutes when he stormed in, ranting. I'd either left him with no money or no keys, I can't remember, but we started having the altercation from hell. Things were being lobbed all over the place – glasses, plates, bottles of red wine (noooooo!), chairs, everything including deeply personal, hurtful insults. The room was beginning to look like a gang of blind burglars had been on the rampage. Chris topped it all off by going upstairs and hurling my full-length bamboo mirror over the balcony of the mezzanine. Seven more years of bad luck came crashing to the floor bringing a blindingly abrupt halt to the madness.

As we surveyed the carnage it was silent. Chris sat down and started sobbing. I knew how he felt and I wanted to sob too, the whole situation was too sorry. But I couldn't, I had to comfort him, tell him it was ok, it was all going to be alright.

The next day he took my mirror to the glass shop to be repaired which was sweet of him. Actually it would have been sweeter if he hadn't have smashed it in the first place but hey ho, it's only seven years. We never spoke about the incident again until some years later after we'd split up. We laughed, albeit nervously, mostly at the idea of him getting into the cab and saying, 'Follow that cab and step on it!', admitting he'd always wanted to say that.

It went on like this for a while. Our poor neighbour, Nina Myskow, who lived upstairs must have hated us. There was already no love lost between her and Chris as he'd had to produce her on GLR and they didn't really hit it off.

So far, not many good times. I had to think long and hard if there were actually any good times, but there were, even though they were few and far between. That wasn't how Chris saw it though.

In January 2010, in an interview for *The Sunday Times Magazine* by Lynn Barber, after she'd told him that I'd described our marriage as 'the marriage from hell', he said, 'Did she say that? I didn't think it was the marriage from hell, I think we had a good time.'

I suppose we did have some nice holidays. We had some lovely times in the New Forest staying in little B&Bs in Lyndhurst.

And I'll never forget boarding a chartered cruiser on a Monday morning in Bray, when everyone else was going to work, for a three-day sail up the Thames with Andy Bird, his wife Caroline and Timmy and Linda Mallett. The weather was glorious and all we did was stop off at various pubs on the way and eat and drink. Negotiating the locks was a nightmare but we got the hang of it. Chris spent most of the time with a wet hanky over his face and under his glasses trying to protect himself from the violent hay fever that was around that summer.

The grand tour of Great Britain was one of the best things we ever did. One day, we stocked up with hummus and chipsticks and took off in the MkII Jaguar up the A5 and decided to drive all the way to Wales without going on a motorway. We had no idea where we were going to stay and we took very little clothing with us. We made it to Holyhead, where if there'd been a ferry to Dublin we probably would have got on it. As there wasn't we drove back through North Wales, and on to the Lake District, where we stayed in the most gorgeous hotel with raging fires and giant steaks. We drove up steep ridges in the Jag – the most unsuitable car ever for mountain driving. Even the sheep, balanced at 45 degrees, looked at us like we were mad. We covered Derbyshire, Yorkshire, Lincolnshire, Suffolk, Norfolk, Newmarket then back to London. It was freezing.

We went on another tour in the summer to Somerset, Weston Super Mare, South Wales, New Forest again and Brighton, which was where we were when Chris got the news that *The Big Breakfast* was confirmed as the new Channel 4 breakfast show. We were in the Grand Hotel and because we'd been away for a while, I suggested going to check if there were any messages on the answering machine at home – I had a remote device thing that allowed me to listen to them. When I heard how many there were I knew something was going down. There were 49 if I remember correctly, so I was gone a while. I listened to them all and wrote them all down. When I heard *The Big Breakfast* one I was so excited for him. He was quite anxious waiting for the news and wanted it so badly so it was a big relief too. Most of the other messages were very important people offering congratulations. I couldn't wait to tell him the news but unfortunately he got a bit cross again because I think he wanted to hear the message first. Straight after, we went home. He wasn't concentrating on anything else at that point. I sensed he was drifting off again. That was around May.

In June he moved out again.

He kept going off to live where Andy D was living in Islington but then kept complaining about having to get up early to move his car and having a small room. It got quite ridiculous and I got sick of hearing it so I moved out too. My flat was rented so I went to live in Leytonstone with my friend Sue who I had worked with at The Children's Channel. He even replaced me on the radio show with a girl who'd walked into the studio one day to be part of the live audience, her name was Alison. I didn't think she was very good but I still listened, I couldn't help myself. I felt like I had been hit by a truck when I suddenly heard him say one day, 'RIP the marriage.' He'd just announced on air that our marriage was over without even having the decency to talk to me first. I couldn't believe it and I got myself into such a state, I was on the verge of storming into the pub where I knew he'd be. But, worried I might just kill him, I rsetrained myself. So I wrote him a note instead. Again. But I never gave it to him. Again.

At the end of my tether I went to see a Relate counsellor. On my own. I was anxious to know if it *was* me, as I had thought and written many times in my journal. Was I was always to blame for the mess? He made me feel that way. Then, in August, I went to see a solicitor about a divorce. I was serious. What was the point? It was over, wasn't it? Then, just as they were about to write to him, he called.

It was just before *The Big Breakfast* went on air in September 1992. It started with a couple of late-night calls then him phoning me on a Saturday morning, asking me to do the 'What's On' for the show. Rachel (his new best friend and star of his *Round At Chris's Live* shows) was standing in for Alison and I thought she was rubbish too. I did it although I don't know why. Then he started coming over to Leytonstone and before long he was suggesting we get back together. I met him in a hotel in Manchester and we had a heart to heart. I asked him if he'd slept with anyone. He said yes. Someone called Jane. I didn't know how I felt about that because I certainly hadn't. I wanted to give it another go in spite of everything that had happened, so we did. We went on a cruise to the Bahamas. It was a surprise and I wasn't allowed to know where we were going, which gave me stress because I didn't know what to pack and took too many clothes because he wouldn't even tell me if it was going to be hot or cold. Anyway, while we were away on the cruise the news that we'd got back together appeared in the paper along with the detail that he'd booked me a 'surprise' cruise as a way of wooing me back. Wonder whose idea that was?

So it was all OK again for a while. Chris agreed that we should buy a bigger house, especially now he'd got the big contract. I spent months looking at houses in Berks, Bucks, Herts and Kent. Everywhere. They were never right and so we rented a three-storey townhouse in Parliament Hill in London. It did improve things, what with him having the job of his dreams, and I was happy to sit back and help him on his way to fame and glory. I threw myself into being a great housewife. Cleaning, cooking, doing the laundry and, after he decided to get one, walking the dog. I was a bit annoyed that it hadn't been a joint decision but after we'd got her I fell in love instantly. Her name was Angelina and she was an abandoned ex-racing greyhound with an adorable personality. I called her Mangie. I was still looking for houses too, and was getting the distinct feeling that Chris didn't really want to buy a house – nothing was good enough and I tell you, I looked at hundreds.

Things started to go awry again when he got a call from Richard Branson asking him to take the GLR show to launch the new Virgin 1215 station. By this time he was earning £200 a show for the three hours on a Saturday. Virgin would pay him £1,000. It would be the first time he'd done something for money and it didn't pay off because he was being paid for by sponsorship and Chris just didn't want to toe the line as far as bowing to commerciality went. Also, he had started to freeze me out. He got new friends in from *The Big Breakfast* to be in his radio gang. I eased myself out gracefully, not wanting to compete with his new chums.

The last show ever on GLR was brilliant; they were queuing round the block to get in. Everyone wanted to be in on it. I thought he was mad to move it and I told him so. Right at the end of show, he said his thanks to everyone. And I mean *everyone*, from his mum to the cleaners and security men. Towards the end of the hour, I could see there were only a few seconds left. *Ah he's leaving me 'til last*, I thought. Nope. I didn't even get a mention as he signed off with an emotional goodbye. He really was an arsehole sometimes. I couldn't understand why he wouldn't mention me after four years and I was so upset I stormed out of the studio managing to slam a slow-closing, super-heavy, soundproofed door on the way. I got in my car and went home while he went to the pub.

It was probably just another giant clue that he didn't want me around anymore. They were coming thick and fast. Another great one was delivered on a holiday to Corsica in the summer of 1993, with Dan and Lisa – two of his new *Big Breakfast* and Virgin Radio friends. On the way to Gatwick we had such a row that he stopped the car and nearly made me get out. We still went. Lisa and Dan were like our marriage crutches for that week (there were always people around, we were never alone) but one day they decided to go off and be on their own and left Chris and me sitting in a restaurant. There wasn't a lot of conversation going on but I remember him saying to me, 'So, what's your plan then?' He was meaning about life. He was obsessed with plans; he always had one whereas I never did. It was something else that irritated him about me, as well as my not having any hobbies.

I just said, 'Well, I'm going to look after you.'

To which he replied, 'Oh right, so I'm stuck with you then?' It was one of those times when someone says something and it doesn't really sink in until much later.

So I just said, in a jokey, jolly way, 'Yep!'

He was probably thinking, 'Shit.'

As soon as *Don't Forget Your Toothbrush* was commissioned, that was it. I never saw him. He had a whole new bunch of hangers-on and I wasn't included in any of it. I did try to talk to him about it, telling him that if I wasn't involved in his work, I had no part in his life because his life was work. He didn't want to hear it and basically told me he didn't want me 'piggy-backing' on his fame. It wasn't what I wanted at all; I just wanted to be involved in his life. I didn't want to be famous – I was happy, for a while anyway, being a wife.

We did buy a house, a really nice house, in Highgate, North London. Three weeks later he was gone for good. It really was RIP the marriage this time.

CHAPTER 15

The First Time I: Took the dog for a half a lager and decided it was time to go

(The Divorce Chapter)

There was huge potential for acrimony but, as far as divorces go, it was quite civilised. It was such a massive relief when he walked out of the door that the last thing on my mind was money, or divorce. I was just glad to see the back of him. Still, however much I hated him, I was hurt and upset. Not visibly, but the sense of failure I felt straight away was overwhelming. I'd tried hard in the marriage, much harder than it had warranted. The whole torturous episode didn't really deserve five minutes, let alone two years, and with the lovely benefit of hindsight we should really have annulled the whole thing the next day.

As I've said, I never really wanted to be married but I wanted to be divorced even less. It's funny because I have friends who say to me, 'Oh well, at least you've BEEN married!' As if that's a better scenario, to have at least one, failed marriage behind you rather than to not have been married at all. Wrong. I, maybe naively, always believed that if you said those words, 'until death do us part', you should follow them though, or at least do everything within your power to try to make it work. I think I did. But when someone makes it completely intolerable, impossible and unbearable and is determined to destroy something, then you have to know when to give up.

That day probably should have been sooner but in the event, it was 11 August 1993, just over one month short of two years after we'd got married.

The thing is, when something is that tiring and difficult, it's sometimes hard to know when to call it a day. I'd been thinking for ages that it shouldn't be this hard and had sat in my flat between rentals and imagined how much happier I'd be living on my own. I'd also been looking at other, bigger flats thinking I might leave him. I'd also spoken to some of the females from couples that we used to hang around with. I wanted to know if everyone was the same. Did they all have to walk on eggshells constantly, wondering when or if you're saying the wrong thing? Were there days of silence when he just wouldn't talk to you? The answer was always no. But still you go on until one day you come across the straw that breaks the camel's back.

A few days before, my mum had come to visit. Now, my mum wasn't a good traveller, she didn't really like being away from home at all but I'd gone down to pick her up because she wanted to see Chris and me, together, have some lunch, something like that. She loved Chris, thought he was an absolute god. I never shattered her illusion; why would I? Anyway, when we got back to the house, she was all eager to see him but he wasn't there, he wasn't home from work yet. He was doing *The Big Breakfast* at the time which finished at 9am and he knew we were taking my mum for lunch so why wasn't he home? Mildly irritated, I left him a note to say where we would be and to come and join us. I made his excuses and took Mum for lunch in one of the pubs in Highgate. It was nice, but awkward because he wasn't there. We waited for a bit before we ordered in case he turned up. He didn't. I really felt for my mum. She quite obviously took it personally and was overcompensating by making excuses for him too. When we got back he was in bed. By this time I was fuming. Mum was staying the night so we just sat downstairs watching telly and talking while he slept upstairs. Later on I went to see him because

I needed to ask if I could use the Porsche the next day to take my mum home. Our other car was a 1968 Mark II Jaguar that was pretty unreliable to say the least. It did always start but you had to open the bonnet and do something – I think it was manually activate the choke – before it would, then it would take ages to warm up, so it was a bit of a chore and I didn't fancy a long drive down to Kent and back in it in case it broke down. He grudgingly agreed.

The next morning at 3am I heard him trying to start the Jag. It was being stubborn and didn't sound like it was going to go. Next thing he comes back into the house ranting that it's dark, it's 3 o'clock in the morning, he's got to get to work (unlike me) and he can't even take his own car, the Porsche. I'd asked to use it for one day. One day only. So I could take my old mum, who he didn't even have the courtesy to come to lunch with the day before, home safely. I was furious with disbelief. And at that precise moment, I knew I couldn't be with him for another minute.

I took my mum home and returned the car to the house. I picked up the dog and went for a walk. We walked up to Highgate to The Flask pub and I sat there with a half a lager, gathering my thoughts, taking stock, thinking how happy I was going to be when it was just me and Mangie Angie the dog. There was no question he would take her, even though it was wholly his idea to get her, so I wasn't worried about a custody battle. When I got home the first thing he said to me was, 'Where have you been?' But not in an inquisitive way, like he was interested. In a kind of accusatory way: 'Where have *you* been?'

I could feel a red mist rising as I said, fairly calmly considering how much I was still shaking with anger, 'In the pub actually.' I might have followed that with, 'Thinking about how much I hate your guts,' but in reality I think I just told him I was leaving, I'd found a flat (which I had) in Highbury and that was it, I was off, I'd had enough.

He then said, 'Yeah, I'm not happy.'

At which point I lost it. I don't remember exactly what I said but

I know it contained the phrase, 'I can't stand you anymore', and that I told him how fucking awful he'd been to my mum while reminding him that I often spent days entertaining his mum while he went off and did his own thing. I then grabbed the dog and tried to get out of the door.

He stopped me saying, 'No, you're not leaving, I'll go,' and for a moment it was like a race to get out first, both getting stuck in the door trying to leave at the same time. I was right, he didn't argue about the dog. He took nothing except the keys to the Porsche and disappeared into the night. He left everything else but days later I packed it all up in boxes and it sat in the spare room for over a year before he sent someone to collect it.

Where he went that night I had no idea and I cared less. I felt like the old me had returned and that a giant weight had been lifted from my shoulders. I was relaxed for the first time in a very long time. I called my friend Jayne who came round soon after and we went up to the village for a meal, although we were more interested in drinking. It was like a celebration even though I should have been lying on my bed face down, sobbing and taking turns with each hand to punch the pillows, left, right, left, right while screaming, 'No! No! No!'

The press didn't click straight away but it was obvious they were going to sooner or later so Chris's PR, Kris Thykier at Freud's decided it was time to put out a press release because that's what famous people do when something calamitous happens in their private life and, by that time, Chris was very famous indeed. I was just ambling along thinking we'd got away with it but no. Kris read the proposed copy back to me over the phone and hearing the words brought back that familiar feeling of hideous angst. I was well aware that this was something that was now completely out of my control.

I'd never really had to deal with the press before, apart from when I was falsely accused of having an affair with Mike Hollingsworth, and a few appearances at film premieres. The thought of such a big story made me feel quite sick. I was so shaken I phoned my friend

Daphne and asked her to come round and bring some cigarettes. Benson and Hedges. I'd given up smoking in 1986 and hadn't smoked since but suddenly on that day in September 1993 I needed a crutch. Daphne was there when the final copy was faxed through. When I saw it I burst into tears and started shaking uncontrollably. I couldn't handle it. I didn't want to handle it. I sat there all night smoking and wondering what to do.

The story wasn't going to be released for a few days; the idea was to get it in on a Saturday when Chris wasn't on telly so by Monday, when he was back at work, everyone would have forgotten about it. I had a few days to sort something out.

My first priority was to get the hell out of the house. So I called Helen and asked if I could hide out and could I bring the dog. She kindly obliged and that night I packed a bag, locked up the house and went to stay with her before the shit hit the fan. I didn't want to stick around to witness the fallout, for there was bound to be some, so I booked a cheap last-minute holiday and buggered off to Cyprus for a week.

I left in such a hurry I forgot to cancel the milk and papers so I asked Daphne to keep an eye on the house for me, although it really wasn't necessary, there was already round-the-clock security in the form of a gang of vultures, I mean journalists and photographers, who'd taken root. They constantly harassed her as to my whereabouts but all she said was, 'I've got nothing to say.' Some smartarse journo replied, 'You've been waiting your whole life to say that, haven't you love?' They stayed there for a whole week on shift in case I came back.

When I knew the coast was clear I went home but it wasn't long before they started stalking me. The first time I noticed them they were in a car at the bottom of the hill by the bus stop at Swain's Lane. I was going shopping. I wasn't particularly dressed up but I wasn't looking my worst. The picture appeared in *Today* newspaper with the headline, 'A WOMAN SCORNED!' and described me as 'trudging' down the road. Actually, I was walking, that's all. There was also a picture of his new model girlfriend.

★ TODAY Wednesday September 22 1993 **3**

TODAY / PRICE OF BREAKFAST FAME

A woman scorned..

Dejected-looking Carol walks alone near her home Picture: PAPPIX U K

Chris and Carol pose with pet greyhound

Cheek-to-cheek Evans and ex-model Rachel

No glitz, no contest by breakfast show wife

by CHERYL STONEHOUSE

BEHIND the severe spectacles, Carol Evans is attractive enough. But the competition is formidable.

Her husband Chris, 27, manic, chubby-cheeked star of TV's Big Breakfast, is lavishing attention on a dazzling, 24-year-old blonde ex-model called Rachel Tatton-Brown.

And 33-year-old Carol seems to have decided there is no point in trying to compete with all that glitz.

She trudges along the leaf-lined streets near her home in Highgate, north London, with an air of resignation, if not downright defeat.

Yet it is only 10 weeks since Evans announced that he was giving up his Virgin radio show to spend more time with her, and save their marriage.

He splashed £350,000 from his £1.5 million Channel 4 deal on a pretty cottage. But last weekend, Evans was dining and dancing with 6ft Rachel, who quit modelling for a Big Breakfast studio job.

Carol and Chris have parted once before, only eight months after they wed, two years ago.

Nutter

"The split was all my fault," he admitted later. "I'm a bit of a nutter."

That first time, he won Carol back with a romantic cruise. Perhaps he thinks that if it all ends in tears, he can run home again.

But this time, it's all a lot more public. The hurt, for Carol, a good deal deeper.

There's an old, old saying that her gallivanting husband might bear in mind.

Something about a woman scorned . . .

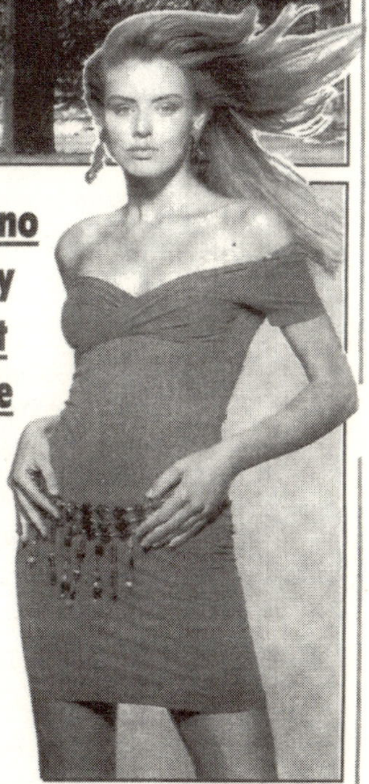

Rachel the 6ft blonde dazzler in her modelling days

EWS TODAY NEWS TODAY

/COP GOES OWNBEAT

star Nick Berry is to
l his clean-cut image in
ritty new show.
lick, 29, who plays PC
wan in the hit ITV series,
artbeat, will play a
ncer with a ponytail in
£1 million thriller.
he pilot show – not yet
d – could replace Heart-
if ratings slip.
t's a vehicle for Nick –
per cent his own show,"
ITV spokesman said.

Monster prices

PARENTS are being charged monstrous prices for Jurassic Park dinosaur spin-offs, says a Labour MP.

Models and other souvenirs from the hit movie are up to 83 per cent more expensive here than in America, according to shadow consumer affairs minister Nigel Griffiths.

His survey found a model of Tyrannosaurus Rex, which is the vicious star of the Steven Spielberg film, cost the equivalent of £6.66 in the US but £12.22 in the same store in Britain.

He said: "Here in the UK, retailers are greedier than T.Rex – ripping off large chunks of cash from children and their parents."

I wrote about the press attention in a letter to my brother who was working in Ghana at the time:

8 October 1993
How nice to get a letter that didn't come from the poison pen of a journalist working for a Sunday Shag Rag. Yes, I'm out, I've come out at last. What a nightmare eh? Well you probably don't know the full extent of the damage or do you get 'The Sun' delivered in Ghana? Basically, I've been hounded by the press for the second time in my life and I'm not even famous! You know, I was actually followed for 4 whole days by a photographer on a motorbike and well, he got some really juicy stuff: me going to buy dog food, me going to the accountant's, me putting the rubbish out, me posting a letter and wait for it, the picture that'll be worth millions, the one that'll trump Fergie's Toe-Sucking Snap, me sweeping the leaves from my driveway! Honestly, they are so stupid. They've offered me everything for 'My Side Of The Story'. Like paying for me to go on holiday to anywhere I wanted in the whole world for as long as I liked all expenses paid and all they wanted in return was a few snaps of me on the beach! Then they wanted to do a photo session in a studio to get some nice 'shots'. So I could have my choice of photographer, hairdresser, make-up person, money to spend on clothes and as the bloke at the door said, 'Yeah, get you in a studio luv, bit o' hair, bit of make-up, make ya look a million dollars luv.' Yeah and I've seen the Sunday tabloid version of 'a million dollars'. They all end up looking like Angie from Eastenders. SO NO WAY. Then the money. The letters always underline substantial sum of money. I wonder. You know I wouldn't do it but I can understand why people do talk to the press because it is tempting and they are very persuasive and some people will do anything for money I suppose. Guess what. They were going through my rubbish the other day. Nightmare. Anyway, only one sensible piece appeared out of all of the mess, and I've enclosed a copy for you. Basically, I wish I'd written it. Thank God for at least one intelligent journalist.

That journalist was Victor Lewis Smith writing in the *London Evening Standard* and I want to thank him personally here for that ray of brilliance during such a hideous time in my life. He had written about how Chris had predictably, after dumping the frump, gone straight for a blonde, younger model. And who could blame him? He was 27 years old with the world at his feet; he could pick and mix in the sweetshop of fame to his heart's content. The last thing he wanted was a 33-year-old wife hindering his selection.

Spitting Image even did a sketch about it. It had him doing a 'Toothbrush' style game show and Chris is asking the contestants who they are. He turns to a vague image of me and says, 'Who are you?', the puppet says, 'I'm your wife, Chris.' He then slaps her away saying, 'Not anymore you're not!' Then the credits roll and they're all for Chris Evans and the song is, 'Leave your wife, leave your wife, as soon as you're famous, you leave your wife' to the tune of 'Ebeneezer Goode' by The Shamen. It was funny.

The other nightmare was the house. We'd only been in it since July but Chris had already got the local builder, Jack, in to knock down the wall between the kitchen and the dining room and rip out the kitchen. So there I was, left in the house, with no husband, no job and no kitchen. I lost so much weight because all I ate every day was a portion of Singapore noodles from the Chinese takeaway down the road.

We dealt with the division of property and the money side very quickly in the Separation Agreement. Communication came from Kirit, his accountant. Chris was basically asking what I wanted by way of settlement. I asked for:

All the equity in the house;

Mortgage paid for two years;

I keep my flat and he keeps his and the cars;

All the money in the joint account to finish the kitchen, decorate the house and buy a car;

Dog maintenance until she died (well, she was his dog).

And that was it. He agreed, the agreements were drawn up and signed with the inclusion of the words 'in full and final settlement'.

It was very fair considering how high he was flying, he had no reason to complain.

This didn't stop him making snide remarks on his Virgin Radio show many years later.

For some reason I logged them in my journal.

> *Chris Evans is speaking on his breakfast show on Virgin Radio. The phone-in this morning* (it's Wednesday 4 August 1999) *is: 'If you could marry again, would you choose the same wife' or something like that. A caller declares, 'marriage is not a game'. Chris says, I know it's not, believe me, I know it's not. Take a look at my bank statement the week we split up. Holly, I don't treat it as a game do I?' For once, Holly says no.*
>
> *Chris is on the radio talking about me again. A caller calls in, 'It's Carol.' Silence. 'Carol from Dundee.' Chris breathes a sigh of relief and asks that no one does that to him again. Anyway, he goes on. He's just played a Neil Sedaka track and so he plays 'Oh Carol' (MY SONG!) and sings along, 'Oh Carol, I am but a fool, when you divorced me, you took all my savings from when I was a little boy.'*

Admittedly I did carry on cashing the cheques for as long as they came to the house – I had a kitchen to pay for and I thought if his agent can't get his act together to re-direct the payments then why should I forward them? I didn't consider it theft; the agreement hadn't been signed yet and we had a joint bank account so technically it was still *our* money.

The surprising thing about finding myself on my own again was the realisation that it doesn't matter how much you want a marriage to end or how relieved you are when it does, you still have to work quite hard to pick yourself up afterwards. It was a nightmare. And even more surprising was that I missed him. This was all made much worse by the fact that my departed ex's every move was in my face every time I opened the paper. In fact, the first time I'd seen anything of him after he'd left was a couple of months later in the newspaper out at a party with his new six-foot blonde model girlfriend, Rachel, my sometime replacement on the radio show at GLR who he'd met working on *The Big Breakfast*. They were all over the place. People would say, 'Don't read it!' *But why shouldn't I?* I thought. I liked reading the paper. On top of that, everywhere I went there were giant billboards of him with his giant toothbrush.

I felt like absolute shit. I didn't even have work to distract me, as I hadn't worked for over two years – the last time was for Big & Good but after it folded Chris didn't want me to work so I hadn't. I didn't really know where to start. So for nearly three months I wallowed, cried and wrote really sad and pathetic letters to Chris that I could never post because I had no idea where he was.

I felt like a total failure and I was living in a new house, that was miles from anyone I knew, spooky at night and had rubble for a kitchen.

I knew the first thing I had to do was get a job and I started talking to people and buying the Media *Guardian* on a Monday. I applied for loads, some completely unsuitable and some for which I was totally overqualified but I didn't care, I just knew I had to get back to work. While scanning the paper one day, I came across an ad for an assistant to the MD of a company I knew of, West One Television. I not only knew the company, I knew the MD – it was my old mentor Jane Kelly. I phoned her straight away. She was extremely hesitant about giving me the job, she knew I could do it but she told me, 'Look, you're overqualified and I know what'll happen, you'll do it for a couple of months and then you'll go off and do something much more interesting.' I told her she was wrong but she knew she was right. I was honest in that I really needed to get my confidence back and in the end I think she took pity on me and gave me the job. I will be forever grateful to her for that. I could start straight away, which was perfect.

By Christmas I'd lost a stone in weight and it was time to go out again. Trouble was, even though I was thin, I looked a total state. I hadn't really done any grooming for quite a while. My legs were like a chimp's, my toenails were growing back into my feet and my hair looked like Neil's from *The Young Ones*. So the first thing I did was get my hair sorted out.

I went to John Freida's salon in London. It was the first time in years I'd spent any money on myself and as I walked out, I felt quite elated, like all the stress of the last few years was now lying on the floor of the hairdressers. I felt so good I walked up the road, intending to walk all the way home, and when I chanced upon a pub, instead of walking right past as I had intended, I decided to go in for a drink. I only had half a lager but it was like a little celebration with myself. It was a big turning point.

I also bought all new underwear and a short, silk dressing gown. They were also both really important moves even though they don't sound like it.

The 'D' word wasn't mentioned until much later. I had no problem with a divorce but we didn't actually do it until 1998.

In the summer of 1995 Chris turned up near to where I was living in Belsize Park. He'd bought a flat there, was going back in the local gym and we became quite friendly. I saw him a few times in the Haverstock Arms just after I sold the Highgate house. He said it had been a mistake to sell it but I told him I had to because I couldn't afford to pay the mortgage. He blithely said he would have carried on paying it. *Great, thanks for telling me now.* So I thought I'd try my luck and ask for a loan to buy a bigger flat. I was living back in my tiny one-bedroom flat that I'd bought in 1990, with the giant greyhound, Angie. I had so much furniture in there it became very difficult for her to walk around and because she was so big she couldn't turn round so she literally had to reverse around the coffee table to get anywhere else in the flat. Poor little Mangie. Anyway, the flat I wanted to buy was £250,000. I had about half of that and asked if he'd either lend me the rest or at least guarantee a mortgage for it. He said no, and no. I wasn't surprised, I hadn't really expected him to go along with it but I thought it was worth a try.

One afternoon when Chris was meeting some of the old gang in a café in Haverstock Hill, he invited me along for a drink. I kind of knew it wouldn't be a good idea but it was a nice sunny day and Suzi, his girlfriend at the time, didn't seem to mind so I went along, got pissed on copious bottles of Becks and when he said, 'So shall we get divorced then?' I said, 'Yeah, I suppose so, one day.' The next day it was in the papers under the headline, 'BECKS WITH THE EX' and the story was that the day before we'd had our 'divorce party'. It pissed me right off and when Chris's solicitors wrote to me asking me to give my consent I just ignored them.

I thought, *he's still trying to control everything, well he can fuck off.* For the first time since I'd met him, I was in control of something. I know it's pathetic but I couldn't help myself. It made no difference whatsoever to me if I was divorced or not. I've no idea if he wanted to remarry but I didn't so I held out until I was ready to let him have it.

I wrote to his accountant Kirit in September 1997 to say if he wanted it I was ready to give him the divorce and that night, as he was giving out a prize at the Comedy Awards, he announced it live on TV and thanked me, which was odd to say the least, especially as he wasn't even receiving an award, he was just handing one out. The Bizarre column in the *Sun* described it as 'astonishing' and also said that 'host Jonathan Ross was clearly amazed'. Jesus, so was I.

In 2009 I was asked by Chris's PA (not Chris) to write a testimonial page for Chris's autobiography. I thought I might do it but I had some questions. Namely: 1) How many words? 2) Is there a fee? 3) Can you give me a guarantee that if I write it, you will use it without any editing? This last question was because I wasn't sure that Chris would like what I'd written and I didn't want anyone changing it or maybe not even using it if I'd made the effort. I got a reply (from the PA again) that said they required 300 words and there was no fee, but everyone else had agreed to do it. There was no answer to my last question so I left it at that.

But even though I never submitted it, I wrote it anyway:

CAROL MCGIFFIN ON CHRIS EVANS

I definitely got Chris too early. He wasn't ready for me, let alone marriage. Back then he was like a big ginger tsunami. Confusing, overwhelming, uncontrollable and would engulf a person with all-consuming power then disappear without looking back, leaving carnage and destruction behind him and acting as though you never existed.

He's obviously much better now though. In writing his book he is finally acknowledging his past whereas before there was no past and no future, only today. It made him so exhausting to be around. Always convinced he was going to die and therefore we must all get as drunk as possible all of the time, except he wasn't; he preferred to be in control.

When we met we had the most fun two people could have had but his eye was always on the bigger picture. During one of our marital sabbaticals I decided to clear out the house of all junk and I came across a list he'd written. It wasn't dated but the things I remember that were on it were:

1. *Get a morning TV show*
2. *Do the Radio 1 breakfast show*
3. *Get Carol and marry it (sic)*

The other things on the list probably involved cars.

All of these things, and more, he'd achieved by the time he was 30 which is admirable but also sad because during his period of madness I speculated that he'd done it all and had nowhere to go, nothing to do, nothing to look forward to. It was probably the only time when he did actually get really drunk.

I don't know Chris now and although we speak on the rare occasions we bump into each other, we're not friends and I don't have his phone number.

I'm not surprised about anything that's happened to him, his success, his fuck-ups and his losses but I wish him well with his new family. I will probably never get to know the new Chris so I'm left only with my memories of the old one. And unfortunately, most of them are not very nice.

CHAPTER 16

The First Time I: Dated a model, an MP and another DJ

(The Dating After Divorce Chapter)

Finding yourself single again after such an intense liaison is a strange feeling. A mixture of relief, sadness and woe-is-me. In other words, I was happy to be free, but sad that I had failed at marriage and a little sorry for myself. Because, despite everything that had happened, I still kind of missed him.

Obviously, after such a tumultuous few years I certainly wasn't looking to get hitched again and nor was I really looking to go dating; what was more important was getting back out there and having some fun. I'd been so bloody miserable for so long I was beginning to piss myself off.

Plus, I was still in a bit of a sexual prime time and I wasn't ready to give up on men just yet. I was still only 33 years old after all.

Luckily, I was looking much better than I had in years because the stress had been lifted and I'd lost weight, but my confidence was still getting a constant battering, what with having to witness the numerous blonde bombshells that were hanging off Chris's arm so soon after our split.

I'd not been out for nearly three months so it was a big effort to actually do it and the first night took a lot of guts, deep breaths and wine. I thought, *if I'm going to go for it I'd better start as I mean to go on* and instead of going 'undercover' in jeans and a nondescript top I put on a skin-tight red Lycra dress that I'd bought in a designer sale years before. I'd never worn it because I couldn't really get into it. Well, I could, but it didn't look good because I was always too fat for it. But divorce or separation can be good for the old figure so when I put it on that night I suddenly woke up and saw my old self again. The booby bit was a bit empty but who cared, my hips were compact and there weren't the usual saddlebags of excess flesh attached to the sides of my thighs. I had snake hips and I liked it.

The other problem was, I had no friends. They'd all fallen by the wayside and the only acquaintances I had were ones that frequented the Haverstock Arms, so that's where I went. I was slightly over-dressed for the pub. The usual suspects were all there, propping up the bar. Used to seeing me in baggy old denim jackets and no make-up they almost fell off their stools when I walked in. Mainly because the dress was short and I had super-sheer tights on and very (for me) high heels on for the first time in years. I had to make a real effort not to trip over my own feet.

It was a successful night. I went to a party and got chatting to a very handsome friend of one of the regulars from the pub. It all felt so good, so normal and so easy.

After that, I got right back into the party mood, going out, meeting new friends and even having parties at my house. In fact, there were always people round and my place became a proper little social hub.

I even had a really great night with one of those blonde bomb-shells that had been hanging off of the ex's arm – Kim Wilde. It was at a hen party for a mutual friend. When I turned up there was a bit of tension in the room over the fact that Kim and I were both there. We'd never met previously but I wasn't worried; I didn't have a problem with her and I wasn't particularly interested in what had gone on with Chris. But I knew as soon as I met her that I liked her. She, at the time, was like me, a good-time girl. It was a wild night in more ways than one. The girl whose hen night it was happened to be very well connected and so we ended up being chauf-feured around town in a Rolls Royce, first of all to Tramp where Kim and I were photographed by a paparazzi. We were in the car, obviously a little bit drunk. I was smoking and gesturing something to the photographers out of the car window, and it is to this day another of my favourite pictures of all time. Apparently, it was featured on the walls of the Paparazzi Café in Kensington for quite a long time, it was that good a shot. The headline in the Bizarre column of the *Sun* was funny too: 'Good Evans It's My Two Exes' it screeched.

3G THE SUN, Wednesday, May 18, 1994 15

BIZARRE

By Andy Coulson

OLD FLAME, but Kim and Carol hardly mentioned their red-headed ex Chris

OH EVANS! IT'S MY TWO EXES

Kim and Carol hit the town together

PICTURE EXCLUSIVE

CHRIS EVANS'S jilted wife Carol and his ex-girlfriend Kim Wilde enjoyed a boozy night on the town together.

They spent more than five hours at a hen party for a mutual friend at the posh Tramp nightclub in London's West End.

Kim, 33, and Carol, 34, rolled up giggling in a chauffeur-driven Bentley.

Then they strolled into the club, arm-in-arm with their pal Louise and another girl.

Carol, a radio producer with Virgin 1215, split from Chris last summer after 18 months of marriage. She still wears her wedding ring.

She hit the dancefloor with Kim, whose romance with the Big Breakfast star broke up at Christmas. Then the girls sat down to enjoy a few drinks.

Carol said: "I'd never met Kim before, but I knew she was going to be there and didn't have a problem with it.

"We ended up having a fantastic time. And we hardly ever spoke about **HIM.**

"I don't know what Chris would make of it—and I don't really care."

Chris, who is on holiday, is now dating Rachel Tatton-Brown, the hostess on his Channel 4 show Don't Forget Your Toothbrush.

WILDE NIGHT . . . Kim and Carol on town

Pictures: BIG PICTURE

£250 DEAL MAKES FANS PHIL GOOD

PHIL COLLINS is selling tickets for his world tour for £250 in a bid to help the homeless.

Fifty Platinum Tickets will be issued for each performance in every country on the tour, which hits Britain in September. More than £200+ from each ticket will go to help the needy worldwide.

Punters will get VIP treatment. They'll sit in on the soundcheck and get a slap-up meal before the show. Phil, 43, who's in South America this week, says: "If you are prepared to put something in, you will get a lot out of it."

Billy slams door on Loyd

BILLY CONNOLLY has turned down three invites to appear on TV's Through The Keyhole with house snooper Loyd Grossman.

He says: "I'd rather be burgled than have Loyd in my house."

★ ☆ ★

JET-SETTERS Take That have been pestered for autographs so much by British Airways staff that airline bosses have ordered them to stop.

Having just flown back from Miami on BA, I would have been happy for the attractive stewardesses to pester me.

■ TODAY'S Bizarre is edited by Matthew Wright

The *JOHN GOODMAN has already been approached to play Fred again in The Flintstones II. But he's waiting to see how the first film fares at the box office before deciding.* BIZ

PETER'S GAY KISS

D:REAM'S Peter Cunnah has admitted having "several strange gay experiences."

The singer—who's back with long-term girlfriend Amy Leigh after eight months apart—told new gay mag Attitude that he was urged to experiment by a female pal.

Peter, 27, said: "I don't know if it's cool to talk about it because of the people involved. But this girl encouraged us. So me and a friend ended up snogging each other—enjoying it was the funniest thing."

The *THE Rolling Stones's Voodoo Lounge shows at Giants Stadium, New York on August 12 and 14 sold out in 81 minutes. They've added a third date on the 15th.* BIZ

After Tramp we went on to a party in a very posh mews house in Mayfair and one of the girls found a bathroom with a giant, and I mean GIANT jacuzzi in it, filled it up, rounded up the hens, stripped off and got in with all the bubbles. A bottle of champagne joined us followed by the chauffeur who must have thought it was Christmas. It was good that he kept his hat on too, it all added to the comedy value of the night. When we ran out of champagne we drew straws to see who would have to get refills from the kitchen. Of course it was me. And the condition was that you had to go naked. Now, bear in mind that this is a VERY SMART HOUSE full of VERY SMART, RICH PEOPLE all standing around politely making conversation in a massive room with low music. Then I emerge from the pool suite, covered in bubbles but naked underneath and walk across a very shiny wooden floor towards the kitchen in search of champagne. And if everyone wasn't looking at me simply doing that, when I slipped, banana-skin style right in the middle of the floor, they certainly were then. Worse still, I was so covered in bubbles that I couldn't get up because I kept slipping over. I was like Bambi on the ice only bigger, clumsier and much, much uglier. And NO ONE HELPED ME! Anyway, the good news is I got the champagne and walked all the way back across the room to join the others once again in the jacuzzi. Luckily, no one had a camera. We rounded off the night driving round London in the Rolls Royce dropping everyone off as it got light. One of the other girls and me, of course, then thought it would be really funny to moon out of the back window of this monstrously expensive, chauffer-driven car, and it was. Very funny indeed.

It was a bit of a coincidence that the first person I had a thing with was called Chris. I'd met him in the Haverstock Arms through a friend of a friend. He was a model. Very good-looking, like a cross between Mel Gibson and Hugh Grant. Trouble was, he spoke like Wayne Rooney. Not that there's anything wrong with Wayne Rooney, or a Scouse accent; I liked it. I liked him, but it was never serious and the minute I saw his car I knew it never would be – he had the worst car I'd ever seen. It wasn't a Skoda but it was something equally terrible like a Vauxhall or something. It was funny because he was such a geezer about town but his car made him look like a joyrider. We weren't really suited as lovers or as boyfriend and girlfriend but he turned out to be a great friend, we had such a laugh together and it was good to be around someone who was so nice to look at for a change. Him and his mate, Ritchie, were both handsome boys, and I loved hanging out with them.

After almost exactly three months I left West One. Jane Kelly was right, and spot on with her prediction. Typical. I felt so bad, I really did, but Jane understood and never held it against me. Well, I don't think she did.

My new job was at Virgin 1215, the station I'd worked at briefly with Chris when he took the GLR show over there. I'd sent a Christmas postcard to John Revell who I'd worked with at Radio Radio, who was now the programme director, saying 'Give us a job!' And so he did.

It was there I met Mitch.

To begin with, I worked with Gary Davies (oooooh, Gary Davies, remember him?) but before long I was assigned to the breakfast show with Russ (Williams) 'n' Jono (Coleman). The hours were a nightmare. Getting up at 3am is never easy, but it's easier when you have a great job and this was certainly that. I also produced *The Big Red Mug Show* on a Saturday morning – it was the show that Chris left GLR for, but now it was presented by Paul Ross and Rowland Rivron, two of the funniest men in broadcasting in my opinion. The show was one of the funniest on the air at the time because we had contributors like Matt Lucas, John Thompson and Tommy Vance regularly doing sketches and characters for us. What a great privilege that was. Working at Virgin was just one great privilege in fact; it was like being in a rock band. There was a staff area upstairs with a bar (a real bar, with booze and everything) all supplied by Virgin and every night most of the staff would decamp to there for a few, then go out to the pub for a few, and at the end of the night either end up back at the staff bar for another few – you'd often arrive in the mornings and have to step over recovering bodies on your way to the studio – or back at my house. A group of us formed a little routine whereby every Thursday we'd all end up back at mine, get really drunk, dance around the living room and then all sleep in my giant bed together and get up and go to work the next day. We called it Double Bed Thursday.

One of that gang was Mitch, a DJ. He'd been asked to return from his very comfortable DJ life in Hong Kong to do the breakfast show on the newly formed station, although he was sidelined at the last minute because someone had decreed that he wasn't right for the slot, which is why Russ and Jono were in it. My guess was that he was far too good, too tall and too handsome and that someone didn't much like the idea of that.

At first I only had eyes for another DJ there. Blimey, hadn't I learnt my lesson with DJs? Obviously not. His name was Paul. He was way too short for me and nothing like my type (whatever that is!) but I had such a big crush on him it was pathetic. But it's always good having a crush on someone at work, it makes going in so much more bearable. I produced his shows for a while and we did get quite close. I have no idea if he knew how I felt about him and I don't think I ever, even drunkenly, declared it, although we were in a mini cab one night when I might have given it away when I had my head in his lap.

He was Mitch's flatmate and so I used to spend a lot of time round there but Mitch always seemed to be asleep. I was always disappointed when he was because whereas Paul was like a naughty mate, Mitch was like a big, clever grown-up who knew everything. And he was really funny.

So when Mitch moved into a flat round the corner from mine we became really good friends. We used to spend so much time together that everyone thought we were a couple and in lots of ways we were. We always linked arms or held hands when we walked. Mitch was always my date if I was invited anywhere and vice versa. He would come down to Kent with me and spend time with my family and I'd hang out at his mum's house in Spain, usually naked. Mitch wasn't one for clothes. He was like a totally unselfconscious kid in that respect. Clothes were annoying. He would think nothing of roaming around his mum's place starkers and she wouldn't even really notice. People would come round and where most people would scream and grab something to cover themselves, Mitch would forget. He wasn't showing off – although he did have every right to – he was just far more comfortable naked than clothed. I envied his attitude and joined in on occasion but I never felt entirely comfortable, I was always a bit self-conscious. If I sat down I would always make sure I was holding my tummy in and would make sure I didn't sit how I normally do, i.e. with my legs open. It was fun being nudie in the sun but I preferred being nudie while pissed at parties frankly.

Mitch was the best holiday companion. We went to Cape Town, Barbados, Paris, Amsterdam, Nice, Sardinia. But no matter where we were going, I would always lie to him as to what time we had to be at the airport because he just did not have the urgency gene. He was so laid back about everything that unless it was work, he had less than zero ability to be either on time or early for anything, especially planes. So, say the flight was at 11am, I would turn up at his house at 7am because I would have said the flight was at 10. He'd still be in bed so I'd have to let myself in and wake him up. Then, within the space of ten minutes, he'd get up, shower, get dressed and pack. He wouldn't have even packed. And this was what I always aspired to: Mitch's packing routine. He would pick up his little backpack then wander around the flat for a bit, rummaging and mumbling, 'passport, camera, shorts, toothbrush, money'. And that really was it. Meanwhile, I'm following with the biggest, most tightly packed, giant suitcase in the world. Even for a weekend. And, like I said, they didn't even have wheels then. Mitch never carried it for me; he'd just stand there laughing, all smug with his little bag.

The best thing about Mitch was his impulsiveness. On 9 August 1999 we were sitting around, doing not much, at his flat. It was the time of the full eclipse and the word was that a certain place in Northern France was to be the best vantage point. Of course people were flocking there and we were contemplating and regretting not booking anything, or getting it organised to go and look at it. After all, it probably wouldn't happen again so close to home in our lifetime. But then Mitch said, 'Why don't we just go? We don't need anywhere to stay, we can sleep in the car!' To which I replied, 'OK, come on then, let's book it, Danno.' I was trying to be a bit more laid back at the time – less five star, more hostel – because Mitch thought I was getting spoilt and accused me of being like girls with ponies. I wanted to be cool like him so I really tried to go along with his bohemian, hippy plans without letting it be known that I was under duress. So off we went in Mitch's 4x4 Jeep, booking the shuttle crossing on the way and driving for most of the night to somewhere we thought was near to the village we needed to be in, where we parked in a field and went to sleep. When we woke up we got back on the road and into a traffic jam for about four hours before reaching the village of Leon where we witnessed the total eclipse of the sun through thick cloud. I wrote:

France – The Eclipse – 9 to 12 August 1999
Originally wanted to leave at 3pm, we made no effort to hurry things along, left at 7pm for France. Mitch just moaned at me for taking literally 7 minutes to get all my stuff together. I know I'm a new woman but I'm not that new! He wouldn't even let me set the video.
Then Mitch bought ham and bread and tomatoes and I had a plate on my lap making sarnies while driving along. Meanwhile, Mitch was making a phone call, taking a photo, opening the window, drinking beer, eating a sandwich, smoking and driving all at the same time! V. funny. Also v. dangerous. Obviously.
Booked the shuttle on the way down there, how cool is that?
Beer makes you speak French.
I got into my 'where's my pony' mode. 'I'm cold, where's the toilet, drive me to the toilet, give me the keys, why should I go out there when there's a perfectly good toilet a half a mile away.' Like a spoilt five-year-old, where's my pony?
Mad couple in the restaurant in Leon. She had two large sherries and he had two large Pernods, then a jug of wine each, then brandies. Made me and Mitch look teetotal they did.
Woke up in the middle of the night and Mitch was snoring like a hog. Begged him to stop snoring and in his dozy state he mumbled, 'Oh no, we're incompatible.'
I'm a changed woman. Moths, sleeping in the Jeep, haven't washed

for two days and wearing the same knickers and I'M NOT EVEN MOANING.
In the Hypermarche Leclerc car park we found a real fur coat from the charity bin! Mitch made me put it on and took a photo.

You always learn things from people but Mitch taught me more than most. He had such an infectious *joie de vivre* and stressed about very little. He was my best friend when I felt low and lacking in confidence. He always cheered me up. He was there for my fortieth and came dress shopping with me and bought me two fabulous pairs of shoes. It's thanks to Mitch that I don't freak out or do a rain dance every time I see a moth now. I even travel light because of him. But the best lesson of all was easing my OCD-like tendencies when it came to cleaning. He wasn't the most, shall we say, *pernickety* person when it came to housework, as there were always much more important and enjoyable things to do.

It was the perfect relationship and we even had sex a couple of times. But there was never any pressure, no checking up on each other; he lived in his flat and I lived in mine. No hassle, no aggro and no stress. Just fun and laughter. I really loved him. But I really don't know if I was ever in love with him. I think the feeling was mutual.

In fact when Mitch and I went our separate ways after nearly seven years of friendship or relationship or whatever it was, I wrote him a poem.

My phone no longer rings
My heart no longer sings
Life was so much fun
Being nudie in the sun
I miss you in the morning
When realisation is dawning
That maybe I was in love with you.

I'm still in touch with Mitch but we don't really hang out anymore. He moved to France with his adorable dog, Alfie. I went to see him a couple of times. He's back now though working as a DJ in Southampton and is also spending weekends back in London which is good news because I miss him.

After Mitch I went out with a young man – a very young man – who completely took the piss so even though he was extremely sexy and quite nice to look at he had to go. For a start, he was a bit too impressed by celebrity and once abandoned me to walk home alone late at night while he stalked my ex-husband, Chris Evans, in a pub. Another time, we were with some of his friends who were all ordering drinks at the bar. When they went to pay he pulled their money back and said, 'Don't worry, she'll pay.' I dumped him there and then and never spoke to him again.

After that little lesson I made a decision. I was talking to my friend Zoë Ball who I'd worked with on *The Big Breakfast* and had become quite close to. She was also not having much luck with men at the time, and we came to the conclusion that what we needed was a grown-up. We needed to stop messing about with these useless youngsters; they were wasting our time and doing our heads in. We compiled a list: he had to be older, richer, emotionally sorted, have a strong personality, no baggage, mustn't work in media, be un-intimidated by our girl-power, not teetotal, own a house and car.

We both got our wish.

She ended up with Norman Cook. I got off with the MP.

Now, remember that millionaire I met when I was in that club with Zoë and Stuart? The one who gave me his phone number that I never called. That's the MP.

Well, he wasn't an MP as such, but that's what I called him, the Millionaire Plumber. He had all the required traits. Except that I hadn't included 'taller' and 'with hair' in the list but I could live with that.

It was 1998, just after I'd been sacked for the second time from Talk Radio and I'd just moved into my new flat in Camden Town (see next chapter – *The Working Breakfasts Chapter*) when Stuart called.

'We're going to New York, why don't you come?'

'I might.'

'Caaaaaaam on, you've got nothing else to do!'

It was true, I didn't. And I'd just sold a flat so I had a bit of money in the bank. I booked my ticket and off I went. We flew Virgin Atlantic economy, all of us. I was surprised by this because the MP was indeed a millionaire so what was he doing turning right on the plane when he could easily afford to turn left? Well, he was on a plumbers' convention and as it was an organised trip he didn't have any choice. He did look familiar and I kind of remembered him from the time in the club. On the plane he was very attentive and kept coming up to my seat to see if I was alright. He was fascinated by my luggage. Having been taught well by the mighty Mitch, I had nothing but a small carry-on bag, like a big handbag. In it I had a pair of trainers, a T-shirt, some knickers and few toiletries. That was it. I would buy stuff when I got there, we were going to New York the shopping capital of the world! He couldn't believe it, 'Is that all you've got? Bloody hell, the girls I go out with have make-up bags bigger than that!' he said, and I'm sure he wasn't joking.

When we got to New York, we did get to know each other better. I gatecrashed the plumbers' dinner cruise up the East River – I'd made a real effort to be ladylike and wore my lovely new suit I'd bought in Barney's earlier that day, but I was jet-lagged and not a little bit drunk so failed, finishing up under the table after too many red wines. Later, the MP and I got a little more lost in each other and kind of forgot Stuart was there. We sat in the bar of the Soho Grand snogging the whole time while Stuart bought Dom Perignon and tipped the staff $50 a time on the MP's credit card.

When we got back I gave the MP my phone number and he called quite soon after. Ooh, he's keen, I thought. I went out with him a few times. We went to Nobu for dinner, I went to stay with him and he cooked, driving to Whitstable to buy fresh oysters and having fine wine delivered. Whenever we went out he'd get a driver and we'd sit in the back of his Range Rover drinking champagne from the fridge. He had two housekeepers and had his sheets changed every day. Yikes, I couldn't possibly let him near my place then.

He was my kind of millionaire. He didn't really do presents, just fun. The only presents he bought me were some bath towels (because I had none) and some potpourri for my fortieth birthday. Yes, potpourri.

I dunno, the diamond ring must have been lost when I opened it . . .

I even got on with his ex-wife. It was all going so well. But then he took me skiing. To Obergurgl in Austria. Another plumbers' convention. I had a good time but I wasn't competent enough for him so he'd just go off and leave me, which was nice. Actually, he dumped me after that trip. I don't know if it was because I couldn't ski or because after too many après-ski schnapps I decided to flash my tits at all his plumber mates. I never gave him the chance to tell me. He tried to and offered to come all the way to London to tell me but I don't see the point of that. Being dumped is bad enough, without someone travelling long distances to say it to your face. Not my style. It was OK, he was too short for me anyway. And old. And bald.

We're still good friends by the way, but the main thing the MP taught me was that I wasn't really ready for older men. I don't mean that in a mean way, but the MP was the first bloke I'd ever been out with, apart from when I was a teenager, who was older than me! I enjoyed all the manners and the rich perks but honestly, he couldn't keep up.

But I didn't learn my lesson and just after my fortieth birthday I went vintage again (see *The Turning 40 Chapter*).

CHAPTER 17

The First Time I: Had the best job in the world and the worst job in the world

(The Working Breakfasts Chapter)

Towards the end of 1994, while I was working at Virgin Radio, I got a call from Rob Jones. He was consulting for a new radio station that was just setting up and set to launch on Valentine's Day 1995.

Rob was my boss at Music Box for a while and then at Radio Radio. I liked him; he was always overacting and he had a bit of the Barney Rubble about him, so much so that I did used to call him Barney. He always spoke like he was telling you a secret and he usually raised his eyebrow as if to say, 'Whaddayasaytothatthen?' This time he was on the phone but I could still see him doing it. In a kind of seductive whisper he said, 'Listen. I'm helping to set up this new station and we've got this guy doing the breakfast show, he's the new Chris Evans, do you wanna come and be the weather girl?' My first reaction was, 'What on earth do we need another Chris Evans for?' But then I thought, 'Mmmmmm, that sounds like a good job, OK then!' I was aware that I knew nothing at all about meteorology so I was probably being asked to do the job partly because I was 'Chris Evans' ex-wife' but then again, Rob knew I wasn't entirely without experience and that I'd done radio before with Chris. Also, he needed someone who had a lot to say as it was for a four-hour show, scheduled for 6am to 10am, five days a week, with no music and to start with, very few ads. Yikes – all that time to fill with, well, the new Chris Evans and me talking.

So I went in for a chat with the programme director, met the 'new Chris Evans', did a pilot show and signed the contract.

The station was Talk Radio UK, the first national commercial speech-only station ever, and it was planning to put itself on the radio map by being different, controversial and outspoken. The presenters were all recruited with this in mind, as were a lot of the big names on the weekend schedule: Jeremy Beadle, Dale Winton, Vanessa Feltz and Terry Christian, to name but a few. The most well known on the daytime would have been Scott Chisholm from Sky News and Tommy Boyd of *Magpie* fame. And there was Anna Raeburn.

My radio husband on this occasion was to be Moz Dee. He was a lovely bloke. We went out for a few beers on the night we met and got on well but we were like chalk and cheese to say the least. But as far as being the new Chris, he couldn't have been more unlike him if he'd tried. He was a child star actor from Ireland, who'd been doing radio in Coventry and who wore a suit with waistcoat and tie to work even though we were on the radio. I could never understand it. That was the beauty of radio after all, no one could see you. I took full advantage of this of course and most days probably didn't even bother to brush my hair. Especially when we were doing real-time practice-run early shifts.

Those dummy shows proved to be a kind of downfall, because what we talked about caused a last-minute panic, which resulted in an eleventh-hour change to the schedule by the station's bosses. The show had already been named *The Rude Awakening* so there was an expectation of us to be, well, rude. But then when we were, they all started running round like headless chickens saying it was all too offensive for mornings and they switched us to the evening, 7-10pm, and the duo who were in that slot, Sean Bolger and Samantha Meah, were put on breakfast. This all happened three days before the launch. I was happy. I now didn't have to get up at 3am and I had an hour less to do on air for the same money. I don't think Moz was so chuffed; the breakfast show is the flagship show after all and whoever gets to do it is considered the station star. Obviously, Sean and Samantha were over the moon. Especially as they were paid gargantuan amounts of extra money in order to shift slots. That was the other reason I was OK with it. Because, with a new station, the breakfast show was going to be the one that everyone would focus their attention on and if anything was to start going wrong, it would be that that would fall first. It was a bit of a poison chalice in a new set-up so I was quite glad to be out of it. And the best bit was I didn't have to deal with the weather.

In the panic, all the production was thrown at the breakfast show, meaning we had no producers. An independent company called Campbell Davidson were drafted in to get our show on the air with its proprietors, Patrick and Clare, as our mentors, managers and inspiration. We met them for the first time on launch day, and went for lunch. Luckily, we all got on like a house on fire and between us had enough experience, ideas and enthusiasm to get a half-decent show together. As a result, we were the only weekday show, apart from Anna Raeburn, that garnered a good review from the fearsome Gillian Reynolds, the *Daily Telegraph* radio critic. Well, I think it was good.

On 16 February 1995 under the headline 'Is all this talk just hot air?' she pondered thus:

> *Talk Radio's* The Dish, *presented by Samantha Meah and Sean Bolger is unremittingly dreadful. Here is a pair with nothing to say, lacking the vocabulary to do it justice. It was meant to be in the 7pm slot but was swapped, last Friday, with* The Rude Awakening, *presented by Maurice ('Moz') Dee and Carol (the former Mrs Chris Evans) McGiffin, originally intended (hence the name) for early mornings but suddenly deemed too risqué at cornflake time. This duo look likely to land the network with its first libel suits, if the various rock stars named in Monday's edition care to send for the tape. It's lively, original, rough as a groupie's grope and there's nothing quite like it on Radio 1. If there were, questions would be asked in the House.*

Which sounded about right. But that was what being on in the evenings was supposed to be about, we had more freedom to deal with more risqué topics.

One of the very first shows we did was about piercings. The

producers had brought in a couple who were, shall we say, ardent fans. The pierced woman had literally hundreds of them; I'm surprised she didn't whistle in the wind. One of her favourite bits to get pierced was a particularly sensitive bit in her nether regions. During the discussion, Moz asked, 'Can we see it?' And without a moment's hesitation she'd pulled down her trousers and pants and was thrusting her metallic labia into our faces. Thankfully it was in the days before webcams. It was horrible. Like the scrap drawer at Ratner's.

In our headphones all we could hear from Patrick and Clare was 'Put it away, tell her to put it away, no, no no, it's not 9 o'clock yet!!!!!' What could we do? It was live radio and in any case, as I said, no-one could see it.

There was a 'dump' button for really big mistakes. This meant that what you said on air, wasn't actually broadcast until seven seconds later so there was a bit of delayed time in which you could 'dump' any dangerous comment. I pride myself that in all the years I have done radio and now TV I have never, not even mistakenly, said a swear word. Well, I hadn't until Patrick had the bright idea of trying to cure my fear of spiders one night. He'd got an 'expert' in arachnophobia on the line who was going to talk me through the cure. So, he dimmed the lights, Moz left the studio and I was blindfolded. Then as this guy was calmly talking to me about the irrationality of being scared of spiders, Patrick snuck into the studio, crawled under the desk and did a giant-spider-crawling-up-leg action with his hand. Up my leg. Well of course I'm going to swear. I shouted 'FUCK OFF!' at the top of my voice before realising that it was Patrick being an arsehole and my seven available seconds of dump time were ticking away. Like a flash I jumped up and hit the button just in time so the actual word wasn't broadcast. Thank God, because I definitely would have been fired before I was if it had.

There wasn't much we didn't tackle and we had some cracking calls. Some of which were too weird to be true but then this was radio, the theatre of the mind; who cared if they were telling the truth as long as they could tell a good story? It wouldn't happen now, the whole of broadcasting is obsessed with not getting caught out doing anything that isn't completely and utterly genuine. Sometimes, that's not such a good thing.

What was scarier was the fact that both Moz and I smoked at the time. The studio was small and we sat either side of a desk that just about fitted in there. There was enough room to spread some newspapers out but that was about it. Guests sat on the end, by the window between me and Moz, so we could both see them. We would get through around 20 ciggies each, every night. And there were no breaks out of the studio because there was no music, just the news and the relatively short ad breaks. Anyone who didn't smoke must have felt like a 1970s tobacco company beagle in the smoking lab. Honestly, with both of us puffing away on our Marlboro Lights it was like a killer smog in there, a real pea-souper. We didn't even notice but it must have been foul, especially as the window didn't open.

Despite being up against peak-time TV viewing the show did well and lasted longer than the breakfast show, which predictably was axed after about nine months. The entire management was also axed and new people coming in always meant that people would be fired. I was one of them. I lasted another few months but was taken off *The Rude Awakening* almost exactly a year later. Moz carried on doing the show on his own and I was given a weekly music singles review show on a Friday night I called *The Singles Bar* which I did for six months. It was supposed to be like *Juke Box Jury* on the radio, but I wasn't really a DJ and I just felt like a fraud. It was good getting all the free CDs though because it was a great time for music. In 1996 Britpop ruled, and the big Blur vs. Oasis battle was in full swing. We had some good guests on. Ant and Dec, who had a single out at the time as PJ and Duncan; DJ giants Tommy Vance and Johnnie Walker; rock and pop gods Lloyd Cole, Kim Wilde and Mike Flowers; comedy geniuses John Thompson, Jack Docherty, Morwenna Banks and Rowland Rivron; and my favourite guest of all time, all-round genius and author, Jon Ronson.

Status Quo would have been on that roll call but one Friday they cancelled at the last minute so I had a singles review programme with no guests and I was half pissed. I'd been in the Haverstock

Arms all afternoon, drinking with Chris Evans and his girlfriend Suzi, on one of our rare moments of friendship. It was a bit weird being out with them both and although I got on OK with Suzi, I didn't have much in common with her. Although I remember thinking how glad I was that he was with her now and not me. I thought for a second he was going to volunteer to help me out seeing as he was being my best friend that day, but no, instead he generously volunteered two of our mutual friends and drinking buddies, Mel Galley (who used to be in Whitesnake) and our dear now departed friend Tony Ashton (of Ashton, Gardener and Dyke fame – 'The Resurrection Shuffle' – remember that?). Anyway, so we all trundled off to the studio, all of us three sheets to the wind, did the show and just about pulled it off. What was really disconcerting though was Chris was all the time crouched down on the floor with Suzi in the studio and I thought, well he's a big bloody celebrity why doesn't he just do me a favour now? But he didn't. We finished the show and they went off and Tony, Mel and me went back to the pub and carried on where we left off.

I got a job as producer on *The Big Breakfast*. Everyone there thought I'd only got the job because I was Chris Evans' ex-wife again. He wasn't working there then, he'd left to do *Don't Forget Your Toothbrush* not long after we'd split up. One of the producers, a girl called Ruth, was assigned to show me the ropes. I noticed she was very stony and abrupt with me at first and she did tell me later that she resented training me because she thought I'd simply got the job because of my history, but we ended up getting on very well. It was a vintage time to be working at *The Big Breakfast*. The number of people who worked there who now basically run TV in the UK and US is phenomenal.

When I joined I only took a year's contract and I was glad I did. The presenters were Zoë Ball and Mark Little who I thought were both good and suited the show. I got on particularly well with Zoë, we were kindred spirits of sorts. I thought she was amazing and she had the best figure of anyone I'd ever met. She was taller than me, about 5'11" and she was a size 8-10 and I modelled myself on her, longing to have thighs as thin as hers (we measured them once, hers were 19" and mine were 23"!). She was very generous too. We lived in the same area of London and I'd go round to her flat where she'd give me piles of clothes. She'd just throw stuff my way, new stuff, expensive stuff that she'd never worn. She liked shopping a lot then and had a wardrobe to die for. Unfortunately most of it was still in the designer bags. She once gave me a brand new pair of Prada trainers, I couldn't believe it. She also took me to Barcelona for the weekend where we stayed at the Hotel Arts. She'd been invited by Pils (the beer company) who were having a party there with Pulp playing a gig in the old amphitheatre in the hills above the city. It was real goosebump stuff watching them in that atmosphere, with that view. She was great to hang out with but she was also such fun to work with, never complained and did anything the producers would ask of her, and she did it well.

Vanessa Feltz was 'on the bed', interviewing celebrities on the bed, and I also liked her very much. She was brilliant to work with too. But when new exec producers and editors came in it was all change. They set about transforming the whole look of the show with a new futuristic and modern look to the house. So, for five weeks, we all still had to do the show, but on a building site.

It was arduous working while the renovations went on, but there was no other way. Mark left first and there was a series of 'guest presenters' in to work with Zoë for a while. My overriding memory of that time was of one of the guest co-hosts, Frank Bruno, on an elephant during one of those stand-ins. Quite how Frank Bruno managed to co-present a two-hour live show was amazing enough, but getting an elephant into the grounds of the house while it was being rebuilt was a tribute to the people working on it.

It was a wonder they achieved so much with the lack of resources, staff and budgets, but they always did. I was the producer of the Friday show. There were two editors who oversaw the day producers, one for each day, and we all had one researcher assigned to us. Guests were booked by a separate team, the set and props were all taken care of and all the regular stuff, i.e. Zig and Zag, was done by other people. But the main 80-odd items per show had to be thought of, written and instigated by two people. My researchers, Emma and Nick, were the ones who actually made things happen.

I was never short of ideas and I was quite proud of some of my items. Of all of the hundreds I must have come up with my favourites were the Great Net Curtain Debate, the Cherry Pip Spitting Contest and a series of little films we made titled, How On Earth Did We Cope Without . . . ? which were short silly films speculating as to how we coped without mobile phones (lots of people using tin cans joined by string getting tangled up), cashpoint machines, non-stick pans, deodorant and remote controls. I also had dogs on human running machines and Joan Rivers on set for most of one show, cleaning a bath while we chatted to her. Zoë, at my behest, once did the whole show from the inside of a giant dog costume. No reason why, it was just funny at the time. But that was probably the problem, it was just funny at the time, or more like funny in the middle of the night when we were sitting there still writing the script, scoffing Pringles and getting mildly hysterical. For such was the nature of the work that you would more often than not get in at 8am on a Thursday morning, and not leave until after the show finished at 9am on Friday morning. I had never felt so ill. And fat. Being up all night and desperately trying to glean energy from greasy Indian and Chinese takeaways just wasn't the way forward and it showed. Then we'd have to be at the house for a 3am meeting to take the production crew through the show we'd come up with. It was always at this time that I was convinced I had the worst job in the world. Every week Emma and I would become hysterical with laughter from sleep deprivation and MSG overload. Uncontrollable giggles would ensue and everyone would get really annoyed. We really couldn't help it. But at least if the ideas were good, everyone would forgive you.

My finest hour was the Ugly Baby competition, inspired by my new little niece, Holly, with full permission from her mum, I might add. I thought of it when Tracy sent me her first official photograph because I couldn't stop laughing. It was terrible. I know all babies are beautiful and all that but in this picture at least, she was ugly! So we launched a nationwide search for the ugliest baby in the land and the response was massive. We had sackloads of entries, which provided such priceless amusement around the office I can't tell you. The competition culminated in a final 10 who all came into the studio as gorgeous grown-up children or toddlers to prove that actually they'd just taken a bad photo. Everyone loved it. It was typical *Big Breakfast* fodder: rebellious, chaotic, different and fun. Holly, who is of course beautiful now, was to be the guest of honour having been the inspiration for the whole thing but unfortunately, her stupid auntie (i.e. me) gave her mum the wrong directions to the studio and they ended up in Barking instead of Old Ford so she never made it.

So, on 2 September 1996 the re-launch happened and it really did turn into the worst job in the world. The house was renovated to look like a Mediterranean mansion with pool and deck to match, big glass swing doors, extravagant balconies and sunken dens everywhere. It was ruined. It would have been lovely in the Ibiza sunshine but in the greyness of London in September it looked depressing and horrid. All the quaint cosiness of the original lockkeepers' cottages had disappeared under a swathe of modernity. The new presenters, lovely people though they were – Sharron Davies and Rick Adams – struggled. The proportions were all wrong for a start. Rick was like a plugged-in-to-the-mains skinny little kids TV presenter trying slightly too hard to be the new Chris Evans (why did everyone want to be the new Chris Evans?) and Sharron was completely incongruous by his side, a picture of sophisticated, Amazonian maturity and towering over her little partner in crime. They were like mother and son.

I left just before Christmas, two months before my contract was up. I didn't get on with one of the editors or the series producer, who said to me, as she asked me to produce all the Christmas specials, 'You have the best ideas but you're not a good producer.' But having ideas was the biggest part of being a producer I thought, at least it was on that show. If you haven't got any ideas you've got nothing to produce? I admit I was crap at the logistical side, but then I thought that was what the director, crew and other floor staff were for and anyway, *The Big Breakfast* was supposed to look as though it was chaotic, wasn't it? OK, maybe not that chaotic then.

Luckily I'd been offered another breakfast radio job at around the same time. Liberty 963 was a short-lived project in London only and on medium wave. It was owned by Mohammed al Fayed who'd bought the station from Lynne Franks and her gang who tried to do a station 'for women, run by women' called Viva. It was doomed from the start as it quickly became known as Vulva. Anyway, once again, I was parachuted in to another strange radio partnership.

Rob Jones was at the helm again, along with my old mucker Mike Hollingsworth, who were both still trying to turn me into a weather-and-traffic-reading dolly sidekick. The main presenter this time was Richard Skinner and I really liked Richard. In fact, I was 'best woman' at his wedding to my lovely friend Deborah who I'd worked with at GLR and Virgin Radio, so working with him wasn't a chore at all.

Before long I was sacked again. Richard was moved and Simon Bates was brought in to do the breakfast show. I carried on doing contributor segments for Simon but I found him a bit patronising so in the end I stopped doing it.

I went back to Talk Radio for the best job in the world, working with Paul Ross, the radio husband from heaven and a joy to work with. He is much underrated and so dazzlingly clever you couldn't help but be impressed by his instant recall and photographic memory. The way he'd quote from films and books of any sort was nothing but astounding. His favourite line from a film was 'Badges? Badges? We don't need no stinking badges!' from *The Treasure of the Sierra Madre*, a 1948 film starring Humphrey Bogart. He said it all the time and it became a real catchphrase on the show. I never got bored of him saying it because it made me laugh every time. He took the piss out of me mercilessly but it was OK because it was always funny. We had both been blessed with fame by association so we laboured the point by highlighting our 'tabloid tags'. His was 'Jonathan Ross's brother, Paul', and mine was 'Chris Evans' ex-wife, Carol'. He was a bit of a rascal in those days too, way before he met Jackie, 'the current and final' as he refers to her being his third wife. I never fancied him but was curious, in the same way I was with Chris, what it was he might have that was such a hit with the girls. But that was it. I made the mistake of telling him that one day. He never let me forget it and took it as a much bigger compliment than it actually was.

Paul was doing the breakfast show on his own and was being produced by Patrick and Clare, the saviours of *The Rude Awakening*. They had faith in me and knew I'd get on with Paul so gave me a slot, once a week, doing a TV review. Paul and I worked so well together the bosses eventually let me back on to do the breakfast show every day. It was a dream team and we went from strength to strength. Every Friday we'd reward ourselves by going for breakfast in the Star Café in Soho where we'd have a massive fry-up and Peroni beers at 10am. We squared it because we'd been up since 3am meaning that in body time by 10am it was 2pm and way past lunchtime! Happy days they were. Patrick and I would usually carry on through the day ending up in the Nellie Dean pub in Dean Street, me usually with my knickers on my head or doing something equally disgraceful.

Often we'd have to go out to junkets to interview big film stars and one such star was the US radio legend, Howard Stern. The interview was one of those great moments in life that you never forget and dine out on until everyone's heard all about it. Well, just in case you haven't, here's what happened. Howard was in town to promote the movie of his autobiography, *Private Parts* and we'd gone to see him. We were like two little kids waiting to meet this guy who was basically the king of talk radio. He was the most charismatic man I'd ever met – really tall with long, Louis XIV curls, a giant nose and really dark glasses. This man was what an awful lot of talk radio presenters aspired to be. He was huge. Anyway, we had our seven minutes or however long it was, then at the end of the interview, I couldn't resist asking him if he was looking forward to going on *TFI Friday* (Chris Evans' Friday night programme) later that day.

Immediately he was interested, 'Why, do you know him?'

'Know him?' I said, 'I was married to him!'

Suddenly he couldn't get his breath. He'd obviously heard of Chris and was intrigued. He immediately had an idea. 'Hey, why don't you come on to the show with me and I can fondle you in front of your ex-husband; he'll hate it, no one wants to see their ex-wife being fondled by a big ugly American like me.' I was loving the thought, and not only because I quite fancied him; it would have been a picture to see Chris's face if I'd turned up to HIS show with HIS guest, the mighty Howard Stern.

I put him straight, 'There's no way on God's earth he would ever allow me near the place so forget it.'

But he persisted, insisting that he could do whatever he liked and he'd sort it out. I knew he wouldn't and so left it at that. When he went on the show, before Chris could even ask him anything, he interrupted him and started telling everyone about his idea. That he'd phoned Chris in the day to ask if he could bring me on with him but Chris had said, 'No, no, no ex-wife, I don't want her here!' Which was probably why Howard carried on going on about me. You could see it was making Chris feel uncomfortable and he kept trying to steer the attention back to an apple-peeling machine that he'd got for Howard because he's from the Big Apple. At one point Stern turned into the interviewer asking Chris what had gone wrong with the marriage culminating the exchange by saying, 'I'll tell you what went wrong, you got famous. I got famous too but I got morals and I didn't dump my wife.' It was priceless TV and I still have the VHS of it, which is a bit sad, I know, but it's just too delicious to discard.

We got loads of press out of it too which should have earned us brownie points but the boss, a guy called Paul Robinson, who I'm sure never really liked our show and would have preferred if we hadn't done so well as far as ratings went, was always butting in, trying to turn us into Radio 4's *Today* programme. We'd do little things to placate him like introducing a book review slot to try and make ourselves sound a bit highbrow. Then we only went and won an award. The New York Radio Award for, wait for it, Best Breakfast Show in the World! I'm not kidding. We thought *they* were. That stuffed him for another couple of months. But in the end he could take no more and gave the slot to Kirsty Young. I was forced to make an announcement on air that I was 'really excited' to be handing the best job in the world over to Kirsty, being the consummate broadcaster that she was. I tried not to hold it against her, but later that day, on emerging from the lift into what we called 'The Hall of Fame' – a display of all the presenter photographs on the walls, I took out the biggest piece of chewing gum from my mouth and stuck it on the end of Kirsty Young's snooterish nose. That made me feel much better although it was super childish and I was wrong – she wasn't a snooter at all as I found out later when I met her at Zoë Ball's wedding.

At least I didn't get sacked that time. Paul and I were moved to weekend breakfast where we continued exactly as before, building the audience up to the point where it was bigger than the weekday breakfast. That still didn't stop Mr Robinson telling me off every five minutes, usually a single letter of complaint that I'd dropped another 'h' or something equally trivial. I couldn't work out what I'd done wrong most of the time. Maybe he'd seen me one day place my daily banana skin on the floor outside his office or something.

Funnily enough, we outlived Paul Robinson as Kelvin McKenzie and his Wireless Group bought the station, which meant another big clear-out. I knew my head was on the chopping block. Kelvin's hatchet man was a bloke called Mike Parry. He called me up on a Monday morning and asked me to come in to the office.

I said, 'I don't need to come in, I know what you're going to say, it's fine.'

He said, 'No, it's not what you think, I need you to come in for a chat, can you come in later this morning?' So I did. I walked in, knowing full well what he was going to say and by the way everyone hung their heads and avoided eye contact the rest of the staff did too, but when I got into his office it was even briefer than I'd anticipated.

'Take a seat.'

As I did, I said, with some attitude, 'What?' wanting to add, 'you revolting little man . . .' and amazing myself at my own restraint.

He didn't disappoint and returned with a, 'You're fired, pick up your cards on the way out.' Cards? What decade was he living in?

I was furious. He must have hated me to make me do that walk of shame right in and out of the office in front of everyone.

It was a shame because they should have had faith in the station – but that's what happens, everyone gives up too easily. The station is still going only it's called talkSPORT now and, funnily enough, Moz Dee is the programme director.

I did more radio after that in the form of a Saturday night show on London talk station, LBC, with the brilliant Nick Abbot, which was another hoot. We talked absolute bollocks but people loved it. Nick got fired first and so I was left doing the show on my own for about six months before I got sacked too. But two years later I was back doing a Sunday morning show which I loved. Three hours all to myself to talk about what I wanted with the last hour devoted to talk about travelling. And yet again, it was short-lived because once more, the new boss wanted me to be Fiona Bruce and kept telling me to 'hit the ground running' – I could never work out what he meant so I always just started the show talking about my week. He got rid of me by saying I could only take six Sundays off a year, the one thing that he knew I wouldn't compromise on, and so I left. The one time I wasn't fired from a radio station, now that was a FIRST!

CHAPTER 18

The First Time I: Pole danced in Stringfellows with the owner, Peter

(The Turning 40 Chapter)

Apparently life begins at 40. I wonder why people say that? Is it because at 40 you suddenly wake up and realise that you probably have less time left than you've already had? It goes some way to explaining why some people go a bit mad. I certainly did. Mad as a hatter. It was like a switch. One minute I was completely sane, having a nice life, enjoying what I had and reflecting on what I'd done, the next minute, whoosh. Where's Carol gone?

It didn't help that 1999 was not only the end of my thirties but also the end of the century. In a way, it felt like it was the end of the world so, accordingly, I began behaving like a lunatic who'd been given 12 months to live, doing things I had never done before and spending huge sums of money on wholly unsuitable, unnecessary items like ridiculous cars. I paid cash for a metallic red convertible TVR Chimaera, which in Greek mythology is a fire-breathing female monster with a lion's head, a goat's body, and a serpent's tail – how very appropriate? They're not girl's cars at all; they have no airbags, no ABS, no roll bar and you needed the strength of Geoff Capes to pull the handbrake on effectively. It was the one and only time in my life that I got done for speeding – I was doing 98mph down the M20 and they sent me a picture as a souvenir and everything. Well, what was the point of having a car that could go fast if you couldn't drive it fast? I live in London and the fastest you can drive there is about 4mph. It was a great car but so mad I should have been sectioned.

I'd never really done milestone birthdays. For both my eighteenth and twenty-first I was working; no parties, no big deals. Being 30 wasn't really an event either. I can't even remember what I did, all I know is I went to see my mum. I always did because of the (mild) trauma I suffered as a child when she left me on my third birthday to go and give birth to my sister, Tracy. Every birthday since then I'd get this inner need to go and see her and I always did. It was like an obsession.

The first and only time I didn't go was on my fortieth. It was absolute confirmation of my insanity, and my unreasonable, erratic, out-of-character behaviour. Because for some reason, this birthday was different and I was determined not to let it pass. I know they aren't supposed to matter when you've had a few – people tell you it's just a number, it doesn't mean anything. Well, that one did. So I had organised a bloody great party and there was so much to do I couldn't get down to see her.

Perhaps it had something to do with it being in the year 2000, because when I was 10, during a discussion at school about what we thought life would be like in the new millennium, I was asked by the teacher, 'Carol, what do you expect to be doing in the year 2000?' I searched for an answer that could compete with the imaginative and ambitious ones given before me but, being 10, my brain could hardly deal with what I'd be doing the next day, never mind in 30 years' time. And anyway, who cared? The year 2000 was light years away. I offered my lazy reply: 'I'll be 40, Miss.' Which when you are 10, seems ridiculous and impossible. At that young age, 40 is tantamount to being dead – all grown-up, with slippers and knitting, a boring husband, a couple of kids and a semi-detached down the road from Mum's. Completely unthinkable and totally hideous. But then 30 years just flew by and the reality was even more unthinkable and doubly hideous. Let's re-enact that scene with the benefit of hindsight having made it to the year 2000 and survived my fortieth birthday party.

'Carol, what do you expect to be doing in the year 2000?'

'I'll be 40, Miss, and on my birthday I'll be pole dancing in Stringfellows with the owner, Peter, Miss.'

How did it come to this?

Well, if I was still alive, and not the slipper-wearing-might-as-well-be-dead-I'm-so-old knitting vision of my 10-year-old mind, then what better reason for a major celebration? And as soon as I made that decision, I sort of began to wish I hadn't. It was either going to be the best or the worst night of my life.

Choosing a party venue is always difficult, but I believe you shouldn't stress or think about it too much because the answer will always come to you. I've just done it for my fiftieth, but more of that later. Back then in the year 2000 I wanted to do something different, something ironic and unexpected. I'd met Peter Stringfellow a few times. He'd been in as a guest on the radio show and I'd been in the club a few times with influential people who'd introduced me to him. Then one day I was sitting watching daytime telly and he came on. Ting! *I'll go to Stringfellows*. It was the obvious venue, London's Premier Nightspot! Dinner and disco-dancing, back to where it all began, like going home. Did I have any idea of the excitement this would generate? Not at all. When the world heard the word 'Stringfellows' all hell broke loose, and I started hearing from friends I'd not heard from in ages. 'Ooooh, I hear you're having a party at Stringfellows. When is it?' When I reached a guestlist of a nice round (and suitable) 40, I stopped answering the phone and set about designing the invitation. I spent ages on it.

See the gorgeous bird in the picture?
Well, it's me and guess what. It's my birthday
on the 18th February and I'm 40. Yes 40.
So come and dine and disco dance with me at
STRINGFELLOWS! Which might sound like
anti-feminist post-modern irony but it's not.
IT'S JUST HILARIOUS!!!

HERE'S THE DEAL
You pay me £25 and you get dinner and booze until my
money runs out and then you have to pay for your own, OK?
SO SEND YOUR £25 BY WAY OF RSVP ASAP TO:

DRESS CODE
Boys: Rich Old Bloke Look (Think Drug Dealer)
Girls: Page Three Look (Think Sam from Eastenders)

8pm TBA Drinks
9.30pm Dinner, More Drinks and Disco

Yes, I made people pay towards it. I wasn't rich enough to pay for 40 people to have dinner and drink themselves stupid at one of the most expensive places in London, but they got a bargain at £25 a head and I paid for all the rest of the drinks. It cost me a couple of thousand pounds still but it was worth every penny.

A table for 40 for a new 40-year-old. Nine couples, 12 single (most for one night only) girls, and nine sad, single, hairy blokes.

The biggest problem is always what to wear. Especially as I'd dictated a dress code. Wallis? Zara? Next? No way. Miss Selfridge, Top Shop, Kookaï, Morgan, New Look – I honed in on all the places where I used to pretend I was buying for my non-existent daughter. I dragged Mitch along as I needed to know what looked tarty as I hadn't worn a dress for years. It went like this:

'What do you think of this, is it me?'

Mitch scanned my face for a clue to the correct answer, 'Yes. No. Can I phone a friend?' Eventually, he said the right thing, which was, 'It makes you look slim.'

'Wrap it,' I said. The shop was Kookaï, my 13-year-old niece's favourite shop, and the dress was £49.99. I rewarded Mitch by letting him buy me two pairs of shoes from LK Bennett, much to the amazement and envy of the assistants who all instantly fell in love with him. We spent the rest of the day drinking beer in Ed's Diner; well it *was* the last day of my thirties.

On the actual day I woke up feeling rather odd, half expecting to jump out of bed and find that I had grown another head – which of course I had, because a huge spot had appeared on my forehead. I tried to sleep in to prepare for the evening but my life was supposed to begin today, there was no time to waste. Luckily the postman had brought packages and lots of cards; if he hadn't his life would not have been worth living. I decided that it was a special time and so it wouldn't be unreasonable to pour myself a glass of wine. It was 9am. I was nervous. What if no one turned up? What if all my friends secretly hated me? I spent the rest of the day wandering around my flat wearing nothing but a bathrobe and my new sling-backs clutching the bottle of wine, which I finally finished off at around 6pm. And so, the big night came, and what I thought would

Getting amorous in Dunkirk – 'I love you mate, you're my besht mate . . .'

Grand Prix – and no, I haven't spelt that wrong...

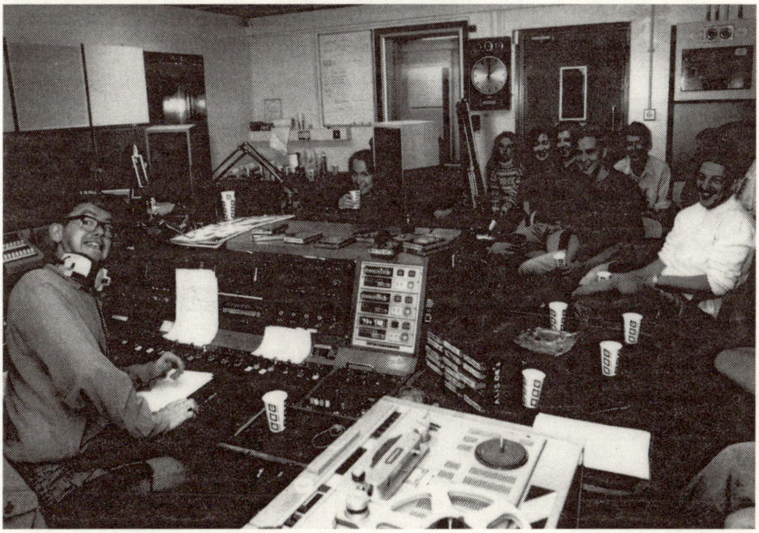

Round at Chris's on GLR with an audience of unchecked strangers and we weren't even scared!

Chris, Andy and me (or is it three lookalike blow-up dolls?) at GLR

With Zoë Ball in Barcelona in 1996

Breakfast with Paul Ross on Talk Radio, the best job in the world (before *Loose Women* came along)

Mr Stringfellow, please! Can't you see I'm pole dancing?

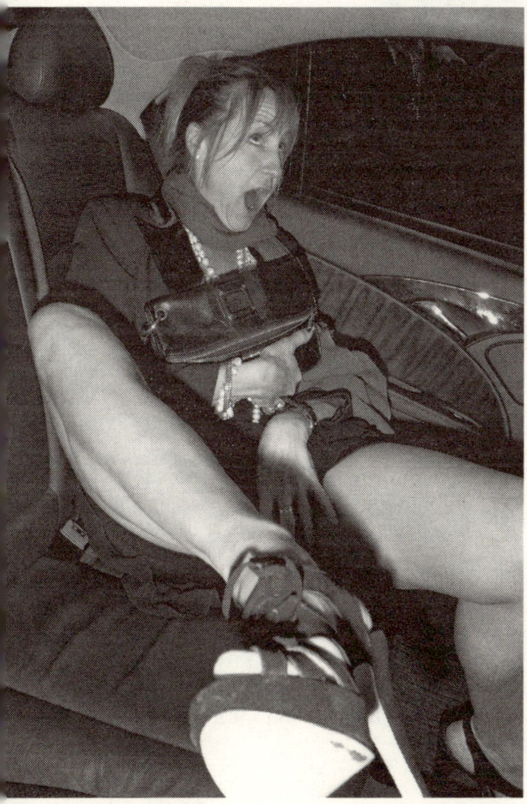

After flashing my arse at the RTS Awards, I nearly flashed something else!

They dared me to remove my make up on live TV – no need, I'd go bare every day if I had my way!

Kaye, Nadia and me in Marbella – they went off to get ready after this picture was taken

The *Sex and the City* premiere – the first time I really felt famous!

Jackie, Coleen, Jane and me before the show 'working' – it's a tough job...

Here's John Barrowman and me outside the *Loose Women* studios cooing over a baby . . . dog

Robbie and me, and some nice body language

'ost *Calendar Girls* gala night with Coleen, Denise and Jackie Brambles, who really let her hair own that night with me in G-A-Y!

Big stage, big ;o, big night – we couldn't believe it. Neither could *Top Gear*

We'd just won an NTA though you wouldn't know it as we don't look 'ery happy . . .

The amazing Sam and Eddie, with Scarlet and me, on Christmas Eve before the tsunami

With the Thai lady who drove me to safety

Our hotel, wrecked by the tsunami

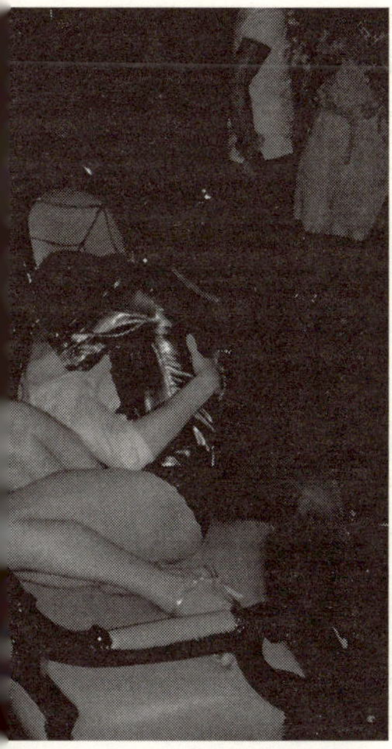

ry public display of affection
he first night we met - well,
ad known each other for at
an hour

Just Engaged! Mark wore his Eiffel Tower hat for the occasion

The two Marks in my life, fiancé and big
ttle brother

Our favourite picture even though we look like extras from *Grease*

At my 50th in Bangkok with the love of my life – a glass of Champagne, oh and Mark!

Nice dress, shame about the hair!

be the biggest headache turned out to be the least problematic and the most pleasure.

Walking into Stringfellows is like going back in time. You feel you are entering an exclusive and secret bordello, an opulent boudoir, all red velvet and chandeliers. It's fantastic. With only two no-shows, and everyone making so much effort, I was relieved and touched. I did my best to talk to everyone, but am pretty sure that I spent about four seconds with each friend. The food was surprisingly good. Peter Stringfellow welcomed us all personally. Everyone drank too much and one of the messages in my guest book (a present, originally a photo album) reads, 'Mate, it's only 11.10pm and you've already got your tits out!' From then on it was downhill all the way to my finest moment. I spotted a gap and a spare pole on the podium where the very sweaty, muscled dancer was gyrating on his own pole. I needed to gyrate too. I was up there like a shot. The audience of random punters were clearly horrified. You could read their thoughts: What is that old woman doing up there? Then, out of nowhere, the Main Man, Peter Stringfellow, owner and proprietor of the club, dismissed the dancer and was up there with me. The punters were even more amazed. So was I, especially when Mr Stringfellow had his hand up my dress (I have the photo!), I couldn't believe it. I looked down on the sea of flashbulbs and suddenly thought that slippers and knitting might not be such a bad idea after all. I probably looked like a nightmare. My brother was sitting at the table below, wailing, 'She's brought shame on the family!' I left there at 4am leaving most of my presents (all later recovered) and some of my dignity (gone forever).

I had terrible post-party blues. They're inevitable, like when you come back from holiday. I imagine that newly-weds feel the same way – all that build-up, organisation, work and expense and then, what? A hideous hangover and the thought of facing the same person for the rest of your life. I looked in the mirror but I wasn't the same person, I looked about a 102. And I felt different, like I'd just cancelled an appointment with Doctor Death.

You see, at the party, I took some drugs. Cocaine. Now before I go on, let me tell you that I had never in my whole life taken cocaine.

At least I don't think I had. I was once offered something in a jacuzzi by a bloke who used to be in *Eastenders* but my friend who knew about these things said it wasn't coke, it was just 'whizz', whatever that was. I'd never even really encountered it apart from at a party in the King's Road in the very early 1980s when there was a mountain of it in a glass bowl on a coffee table in the middle of the room. Next to it was a little tray of cut-down straws and occasionally people would just walk up to it, pick up a straw and take a giant snozzle. No one was taking any notice. Except me. I was intrigued to say the least; I had no idea what they were doing. Because when I was growing up the hardest thing you'd ever get – and they weren't easy to get – was a tablet of speed. I think they called them 'blues'. I only tried half a one once and didn't feel any different so didn't bother taking them again. Cannabis was fairly popular though. There were a lot of old hippies hanging out in the pub I was frequenting at the time and everyone always stunk of 'dope' as we called it. I did get into smoking a bit. I used to hang around with a group of (mostly) blokes in a place called 'The Bizarre' which was nothing more than the house of one of the blokes. The door was always open and people would just walk in and out, listen to music, get stoned, sometimes crash out. I slept there quite a few times, mainly because I was too stoned to move. Dope was OK, I thought, it didn't give you a hangover and it made you laugh. The downsides were that it made you fat because you wanted to eat all the time and sometimes you saw things. One night I was driving home (I know, it wasn't big and it wasn't clever but I was 18 and quite stupid) when, as I came up to the roundabout at Plains Avenue, I thought I saw a house on fire. When I got in I told my mum who sensed I might have got it wrong and dragged me to the corner of the road to check. There was no fire of course. Luckily, I hadn't phoned the fire brigade. I gave it up after that and have never done it since. Apart from when I was in St Lucia in 1997 but as they say, when in Rome . . . (see *The Winning Chapter*).

As to the cocaine at my fortieth , I thought, *oh why not?* After all, you have to try everything once, don't you? And it was my birthday. And at the time I was running out of power, just like those little bunnies that don't have Duracell batteries in them. So I went and took it. It didn't feel right huddling over some scuzzy toilet and I wasn't very good at it because I kept blowing it all over the place. For the life of me I can't tell you if it did anything except keep me awake for a bit longer and stop me going home – meaning my poor brother had to sleep in his car because I had the keys, even though I was convinced that I was the one that couldn't go home because he had them. Anyway, luckily it didn't really suit me. I certainly didn't get that rush that people describe and I didn't really like the horrible taste of chemicals sliding down the back of my throat but the worst thing was, I felt absolutely shocking the next day; not just shocking, quite depressed. Overnight I had turned into a 40-year-old pole dancing junkie and all I had to keep me company while I attempted to come to terms with my new age was a bottle of vintage Bordeaux and a little bit of coke left over from the night before. So I made myself feel worse by finishing them both off while listening to Glen Campbell records and sobbing.

The madness continued throughout 2000.

In June I went on a long weekend to Marbella with some girlfriends. It was a proper hen-style girlie holiday and we wore cowboy hats and everything. Staying in Puerto Banus, we did nothing except sunbathe on the terrace during the day and go out and get slaughtered and pull blokes in the evening. Well, not all of us pulled blokes – only the single ones of course. We'd hang out in Sinatra's, the well-known meat-market on the port which is where we met David Coulthard (not the real one, but a good lookey-likey) and Bradford and Bingley. One of my mates ended up snogging David and I ended up with B&B. I was going to go back with him but I thought it might look a tad easy so I dragged him back to our apartment. Or so I thought I had.

We were staying in an apartment complex in an area that consisted of nothing but tall apartment buildings either side of the full length of a pedestrian street. And it all looked the same. Even more so if you've been knocking it back in Sinatra's all night. So, after ringing about 20 doorbells and going up about 30 flights of stairs, I still couldn't find our apartment. The office was closed because it was so late so I couldn't ask and anyway, even if I could find it, I had no key and the girls would be comatose too. Bradford and Bingley got bored at this point and thought I was leading him a merry dance pretending not to know where I lived. I told him to bugger off then because I had bigger problems than him in that I was absolutely bursting, desperate for a pee. I tried another staircase, went to the top floor (I knew that much) and rang the doorbell. Some old bloke answered it wearing a towel wrapped round him. 'Oh, sorry, wrong apartment,' I said, a tad embarrassed and slightly despairing. I sat on the stairs, almost crying with desperation. What the fuck was I going to do now? If I went downstairs and walked around the streets I'd get picked up by the police for being a hooker. I weighed up the situation. The old bloke who answered the door, did he look like a serial killer? No. Would he let me go to the loo? Christ knows. I had no idea who else was in the apartment with him. There could be trouble ahead but if I didn't get to a toilet I was going to piss myself. I rang the bell again. He answered.

In my best apologetic, if slightly drunken tone I said, 'Look, I know I've got the wrong apartment but I've kind of forgotten where I live and I am so desperate for the loo, can I please borrow yours?'

He smiled a very reassuring, friendly smile and said, 'Yes, of course, come in.'

I then burbled and rambled on and on about how sorry I was and how embarrassing it all was and told him that the girls had locked me out because I didn't have a key and they were all passed out as he led me into a bedroom where the toilet was. He said it was his room so no one else would come in. On the way to the bedroom I spotted the couch.

'Whose is that?' I asked, innocently.

'No one's, why?' he enquired.

'Nothing.'

As I walked into the bedroom I saw the two single beds and thought, 'What a waste.' As I used the bathroom I debated whether or not I should ask if I could just stay the night but what if he was a murderer? Sod it, I had no choice and I needed sleep.

'Who's sleeping there?' I asked as I pointed to the unruffled other single bed.

'No one, why? he said.

'Can I sleep there?' I asked cheekily.

Amazingly he said yes and I lay down on it in all my clothes and shoes and was just dropping off when he started a conversation. *Oh bloody hell, here we go. He gives me a bed for the night and now I have to have a chat do I?* I made the effort and actually he turned out to be quite interesting. As the conversation went on he offered me a massage. Now, forgive me this, and I can't believe I said it, but I did because I'd turned 40 and gone mad, remember. And I was a bit drunk. I said, 'No, but I'd quite like a shag.' Oh my God, this was a total stranger that I'd met about an hour ago because I needed to use the loo! But even in my madness I sent him in search of protection; I was never so mad that I'd indulge in unsafe sex with a stranger who'd just lent me a toilet.

After about three hours' sleep I was rudely awoken and ejected from the apartment. I wasn't surprised, I could also have been some sort of nutter. It was his friends who insisted I leave though, because they thought I was a prostitute and were worried I might rob them. I certainly looked like one at 9am wandering around Puerto Banus with a short black dress, high heels and a pink pashmina. After a few sober attempts I located our accommodation. As I walked in, all eyes were on me as if to say, 'Come on, what happened?!?' Well, I was in no mood to regale and entertain them yet, I was knackered and needed sleep. I ignored them all and went and got my head down for a few more hours.

Getting up with a moral hangover is always worse than the effects of booze, but when you're mad you don't get any sort of hangover at all. Rather than feel ashamed of myself, as I should have done, I got up almost beaming with excitement at the story I was about to tell. As I walked out on to the terrace we all burst out laughing before I sat down and everyone sat around crossed-legged and eager. I was like the *Jackanory* queen. Well, of course, everyone fell about. I suppose it was funny in a sick kind of way but I wasn't really proud of myself, I just thought, 'Well it's done now, there's no use crying over spilt milk is there?'

So that should have been that, but it wasn't. In another out-of-character gesture, I must have given the old bloke my mobile phone number and in the cab on the way home from Luton Airport, he called. He sounded nice but when I asked him, as you do, if he was married he hesitated for a long time. 'So that's a yes then?' I said. Now, normally, I wouldn't go near a married man and it would make no difference that he spouted out all the usual married man guff. 'We never sleep together, I hardly see her, we've drifted apart, she's got her own life.' You know the story. But even though I had no idea what he looked like, because I couldn't remember, I agreed to see him again in London and arranged a 'date'. See? I told you I was off my rocker.

I hadn't been on a 'date' for God knows how long. In fact I don't think I have EVER been on an official and grown-up date. But as he was older (he was 50 at the time; well, he said he was) he wanted to do things properly and offered to take me to Annabel's, a really smart club in London that is always full of really posh people and actually looks like your nan's living room. I said, 'No way, too much of a date for me,' imagining him in a tweed jacket with his top shirt button open and casual loafers with no socks, dancing opposite me, in a prom dress and kitten heels, to the Bee Gees. 'Let's just have dinner instead.' I arranged to meet him in the bar of Claridges Hotel in Mayfair and took my friend Vivien along for support in case I got stood up. Vivien and I were hysterical at the fact I didn't really know who I was meeting and every guy that walked in the door we'd both look at each other and say in unison, 'Bloody hell, I hope it's not 'im!' It was too funny. Anyway, so then this bloke walks in wearing what looks like a safari jacket and he looks vaguely familiar. I'm thinking, 'Oh God, no, not a safari jacket!' And, right enough, it was him. But he wasn't wearing a safari jacket, just a light-coloured blazer. Phew.

So we went to Langan's Brasserie, a safe place for a first date and, more importantly, they don't mind you getting a bit drunk there. It all felt so bizarre that I got completely shitfaced but I carried on seeing him for quite a while. I thought it was about six months but after looking into it, I think it was longer than that. We had a good time though. He took me to Paris and bought me nice presents. I even cooked him dinner. He was really kind and thoughtful but it just wasn't right and I wouldn't do it again.

The last sign of lunacy was in October 2001 on a trip to Barcelona to see Depeche Mode. I wasn't particularly a fan but my neighbour, Sue, knew Andy the keyboard player so I went along for the ride. I'd been to Barcelona before (with Zoë Ball) and I loved the Hotel Arts, where we were staying this time. Sue brought a work colleague, Peter, along. I'd met him before and thought he was quite handsome but no more than that. Anyway, on the first night we all went out and Sue, being slightly more drunk than me, went back to the hotel. Peter and I ended up in the bar talking about sex. After about five minutes and with a complete lack of judgement, I said to him, 'Fancy a shag?' Oh well, don't ask, don't get, as they say. Of course he's a bloke so he said yes and so we went up to my room. The rest didn't entirely register due to excess alcohol but I know that we did it in the bathroom where he had to stand on tip toes and the soap went careering down the bin shute.

Shame it wasn't a bit more memorable as that was to be the last time for almost seven years because, shocked at my own promiscuity, I decided it was time to give it a rest and spent the next couple of years simply having a laugh and as much harmless fun as possible with my new best friends, Scarlet and Eduardo. Scarlet had just split up with her husband so, being newly single, all she wanted to do was go out, go on holiday and party, so that's what we did. I'd met them both earlier that year, again through my neighbour Sue. I was at a party and we were talking about holidays. I was going to Cape Town on my own and they took pity and said, 'Forget it, come to Thailand with us!' Trouble was, I don't think they really meant it and they certainly didn't think I would go, but I went anyway, had the time of my life and fell in love with the place. Little did I know that three years hence, it could well have been the end of me (*The Tsunami Chapter*).

CHAPTER 19

The First Time I: Saw my bum on the news

(The Loose Women *and Fame Chapter)*

The first time I ever appeared on telly was when I flashed my bum at a live news crew outside The Rubens Hotel in Buckingham Palace Road in 1982. I'd been drinking with some friends in Carriages Wine Bar next door and they stupidly dared me to. My mum saw it and tried really hard to be cross but couldn't help laughing. I know, it was a pathetically childish thing to do, but I was only 22. But perhaps that starring role was to be the start of something big? And I don't mean my arse.

Probably one of the reasons I did lose the plot during my fortieth year on the planet was because I didn't really have any work. I was doing the radio show on the London station, LBC, on Saturday nights and I was doing a monthly column for the now-defunct glossy magazine *Woman's Journal*. The only other work I had was the odd travel piece for them where I'd get to go on what they call a 'Press Trip' – a paid-for jaunt for a bunch of journalists who'd all go home and write nice things for their publications. That was a good little gig; I got to go on safari in Kenya, did a cooking course in Normandy, sampled a spa in Las Vegas, had a cycling holiday in Tuscany, did a feature on designer toilets in Valencia, and went to Bermuda. But it all ended when the mag folded, so I was left only with one radio show a week which paid £100. It was the best of times and the worst of times in a sense because I'm very good at doing nothing and would be very good at not working at all if I had endless pots of cash, but sadly I didn't. I was having a riot fun-wise but it wasn't cheap, because when I wasn't working so much I'd go out all the time, knowing I didn't have to get up in the morning. I was financially OK-ish. I'd sold a flat two years earlier but that cash was dwindling, especially as I'd bought another, more expensive, one with most of the proceeds. And the mad mid-life-crisis car. I had no idea what I was going to do. Stop going out for a start. But that wouldn't exactly pay the bills (except maybe for an extra week) and it would only make things worse because I'd be miserable. I could re-mortgage, but then how would I pay the newly increased mortgage? With the money I'd just borrowed from the mortgage? Where was the sense in that? I had no idea. I knew I had a few PEPs that I could fall back on if I needed to so I just carried on, business as usual.

I spent my days either going out for lunch or watching daytime TV – in particular, a show that had started in the latter part of 1999, called *Loose Women*. I watched it with utter disbelief. Not because it was awful or anything – it was good – but because I wasn't on it. *Hang on*, I thought, *I obviously didn't get the message*, and went over to check the answering machine. Nothing. I'd been dying for a show like this to come about. Feisty women, talking about stuff, both trivial and important. Why wasn't I asked? This is my show!!! I realise that sounds terribly immodest but that's what I thought. Here was a show with women of a certain age being allowed to speak and express an opinion. That's what I'd been doing for years on the radio. But in my typical, unambitious, do-nothing way, I did nothing. What I should have done was call up my agent immediately and berate him with force as to why I hadn't even been suggested. Trouble was, I didn't have an agent, but then what did I want one for? I didn't have any work. My jobs on the radio and at the magazine both came straight through me, so why would I want to hand over a good chunk of what precious little I was earning to an agent? I answered my own question in my head: *Er . . . because then you might have been put forward for this show?* Yes, alright. Maybe that was my mistake.

Still, I watched it and enjoyed it. There was a good choice of panel, including Kaye Adams, Nadia Sawahla, Philippa Kennedy, Jane Moore, Karren Brady and a host of others, but secretly I couldn't help thinking it might be better with me on it.

It ran for two series and while I was sitting around on my getting-fat arse waiting for the third, quite out of the blue, the phone rang. It was Monday 18 September 2000. It was a woman called Suzan Price. The conversation went like this:

'Hi, is that Carol McGiffin?'

'Yes, speaking.'

'Oh hello, it's Suzan Price I'm calling from Granada Television, we're making a new series called *Live Talk* which will have four women talking about the issues of the day and it'll be on every day at lunchtime on ITV. Do you think that'd be something you'd be interested in doing?'

I knew she was talking about that *Loose Women* show but she seemed to be calling it something else. I was a little confused but I just presumed I'd misheard her. Anyway, if she'd been standing in front of me I would have bitten her hand off. Of course I said yes and she told me she'd call me back with some dates to see if I could do them. She called back less than 10 minutes later to ask if I could do the first show which was next Monday. Could I do it? Gulp. Of course I could, I wasn't really doing much else. Before I put the phone down I asked her, 'Could I just check with you, is this the same show as *Loose Women*?'

She told me, 'Well it's the same sort of format but it's a different show. This one will be more serious and talk about more current affairs topics. Oh, and it will be shorter, half an hour long.'

I couldn't quite take it in. Did that just happen? Did I just get a job on that show that's now called something else? I think I did. Bloody hell, what a great day. I phoned my mum and then I went out to celebrate with Mitch.

Most people don't believe it, but I never really wanted to be on TV. I'd spent most of the 1990s doing radio and because it was talk radio and I was known to be a bit of a gobshite, I did get asked to do TV debate programmes like *Esther* and the like, but usually it was the night-time versions like *Central Weekend Live* where the subject would be 'Do White Van Men Drive Like Tossers Because They Have Small Penises?' Or something equally provocative. Sometimes I did them, driving all the way to Birmingham just to be sick with nerves and make a complete tit of myself. Every time I did them I would walk out of the place and want to kill myself. They were usually bun fights anyway, so sometimes you didn't even get a chance to say anything at all. I only did them for the money but sometimes it just wasn't worth it for £100.

I did one once about breast implants. There were two sisters on there who had inflatable implants and the valves were under their armpits. So if they were in a big tit mood they'd get the pump out and blow. Hey presto, massive boobs. I couldn't believe it. I couldn't take my eyes off them. In fact, one of them nearly had my eye out while she was pumping. As usual the show turned into a scrap with the 'natural' girls pulling out the hair of the 'fake' girls. It was hysterical and at least that time it was worth driving to Nottingham or wherever it was for the 100 quid. I also did a couple of those shows where you just sit in a room and pass comment on the '40 Worst Celebrity Nose Jobs' or something even more meaningless.

Right at the start when I got my first job in television at Music Box, I'd originally gone there for an audition for a job as a VJ (video jockey). As you know, I was reluctant but I gave it a go because I just wanted to work there. Even when I was working there, I did more screen tests and was always crap. Other people seemed to think I'd be good on TV, 'Oh go on, you'll be brilliant at it,' they would always say. But every time I tried, I just made a fool of myself. I've still got them all on VHS and they are simply awful. I don't know why I keep them.

I also did screen tests with Chris for his BSB show, *Power Up*, and for *The Big Breakfast*. I looked shocking for that one and needless to say I didn't get it, but I was relieved – I'd worked with him long enough on the radio to know that it wouldn't have been a good idea. Shame though, we could have been the Richard and Judy of breakfast.

Before *Live Talk/Loose Women*, the only times I'd accepted the challenge of actually doing a bit of proper TV presenting were the hilariously bad St Lucia report (see *The Winning Chapter*) and a stand-in stint for a sick Steve Blacknell on a programme called *Off The Wall*, also for Music Box (I did OK but it took forever to film because I wasn't good at remembering what I was supposed to say). Then, in the summer of 1998, I did a stand-in job at the Whitehall Theatre for *The Jack Docherty Show* – called, while he was away, *Not The Jack Docherty Show with Carol McGiffin*. Both of those times were down to the same woman: Alex Jackson-Long. Remember the post girl at Music Box? Well she had become extremely important (and still is!) and she was convinced that one day I would be on telly and be famous. She really believed in me and was a kind of mentor for a bit. Unfortunately for Alex, both times I took up the challenge at her behest I managed to prove her wrong and she went on to produce other unknown stars such as Dom Joly, Louis Theroux and Armstrong and Miller. She was eventually proved right about me of course, but I don't think she thought it would take 20 years.

My appearance on *Off The Wall* wasn't bad. I had a look at it recently – it was a round-up of films, music, what's on and stuff like that, an hour-long show of links and clips and music videos. At the start a title caption came up, 'Presented by Carol From the Office', because that's what I was. I was the production manager sitting there all day dealing with budgets, booking crew and doing cost reports.

Not The Jack Docherty Show was a much bigger deal. This was a night-time chat show that aired three nights a week on Channel 5 on terrestrial telly. Again I pulled it off, but I wasn't much cop, and because I was a radio person, no one in the audience had the slightest idea who I was so they mostly sat there with really long faces. I didn't look very good either. You see, working on the radio is probably the least sartorially important job you can possibly do. That was why I loved it so much, because at the time I just didn't care what I looked like, and it showed. They gave me a bit of money to buy something, as I had nothing really suitable for TV, so I bought a couple of suits. A black shiny one and a navy-blue one. Not very flattering as they were both way too small and I looked a bit fat. TV makes you look fatter anyway but I was quite plump then, at least a stone heavier than I am now. That's what doing an early morning radio show did for you. You had permanent jet-lag and you'd try and compensate for it by eating. Eating anything in the hope it would bring energy. Then you'd drink loads of coffee to keep yourself awake and your digestive system would go completely skew-whiff because it didn't know what time it was. So overall it wasn't good for the appearance.

Given all of that, I can't believe I agreed to do it, but at the time the radio show was going well and because we were on for four hours a day, five days a week I was on a bit of a roll so just went for it.

The TV job made a nice change and for five minutes I thought I could be the next David Letterman. I went in during the day despite having to get up at the crack of dawn to do the radio show, got involved with the writers, came up with some ideas and raked in some showbiz friends as guests. I had to do this because it was proving difficult to get anyone to be interviewed by an unknown host. I got my friend Zoë Ball, Jamie Theakston, who I knew from *Live and Kicking* and through Zoë and, of course, Paul Ross came on too. Other guests I interviewed were Sean Lock, who was lovely, Edwina Currie, who I was surprised to find I liked, Debbie Currie, her daughter, and once again my friend the broadcaster Jon Ronson.

Anyway, I enjoyed my little foray into TV but I didn't get another chance. The other two guest hosts went on to much greater things indeed. Melinda Messenger was one and she got the whole show after Jack left. And the other one was none other than Graham Norton. Enough said.

So that was always my problem with TV. There wasn't a suitable show out there for me but when *Loose Women/Live Talk* came along, I knew it was perfect because, as I had proven time and time again, I was better at just being myself and giving an opinion. I wasn't great at 'presenting' stuff, especially other people's words and scripts.

I'll never forget that first show. Monday 25 September 2000. I'd only had a week to psyche myself up, get in 'the zone' as they say. Luckily I wasn't looking my worst because I'd been seeing the married man since May and so I'd been paying attention to my appearance. My hair had been highlighted for the first time in my life, I wore make-up and I bought nice clothes. On that day I pondered about what to wear for hours. It also baffled me as to why I suddenly just got that call. How? Who? What? The only clue I had was when a friend of mine, Graham Jackson, who worked at ITV, told me he'd ambushed the boss of daytime in the lift. Graham bothered him all the way up to the top floor of the ITV tower about how they should have that Carol McGiffin on that *Loose Women* show. I don't know if that had anything to do with it – but if it did, thanks Graham.

I got up so early on that Monday morning I hardly remember going to bed. I had to get a flight from Heathrow at 6.30am so that meant I had to leave the house at 4.45am to get a cab to Paddington then the Heathrow Express, pick up my ticket and get to the gate by 6.10am at the latest. If it hadn't been so early in the morning I wouldn't have done it in that time.

Oh God I felt so important, flying BA Business Class, seat 1a. I'd never flown to Manchester before but I'd got the train and driven, both of which took between three and four hours depending on the time of day, traffic, state of the trains. The flight took off, the cabin crew went into fast-forward, served everyone breakfast and tea and coffee twice, and then we landed. All in 35 minutes. As soon as we touched down there was like a dawn chorus of mobile phones being switched on prematurely. Wow, these people were all going to work, on a plane, on a Monday morning. I was in my element and it felt so good I was absolutely certain it wouldn't last.

Walking into the studios in Manchester was something else. All the pictures around the reception of all the big ITV stars looked down on me and I thought, *what am I doing here?* I was escorted up to the office where the other panellists were already gathered. I knew Nadia wasn't going to be there but she still intimidated me;

well her and Kaye together, they were such a double act on the show that sometimes you didn't really notice that there were two other women there. That day's line-up was Kaye Adams, Emily Symons and Anne Diamond, which felt a bit weird. She had since split up from Mike (see *The Winning Chapter*) but I never really knew what she believed. She was always pleasant to me but, for all I knew, she might have wrongly thought something had gone on between Mike and me, so I had no idea how I would be treated by her.

I don't know why but I expected a big friendly welcome from everyone because this was a new show and surely everyone would be buzzing with excitement. Wrong. The only friendly person I encountered that morning was the editor, Suzan, who at least seemed pleased to see me. I was getting very nervous and feeling a little bit out of my depth but I had to go through with it.

The morning flew by. I couldn't believe you could have such a long meeting for such a short show. Then there was all the messing about with make-up but it was all new, so being in the make-up room with all the pictures of stars (from *Coronation Street*!) up on the walls made it exciting. I was given a top to wear; it was a plain, pink, V-neck long-sleeved T-shirt. It was horrible, I hated pink, but I didn't say so. The next minute it was time to go on air. My nerves were driving me mad. How could I be this nervous when I'd been confidently doing four hours of live talk radio every morning for years? I was sweating and the pink top was showing large sweat patches so I put big clumps of toilet paper under each arm to absorb it. At the same time I was shaking as though I was cold. I hated it and I thought, 'What am I doing? I can't do this, I can't be on TV,' as I looked at the others who were all as cool as cucumbers.

As a result I hardly said a word. In fact, I froze. I watched Kaye fluently put the case for discussion, making jokes, having banter with the other panellists. But I was hearing nothing, not even in my earpiece (which I hated, still do). The guests came and went and I said nothing. I felt embarrassed and sick and when I walked out of there to get the flight home, I was convinced it was for the first and last time. I phoned my mum straight afterwards thinking she'd say something that would maybe indicate that it wasn't quite as bad as I'd imagined but all she said was, 'Yeah, it was good, but you didn't say much did ya?' Thanks, Mum.

When I watched the show back I was mortified at my muteness but was more horrified to see that I had a giant roll of fat hanging over my trousers as I walked over to the sofa area. Suddenly the fact that I'd said precisely nothing didn't seem to matter at all.

Anyway, they did ask me back and I got better and ended up getting on really well with Kaye and Nadia.

I loved those times in Manchester because I loved getting out of London. Even the early mornings and the travelling I enjoyed. Kaye and Nadia, because they were on every day, lived in a rented flat during the week and if I was staying over we'd go out to some of the bars along Deansgate or end up in the Press Club.

One time, when I'd stayed at their flat, we were walking down to the studios and Posh Spice drove past in a 4x4 and hooted and waved. Then once when I was shopping in the Trafford Centre I saw her and David shopping together. Posh was pushing a pushchair and no one was taking the blindest bit of notice of them. Maybe they were look-alikes who were always there as a decoy for the real thing. That was the extent of my celebrity sightings – apart from the guests we had on, of course. We used to get a lot of *Coronation Street* actors on in those days, but I suppose that was understandable because they were just round the back. The first show had Lee Boardman and Jane Danson on.

After the second series of *Live Talk* nothing happened and the entire format disappeared for over a year. I was slightly peeved to see it return again as *Loose Women* in September 2002, without me again. It had changed a bit as well: Kaye wasn't on every day and there were lots of different women. I hated going out and having people saying to me, 'Oh, why aren't you on that show anymore?' I'd just say, 'I dunno, face doesn't fit anymore I suppose.' And that was probably exactly it. The hardest thing to deal with was my mum. She would work herself almost into a rage because I wasn't on. 'But you were the best thing on it! I refuse to watch it anymore if you're not on!' But I know she did and well, she would say that wouldn't she, she was my mum. She was more upset than me about not doing it and I really felt for her. She just wanted to be proud of me.

I did feel like a bit of an outcast for a while and didn't do much work at all for nearly two years. Financially I was still fine because I'd sold my PEPs (at the worst time) so I wasn't destitute but I needed to do something with my time. I went for a couple of producer jobs that friends had put me up for, but I just became completely hopeless in meetings as I felt like they were looking at me thinking, 'Mmmm, didn't you used to be on the telly?' So I gave up on TV for a while and took up painting and decorating and did a whole house for a friend for £50 a day, just to get me out of the house. I hated it so went back to doing nothing. I did a lot of writing during that time and a lot of pondering.

18 October 2002
Oh my God, how terribly wrong it's all gone, it so wasn't meant to be like this. Spending my days plucking stray hairs from my bikini line and eyebrows, checking for emails that no one has sent, avoiding talking to friends as they might ask what I'm doing at the moment.

In early 2003 the show returned – with me on the panel. I went (very gratefully) up to Norwich, where it was now being filmed. I'd heard that the bosses were giving the show one more chance and there was a new production crew and a new editor in place. Again there were new panellists: Sherrie Hewson, Claire Sweeney, Kerry McFadden (Katona), Lisa Rogers, Sarah Cawood and Jayne Middlemiss among loads of others.

That series ended at the beginning of September 2003, by which time my mum was in the final stages of cancer and was close to dying. I carried on working because I knew how much it meant to her, but drove down to Kent after every show and drove back again when I had to. It was the hardest thing I've ever had to do, put on a smiley face and pretend that nothing was wrong.

She died three weeks later. Luckily the show didn't come back until June the following year so I had a good eight months off to compose myself.

Series 6, in my view, was the turning point. It was in London and the set had a big glass backdrop with a live view of the Thames. The set was funky and colourful and there was once again a new editor.

I'd had an epiphany in that time off. I'd taken a good look at myself in the mirror and realised I needed a bit of a makeover. All the time Mum was ill I don't think I thought once about how I looked and I did look shocking. When they do compilations of past shows I can't watch myself, I don't look like me. So when I came back I had new clothes, new hair, I'd had my teeth whitened, had a health check and started wearing dresses and jewellery. Kaye didn't recognise me.

Now a lot of people recognise me because *Loose Women* is still going strong and is arguably stronger than ever. We're now in our fourteenth series and on nearly every day of the year. Which is probably *why* a lot of people now recognise me and indeed all of the girls. It's nice. People are nice. Most of the time. I genuinely love talking to people and saying hello and even if I'm not in the mood, I'll get in the mood.

I can't say I don't like being famous but I also can't say I do. I'm not being disingenuous when I say I really don't think about it because I do everything the same as I always have. It hits you now and again though, like when I'm walking through Bangkok Airport and people come up and say hello. Being recognised while you're on the other side of the world is the weirdest thing.

There's no denying it either, fame carries with it a lot of perks. But I don't capitalise on a lot of the trappings. For example, I really don't like to have a lot of free stuff. Some celebs I know never pay for anything, they just 'make a call' and it gets sent over. They think I'm mad because I pay for my own holidays, clothes, CDs, everything. I have had a couple of things but I always feel beholden to the giver and sometimes it turns out that they think they own you just because they gave you a free fake tan. Quite often, it's just not worth it.

The other tricky thing is hospitals. I use the NHS. I get stick for that because people say, 'But you can afford private health insurance.' Well, that may be so, but as far as I'm concerned no insurance is worth the paper it's written on and I can't be bothered fighting them when they find a reason somewhere in the reams of small print why they don't want to shell out. And anyway, I pay my taxes so I'm as entitled to use the NHS as much as the next patient. Trouble is, when you're on television and people want to be nice and come up and say hello, it's always when you're sitting in the bum clinic waiting to have a camera shoved up your arse or something like that and as everyone's there for the same reason I'm always tempted to say, 'Ah, you're having an anal photoshoot too, are you? How lovely.' I've thought about a disguise but it never works, people just stare more. I've learnt to switch off from it now though. I just think of the slogan they use on the Channel 4 show *Embarrassing Bodies*: 'There's no shame, we're all the same.' And it's true.

The other strange thing is that people seem to think it's totally acceptable to question everything you do. I was on my way to Luton Airport once and this bloke walks up to me and says, 'What are you doing on a train, I thought you'd go everywhere in a limo!' I'm not Simon Cowell for Christ's sake, why shouldn't I get the train? And shopping too. I genuinely like to shop for bargains in the Poundstretcher and quite often I'll get someone say, 'Urgh what you doing in here, thought you'd go to Selfridges or somewhere like that.' Eh? For wipes? Or envelopes? Or cheap bog roll? I don't think so.

I do feel a bit sorry for my family. My poor sister gets harangued all the time by people asking about me, which is understandable, but a bit rude. What about her? Do people ask about her? No! Just before last Christmas she was in a supermarket and one of the cashiers looked at her card and said, 'Ooh, McGiffin, are you related to Carol McGiffin off of *Loose Women*?'

'Yeah,' said Kim. 'She's my sister.'

'Ooh, it must be brilliant having a celebrity coming round for Christmas,' the girl replied.

Kim was well put out and snapped, 'But she's not a *celebrity*, she's my SISTER!'

Celebrity is a strange word. It is applied to all sorts of waifs and strays now who appear on the television for whatever reason, including me. I don't think I deserve the moniker and I don't really see myself as a celebrity, but I do often get called one. And I often get called on to be one even though it almost always makes me feel uncomfortable. I've done two public speaking engagements: one corporate job, which was years ago and totally mortifying because no one there had ever seen *Loose Women* so had no idea who I was; and a charity 'luncheon' that I thought would be in a room for about 20 people, but it turned out to be 300. The best thing about that was that they'd all actually bought tickets so I guessed most of them might have wanted to hear what I had to say. I was asked to speak for 15 to 20 minutes before doing the raffle but I ended up enjoying myself so much I spoke for a whole hour. It didn't seem like that to me, although it probably did to the ladies in the room. No one heckled though, thankfully.

I also try not to *behave* like a celebrity. I never wear sunglasses at night, and even though I've been asked many times, I would NEVER do a deal with the paparazzi like some 'celebs' do where you tell the snapper where you'll be, he takes the pictures and sells them then you get a slice of the action, so to speak. No, that's not me.

The only time I really *feel* like a celebrity is if all the *Loose Women* go to an awards dinner or a party together. The *Sex and the City* premiere was the first big one. Jackie Brambles, Sherrie Hewson, Andrea McLean, Jane McDonald and me all went. To get into the spirit of my then role model, Samantha, I wore the shortest dress ever (Kate Moss for Topshop) in bright orange with super-high heels. Jackie made sure she was walking very close behind me the whole time in case anyone tried to get an up-the-skirt picture! The crowds were amazing; so excited, even at seeing us. There was a moment where we were on the red carpet at the same time as Sarah, Kristen, Kim and Cynthia and there was a group of lairy fans hanging out of the pub shouting at the top of their voices, 'Carol! Carol!

Carol!' I looked round to see if Carol Vorderman, Smiley or Thatcher were behind me but no, they were shouting at me. I was so chuffed I wanted to go over to SJP and poke her and say, 'Look, they're shouting "Carol", that's me that is,' but I didn't want to spoil her night.

I've been up a few red carpets now. The latest and the most amazing night we had was at the National Television Awards. *Loose Women* had never even made the long list before – there are about 30 shows on this and people vote for their favourites to make a shortlist of four – so to be voted the most popular factual programme beating such amazing shows as *Top Gear*, *Come Dine With Me* and *The Apprentice* was really something. A lot of people said we shouldn't have won because we're not 'factual' but we're not fictional – although as soon as you say the word 'factual' people assume it must represent documentaries, history programmes or *Newsnight*. Well, it goes without saying that if they were popular then they would have made the shortlist and won instead of us.

The NTA was our sixth award. Since 2007 we'd been up for seven and only lost one. That was the RTS Award – *Come Dine With Me* got that one. It was a funny night though and one that we'll not forget for a while. Of course we were a bit disappointed at not winning but we were going to have a good night anyway and all went to the party afterwards. It all started to go wrong when Coleen and Jackie were standing out in the lobby waiting for cars to go home. I went over for a chat and saw how many snappers there were outside the glass, it was unbelievable. I turned to Jackie and Coleen and said, 'Look at them, what are they expecting to happen?' Everyone shrugged their shoulders and carried on talking. So I said, 'I'll give them something to photograph,' and with that bent over, lifted up my dress and flashed my bum at them. They were a long way off and there was glass in-between so I thought it wouldn't be too much of a cellulite exposé. Well, they went mad. So did Denise Welch. She rushed outside and demanded to see the evidence at which point she came running in to the editor Emily, saying, 'Emily, I can't flash, this dress is too tight, what am I going to flash!' She was being serious! Because I had flashed my knickers, she just had to do it too so she went outside and flashed hers. Problem with that was, she was wearing flesh-coloured long-johns, or Spanx as they're better known. She looked even worse than me. When I left to go home the snappers were shouting, 'Come on Carol, give us another flash!' So I did but it was a bad move – bright flash and close up, not good for the dimples and my saggy bottom looked like it had had a couple of puppies ears sewn onto it. Then when Coleen and Andrea left, Coleen thought it'd be funny to put a pencil down her cleavage as she got in the car and Andrea's dress flapped out revealing one of her boobies. It was comedy carnage. The next day, the *Daily Mail Online* ran all of the pictures under the headline, 'Loose Women Run Amok at Awards!' We'd hardly run amok but it was priceless nonetheless.

Now, whenever we leave parties or whatever, we always get trailed by photographers and, trust me, having a load of backward-walking paparazzi trailing you around the West End is enough to make anyone feel like Posh and Becks.

I feel like I have to be careful though. A lot of people say a lot of nice things but at the same time a lot of people say pretty horrible things, so you have to take the rough with the smooth. I'm always aware of not letting anything go to my head. I've seen some casualties of that and it's not pretty. I say it's best not to read anything about myself and just to do my best to keep on being me. That's all I can do really.

I'm very happy being a *Loose Woman*; it is the ultimate job and I love it. Believe me, I know how lucky I am to be doing it. But, it is a real job. Many people think we turn up at 12.15pm and go on air at 12.30, but it's not that simple. For the live show, work starts at 8.30am with the meeting where we discuss all the possible topics we might talk about on the show. Then we all go to make-up, which is my least favourite aspect of the whole job. You might think that's mad, what girl wouldn't like to sit in a chair and be made up by people who really know their stuff every day? Er . . . me. It's so annoying for Lee, Donna and Linda, the make-up team. There they are, trained experts in their field who put so much into what they do, and all I do is sit there grimacing, tutting and trying to look anywhere other than at myself in the mirror. And God help them if they try and touch my hair! I don't want my hair bouffed up – I'll leave the big hair to Miss McDonald, that's Jane's domain. As a result I often end up on the telly looking less than perfect with more than one hair out of place. The girls just shake their heads at me and proffer the comedy comb (a giant kid's comb with big gappy teeth) in desperation. In fact, Donna calls me Worzel Gummidge. It's a fair comment.

A lot of people work very hard behind the scenes to make *Loose Women* what it is. I call them 'the kids' because they all seem to be so young. I joke with them that all they do all day is 'drink lattes' and 'go on Facebook', but they don't. Well they do, but not all day. A lot of the success of the show has to be put down to Karl Newton who joined it as a producer in 2003 in Norwich. When he first called me up to ask me back I thought it was Carla and every time I spoke to him until I met him I called him Carla because, to put it bluntly, on the phone he sounded like a woman. When I did finally meet him I looked at him blankly, like, 'Who are you? Where's Carla?' because he is, in fact, a man. I was so embarrassed but he didn't mind; he said he was used to it as he has an alter-ego character that he used to perform in drag clubs called Lady Lola. He doesn't do any of that now, of course; he's a very grown-up, responsible and important editor. One of those types that has an overall effect on something, even though on the surface he appears to do very little. Since he became editor, and then executive producer, of *Loose Women* it has transformed and become even more successful. He's now doing the same thing with *This Morning* with some subtle changes. Most people wouldn't notice his stamp but I do. He can be a bit of a bitch at times but I like him. A lot.

Then there's Emily, our current editor. She is your typical Liberal-leaning, university graduate, TV type. As you can imagine I lock horns with her quite a lot, especially when she repeatedly tells us not to do things that I would never dream of doing. It's not her fault, she has to because it's her job to relay what the lawyers flag up. For instance, when Twiggy was on, she said, 'Right, don't ask

Twiggy what it's like to be in the Marks and Spencer's adverts.' Like we don't know it's a commercial channel and our competition gives away M&S vouchers. As soon as she says, 'OK, a couple of compliance issues,' I tune out. I phoned her at the weekend once and I said, 'I bet you're in a coffee shop in Islington drinking a latte and reading the *Guardian*.' Naturally, she was. But she knows I love her really.

Having been on the show nearly 10 years I can't count the number of women I've worked with on there, and there isn't one I haven't got on with. I particularly miss Kaye Adams and Jackie Brambles and I'm still friends with them both. Of course there are some I get on with more than others, but that's a lifestyle thing. We don't really hang out together much and we don't all live in a house together like The Beatles. In fact, the only time we socialise all together is at work or awards dos. We all live all over the country so it's difficult, but if I do anything outside of the show it'll be with Sherrie or Denise who both came to my fiftieth in Bangkok.

Sherrie and I have also been to Marbella together. We went for the opening of Jean-Christophe Novelli's new restaurant, which has since closed down. Apparently, we caused virtual mayhem there and word had it that we weren't welcome in Marbella anymore. But it was all down to one disgruntled local who took exception to me falling asleep in my tuna steak and being carried out of the restaurant after a late dinner. In my defence, I didn't want to go because I'd had enough and I needed to sleep, so I tried to hide away in my room, but they came knocking and knocking and wouldn't leave without me. Anyway, we met some lovely people there so hopefully we're not really banned.

One of the best things about working on the show is getting to meet so many great guests, especially musical ones who perform at the end of the show. It feels like we're at a private little gig being so close to them. It's difficult to single out favourites but I'm going to try. Without a doubt, Neil Sedaka singing 'Oh Carol' to us around the piano is my all-time finest moment on *Loose Women*. The song was released in 1959 when Mum was expecting me and she loved the song so much she named me after it. So to have him there, in the flesh, singing it (mostly to me) was bittersweet in the extreme because she'd passed away not long before. Another of her favourites, Simply Red, were also amazing. Imagine these giant-stadium-filling 1980s legends in our little studio belting out their most iconic track, 'Money's Too Tight To Mention'. It was surreal.

Robbie Williams was another 'I have the best job in the world' moment too. Robbie was probably my favourite guest ever because he loves the show so much that he actually asked to come on to do his first TV interview for his new album. I hope he doesn't mind me telling you but in the week before, because he's quite a nervous creature, he wanted to familiarise himself with us. He already knew Kate, Denise and Sherrie, who knows his mum, but then he asked his agent to get my phone number so he could have a chat. Now, I'm not normally starstruck but when I listened to his message on my voicemail I went back to being a teenager again. He'd called during a show so when I called him back afterwards and was 'having a chat' someone knocked on my dressing room door. I said, 'Hold on Rob,' (Rob!) and went to the door, answered it and said, 'Yeah, can you come back. I'm just on the phone to Robbie Williams . . . ' The runner looked at me as if to say, 'Yeah right, in your dreams!' But I was, and he was lovely. We chatted for ages and when he came on the show he was given the rare privilege of staying for two parts. As far as I can remember only Joan Collins and Bette Midler have enjoyed the same benefit. Oh, and Joan Rivers, but she was dragged off in the break for calling Russell Crowe 'a piece of ******* ****' so she never made it to the second part.

And then there was Russell Brand. He wasn't booked to do the show but he was in the building for *Have I Got News For You?*. I'd located his dressing room so that I could avoid it as I really didn't want to meet him. He was the object of my fantasies and I didn't want to appear like a gibbering schoolgirl in front of him after I'd said I'd pay him for sex and talked about him endlessly on the show. But that didn't stop me fantasising in my dressing room. I was lying on the sofa in there imagining a knock at the door. I would shout the code out and he'd swagger in, all black boots, skinny jeans and hair. Straight over to the sofa where he'd ravish me while neither of us spoke a word. Lovely. Anyway, I succeeded in avoiding him all day and was safely ensconced in my seat on the *Loose Women* set, doing the show and during Part 3, Denise, who's anchoring the show, asks, 'Carol, would you fart on a first date with Russell Brand?' I say, 'Well no, not on the first date.' And at that point, the audience gasps and they're looking at the guest entrance arch. I turn around and there he is, standing there, smirking his very attractive and sexy smile. I had no idea but the exec producer, Sue, had been to see him in his dressing room and persuaded him to come on as a surprise for me. But I hate surprises, especially when I'm not ready and I wasn't ready, I was wearing the wrong top! Anyway, he was really sweet and made me kiss him. He smelled really nice, really aromatic scent mixed with a whiff of garlic. Perfect.

I met him again when I had to go and interview him about his film, *Forgetting Sarah Marshall*, at a hotel in London. He flirted relentlessly and was being suggestive and very funny. But mid-interview, just as I was getting into my full Barry Norman swing, he blurts out, 'Did you get a cheese head of me? My mum told me you had a cheese head made of me.' I explained that I hadn't but that a viewer had sent it in as a present for my birthday but he continued, 'Why cheese?' I said, 'Well, I like cheese and I like Russell Brand, that's why.' He came back quick as a flash, 'Yeah, well I like sex and I like animals but I'm not about to mix those two things together am I?' I had no answer, which was just as well because I couldn't speak for laughing. At the interview he gave me a flower and kissed me again on the lips. Unfortunately the camera had been switched off so no one believed me.

What I also love is when we have bands like JLS on. I love the thought of the *Loose Women* being 'down with the kids' – it makes me laugh. McFly have been on a few times and we've also had The Saturdays, Pixie Lott, Taylor Swift and The Script (really couldn't believe that one!)

My other favourite guests are always the ones you don't expect to see on *Loose Women* like Germaine Greer, Janet Street-Porter and Clive James, guests who're probably more at home on *Newsnight Review*.

My wish list of people who've never been on are: Pet Shop Boys, David Bowie, Chris Moyles and Hard-Fi. But my number one wish is Victoria Beckham. All the other Spice Girls have been on and Mel B and Emma have both been panellists. I ask them every time to tell her we're alright and we won't be horrid, but she still hasn't been on, even though she's done our US counterpart, *The View*, a couple of times. Also I'd love to see the Queen on *Loose Women*, but somehow I don't think that wish is going to come true.

I think we all knew we'd kind of arrived when we were invited to be guests on the *Friday Night with Jonathan Ross* show. For years I'd watched it, wondering what it might be like to sit in the green room with really famous people, trying to look cool as they all do, so when we heard we were booked the nerves kicked in almost immediately. I must have spent a month wondering what to wear. Coleen, Jane and me were the lucky ones, especially when we heard who the other guests were. Only Tom Hanks! And Dizzee Rascal! So not only were we mingling with a Hollywood A-Lister but we were also down with the kids, all on the same night! Tom (Tom!) was so normal he took my breath away. No entourage, no airs and graces, and so natural with everyone. I wasn't a fan before but I am now. He paid us a huge compliment by saying, 'They're the type I was too shy to approach when I was younger,' and when talking about his film, *Angels and Demons*, he said 'that should be the new name for *Loose Women*.' At least I think it was a compliment . . .

It's not just the big things like *Jonathan Ross* and awards and phone calls from Robbie Williams, though that make it the best job in the world. When I look on YouTube at some of the daft things I've had to do it does make me smile. Like I had a little faux part in *The Bill* with Ben Shepherd; went on a survival course when Bear Grylls was coming on; hula-hooped (more than once) and dressed up as a teenage rapper. I sometimes moan about having to do things like that but they do usually end up being funny, and I always laugh in the end. I thought we also made excellent Spice Girls with Coleen as Geri, Jane as Scary, Jackie as Baby and me as my favourite, Posh. Even Mel B and Emma were impressed.

I think I'm even luckier that *Loose Women* came to me relatively late in life, because being 40 and being on the telly for the first time prepares people. It means that if you can sustain it for at least 10 years, by the time you're finished, no one's really surprised that you look old. I've never thought it would be a good idea to peak too early anyway. What's left to look forward to when you've done everything you want by the age of 30 and you can't now even get a job on the shopping channel because everyone knows how gorgeous you were when you were young? And I'm glad I didn't have that *X-Factor*-type desperation that every young person seems to have now to be famous, because there won't be any of those haunting videos of me in a baked bean advert just waiting for my big break.

No, I'm glad I'm where I am and I'm glad I've been where I've been. In fact, I wouldn't change a thing.

CHAPTER 20

The First Time I: Lost someone I loved

(The Mum Chapter)

I've been dreading writing this chapter and have started and restarted it about a dozen times. I just didn't know where to begin, there's so much to say.

My mum was without doubt the most influential and important person in my life and when I lost her my world fell apart. I know it's a cliché but I don't care, it did.

You see, I'd never known anyone I'd loved to die before her. In a weird way I consider myself lucky that I was quite old, 43 when that happened. The only other people I was close to were my grandma and grandad, her mum and dad, but I wasn't even that close to them and anyway you kind of expect your grandparents to die because they're so much older than you. For some reason you just don't ever think your mum is going to die. Especially not how she did, anyway. Why couldn't she have had a heart attack in her sleep? Or just died of old age? But no one does that anymore, do they? It always has to be some kind of vile, cruel cancer that eats them away from the inside until they scream with pain and gasp for their last breath.

That's exactly how it was for her six and a half years ago.

When that happens it takes a long time to remember how they were in the good times rather than how they were the last time you saw them. But eventually those horrific memories fade and are replaced by the affectionate ones of old.

She was sitting in the kitchen at Week Street, drinking milk from the bottle with a straw, having her hair done and smoking a fag. It would have been either a Player's Navy Cut or a Senior Service, no tips for her – she was a hardcore smoker even though she was pregnant with my sister Tracy. It must have been late 1962, making me two and a half. This was my earliest memory of her but, right up until the day she died, she denied it ever happened. We argued about it endlessly, but in an affectionate way of course. That image is very clearly etched on my brain so how could I possibly have made it up? Her defence was that she never drank milk, she hated it. Indeed she did, apart from in tea (and still not much because she liked it thick and orange, like a builder) she couldn't bear the smell of it. Ditto peanut butter – 'Urgh, reminds me of the war, makes me feel sick, get it away!' – because I used to try and make her smell it. Tuna fish was another one. 'Expensive cat food,' she'd always say whenever I opened a tin.

She knew what she liked, my mum, and she never deviated from it. She ate and drank the same things all the time. Meat and two veg, sausages, pies, fish and chips, chicken curry from the Chinese takeaway, and roasts. She only ever drank two drinks: builder's tea and gin and tonic. I don't think I ever saw her drink a glass of water. She loved her gin and tonic and bloody hell, could she put some away. Funny thing was I never once saw her drunk. She had amazing control and never lost it.

Mum was one of two children, her brother George was two years older. Her parents, Leonard and Ellen, were fairly 'well-to-do' as they say, doted on their kids, and lived in detached houses with names, down sweet little cul-de-sacs in Surrey; I think she had a pretty protected, uneventful childhood. The only indication of trauma was some jealousy from her mother towards her. She told me that she'd once threatened her with a knife for being late home. Theirs was a typical mother/son and father/daughter family. My grandma doted on George and he could do no wrong while my grandad did the same with Mum – which was what, my mum thought, provoked the jealousy. It was sad because there was real love between them; my grandma kept a drawn portrait of her daughter by her bed until the day she died and I know the love and respect was reciprocated, but it never showed. There was distance between them and although we'd make regular visits to their house you could tell it was a strained relationship and Mum always seemed anxious to leave. I loved their house, well, it was a bungalow with an attic converted into a bedroom. It had a piano and a dining room with a permanent swan-like centre piece and a dresser with really expensive china and solid silver cutlery in. There was a big boxed gramophone that looked like a sideboard that had a TV in it but it was never open. Most of the action took place in the kitchen, with its wood-burning stove and 1950s freestanding cooker. Grandma was always either boiling flannels (yes, on the stove in a saucepan) or making jam, scones or rock cakes, which were yum. It was in Upper Warlingham right above the train station so you could always hear the reassuring rumble of trains, sometimes steam trains. They had a big deck overlooking the downs where we would sit for hours watching the gliders, marvelling at the plane that flew without an engine. The garden was sloped and the bottom half was my grandad's pride and joy, his vegetable garden. He grew everything there: potatoes, onions, carrots, peas, runner beans and the sweetest, most pungent-smelling tomatoes I've ever known. It's such an evocative memory, the smell of those tomatoes, that every time I smell anything like it (which is rare because tomatoes just don't smell of anything anymore) I am transported back to that garden and that greenhouse and my grandad with his trousers pulled up too high by his braces and his thick crop of white hair and smiley face. When Mum was evacuated during the war and they were trying to relocate her parents, she had to describe them. She declared that her mum looked like Gracie Fields and her dad looked like the bloke on the Player's fags packet. And they did.

She was a model 1950s girl. Went to school, no qualifications, attended Pitman Secretarial College, worked at Unilever House as a secretary/typist where she met my dad (he was the post boy), got married, gave up work and had four children. Given her upbringing, she was destined to live a privileged life. After my dad, however, she ended up working in pubs and clubs and living in near poverty. But when he left she just got on with it; she picked up the baton of life and ran and ran and never stopped. I don't think my grandma ever really accepted the life she ended up with; she certainly never liked it, it wasn't good enough for her Heather. She hated my dad right from the start and was against the marriage. But Grandad was determined to see her happy, which Mum was with him, and so he gave her the wedding she'd always dreamed off. She looked beautiful and she was happy. She couldn't believe it, my dad was so handsome.

I don't know how she did it. She might have been born never wanting for anything, but when the going got tough she just got going. She had had four kids and she was going to make sure she brought them up as bloody well best she could, all the time having to cope with the stigma of divorce and being a single parent in a time when it simply wasn't the norm – in fact, it was positively frowned upon. But going home to her parents and asking for help (and admitting her mother was right about my dad) just wasn't an option. Her attitude was, she'd made her bed so she'd better lie in it. She took the view that her kids didn't ask to be born so she set about dedicating her life to bringing us up, possibly, at times, sacrificing her own happiness in the process.

I think she did a great job and actually, if my dad had been around I think things might have been very different. According to my mum he was very strict and we might not have been allowed to be ourselves with him around. We were brought up well but we all had a certain freedom that allowed us to develop into our own characters. As I've said, Dad would definitely have made me go to the grammar school after passing my 11 Plus exam which would, without doubt, have changed my character, my personality and my path in life. So I'm not sure I'd be 'me' if he hadn't gone because my mum, although a strong disciplinarian, was also very aware that kids have to grow up and learn their own lessons, learn from their own mistakes, be independent.

She did wallop me a few times. I deserved it. I can remember each and every time and exactly what I did. And all of those things I only ever did the once. So, to use another cliché, it never did me no 'arm.

The first time was at the bus stop in Maidstone High Street. It was dark, we'd probably been Christmas shopping or something, I remember the lights. While we were waiting for the bus I was sitting on the step of the TV rental shop. Being young I was obviously bored so started poking my tongue out at a random bloke standing in the queue for the bus. When Mum saw me I was aware of the red mist rising and she came over, grabbed my hand and walloped me all the way up the stairs of the bus. I was like a football and she was playing keepy-uppy with her hand, all the time screaming, 'Get up them stairs, how dare you be so rude? Go on, get up them stairs!' It sounds shocking just writing about it, but only because it's something that would, if it happened now, definitely bring the social services round with a cage to take the kids away and handcuffs for my mum. It bloody well hurt too! I don't know if it was a reasonable beating but when you think that she was on her own, with loads of shopping, four young kids under six in tow, having to get on a bus where there were no seats left downstairs, you can kind of understand her wrath on that occasion. But sure as hell, from then on, I bloody well knew that poking your tongue out at a stranger was rude and I never did it again. And it stayed with me too. There's an ad on TV where a woman on a bus pokes her tongue out to a young kid who does it first. I don't recall what it was advertising but it annoyed me intensely every time I saw it because it was saying that it was OK to poke your tongue out, and it isn't!

Another time I got a wallop was when I called my sister Tracy a whore. I didn't even know what it meant.

My mum was tall and a natural redhead. When she was younger she was a very beautiful young woman, but in her thirties, after a few years on the council estate and having got right into working in pubs, she turned into Elsie Tanner, wearing a headscarf over her big hair, bright red lips and she always had a fag on the go. When she got much older she morphed into Mavis Riley because she always had that really kind but scared and apologetic look about her, although she was neither.

Some of my fondest memories involve my birthdays. As I've said, I had a subconscious need to be with my mum on my birthday and

I never missed one until my fortieth. Actually, I hadn't even noticed this until she pointed it out to me. The reason was that Tracy was born on 22 February and my mum left to go into hospital on the 18th, my third birthday. Apparently I went mad, nearly tore the house down, and all through my life I never quite got past it. So on my birthday I always made sure I could go and see her and often we'd just go into town, have something to eat, do a bit of shopping, drink some tea. Sometimes we'd go down the coast to Folkestone or Hastings. Or she would come up to London to see me and we'd just wander about aimlessly doing not much, but it was important and it was always special.

I had 100% respect for my mum. I never wanted to let her down, disappoint her, embarrass her or show her up though I probably did many times. And it's my greatest regret that I couldn't even begin to do as much for her when she was dying as she'd done for me over the years.

You see, as soon as I got the news that her cancer was terminal and nothing could be done I went into shock and didn't come out of it again for about four years. For about six months before she was diagnosed everyone was in denial. She kept complaining of different, weird and unusual ailments and symptoms like feeling faint and having chronic, debilitating indigestion. She'd always say it was down to Chinese food and she stopped eating it. Then she even gave up smoking for a bit; that was a real sign that something was wrong. She was a dedicated and determined smoker all of her life and not because she couldn't give it up, she didn't want to give it up. She loved it, pure and simple. Deep down I think we all knew that something was dreadfully amiss but everyone, including my mum, buried their heads in the sand and hoped it would go away. I knew it was serious as soon as she went to the doctor's. She never went because she hated it, was scared of it and preferred to suffer in silence. The last time I'd known her to seek medical help was with a kidney infection in about 1975. But suddenly she was there all the time. We'll never know what went on in that consulting room but quite how it was never picked up that she had aggressive, invasive cancer until five months before she died is a real mystery. She was treated for high blood pressure, indigestion, constipation, had chest x-rays, scans, everything, and yet no one ever mentioned the 'C' word.

It took an MRI scan to reveal the extent of the damage. It was lung cancer which had already spread to other organs. The doctor said it was a 'type of lung cancer not normally associated with smoking'. So was it mesothelioma, the lung cancer caused by asbestos? We don't know because Mark couldn't remember all of what the doctor had said, he must have just been in shock. Anyway, what we did know was that it was too late to treat it even though they did offer her chemotherapy and radiotherapy that might have given her a bit more time but she refused it, thinking that what time she did have left would be made worse by constant treatment. Maybe if everyone had been more honest, more persistent, it would have been found sooner, before it had spread. But even then would she have had the treatment? Maybe not. Like I said, we'll never know.

I was in Norwich doing *Loose Women* in the summer of 2003 when I got the news. Mark had been to the hospital with her to get the results of the MRI. Deep down I think I already knew, but hearing the actual words over the phone was still like a stake through the heart. I couldn't bear it. I felt real pain. Real, stabbing, aching, thumping pain. It was like being blown up by a bomb and surviving.

I wanted to get in a car right there and then and rush down there. The next day, right after the show, I did. But what to say? I had no idea how to handle it and almost reverted to being a scared child again. I felt guilty for not having spent more time with her, for going away for the last five Christmases. When I told her I'd stop work early – the series had another four weeks to run – she nearly had a fit because she didn't want to make a fuss or be a burden and anyway, she loved *Loose Women* and knew, even before I did, that it would be really successful one day. She was its and my biggest fan, without doubt. It was the one thing, she said, she really looked forward to every day, so I had to carry on.

It was tough, impossible almost, but friends who'd been through it told me of this parallel universe that you slip into so that's what I did. I did my job, held back the tears and, as soon as I could, went back to her.

That whole summer she spent outside. She lived in a small, one-bedroom bungalow in Leeds village in Kent. She loved it. When she moved there it was the happiest she'd been throughout her life. No responsibility, no work and free of the men who I felt had blighted and ruined her life. She also had Angelina, the dog I'd inherited from my marriage. Mangie Angie had had to retire to the country on account of the fact that I'd moved into a 'no pets allowed' apartment which also had very shiny wooden floors that she couldn't stand up on without doing a 'Bambi'. The dog was great company for Mum and she really enjoyed taking her out for walks as, since the village shop had closed, she had no need to leave the house until Angie came along. She stopped driving when she moved there too – she'd never liked it – and Tracy used the car on the condition that she'd take Mum shopping once a week into town. So she was happy but still she worried about us, but nothing was going to change that even though we were all over 40. Also, away from the estates and the pub life, she had peace and quiet and the love of her life, her garden. And she had a few quid after my grandma died and left her some money so wasn't a struggling OAP. She told me repeatedly that she wasn't ready to die and the unfairness and injustice of it all made her more angry than upset.

I found out more about my mum in those months before she died than I had in my whole life. She never really talked about herself; it wasn't about her, she just wanted to know about us. She was the most unselfish person I'd ever known. She was also extremely stoic and private, but that was OK – she was my mum after all, not my best friend. She was, quite simply, a real tower of strength.

13 June 2003
I started thinking a lot about what I could have done differently. Aware that all these thoughts are about me and how I felt and how I was trying to clear myself of guilt before she died, was I thinking of her? I want to ask her if there's anything she thinks I could put right before she goes? So the only thing I can think of is that in the last two years when I've done very little work, I would get tetchy if she'd ask me if there was anything coming up. But then I realised, after some

thought, that I was short with her because I felt I was letting her down. She just wanted me to do well so she could be proud of me and I was sitting on my fat arse doing fuck all and waiting for the phone to ring. I was very annoyed with myself but I'm going to tell her that only if she asks.

Strangely enough, the most intriguing thing came in the form of a film. Mum had it on VHS and had obviously had it for a while. It was called *All That Heaven Allows* and starred Jane Wyman and Rock Hudson. I'd never heard of it. While we were sitting there one day, out of the blue she said, 'Do you want to watch a film?' It was odd; she only ever watched soaps, as far as I knew. But she put it on and we watched it. The story is about a wealthy widow who sacrifices love to please everyone else including the class-obsessed gossips (he was 'beneath' her because he was a gardener) and, more poignantly, her children. What was she saying to me? I sat there, confused and a little bit guilty. Did she have some great love that she passed on because of us? Did we object to any of her suitors? I had to think hard. I asked her why she'd shown me now, and not before. She just shrugged her shoulders and her eyes filled with tears, just as mine are right now as I write that. And then she went to sleep. I've still got that VHS and I keep meaning to watch it again but I can't. I'm still bothered by it and I think about it a lot. I'm sure we never objected to any of the men she hooked up with, not even her second husband who we all had doubts about right from the off. And I'll never know if she had a great love that she missed out on because of us.

The only possible conclusion I've managed to draw resulted from something my sister said recently. Kim has two children, now aged 27 and 25, she loves them dearly. But she admits, very honestly, that although she can't and she wouldn't change a thing now, if she had her time again, she wouldn't have children. Not that they bring her great unhappiness but if you're the type that my mum and Kim were then they do become your life and you can never stop worrying about them. And only when it's too late can you really start yours. I don't know if my mum felt like that but after watching that film, I wouldn't be surprised.

She certainly had men in her life. Kim and I think that some of them were more financial affairs than love affairs.

Certainly the greatest love of her life after my dad was an expat called Frank. She met him while he was on leave from working in the Middle East as an engineer. Whenever he was away, he wrote to my mum every day. I know this because I used to regularly go to the bottom drawer of mum's dressing table, formerly the bottom left-hand side of the wardrobe, where she kept an old tan-coloured, plastic handbag which was stuffed full of letters from him. Proper handwritten love letters. One for every day he was away. I never told her I read them and I feel really disloyal now coming out about it but, in a way, they humanised her for me. After my dad left, she was just my mum, who cooked and cleaned and worked. When I was younger, I'd seen her snogging a bloke I thought was just a family friend in the hallway (not Frank, this was way before) and I remember being truly horrified because she was my mum and she wasn't supposed to be doing things like that. It didn't seem right. But when I found the letters I was older and I felt happy for her. Whenever Frank was on leave he'd come home and we were all thrilled to see him, he'd always bring us presents. And they'd be like a young couple, always playing the same record, Dusty Springfield's 'I Only Want To Be With You', really loud. They'd dress up and go to the pub, usually the Albion in town. They looked like a right pair of spivs 'cos my mum had really big hair and Frank had the most gravity-defying quiff I've ever seen. She was very happy with him.

One Sunday night, while we were all watching *Sunday Night at the London Palladium* there was a knock at the door. It was one of the neighbours, obviously a nosey one, who'd come to tell us that Frank was walking down the road. He wasn't due home so the whole house exploded with excitement and even though it was a rare treat that we were allowed to stay up to watch *Sunday Night* . . . we ditched it in favour of running down the road to greet him. He was as excited to see us as we were to see him. I only found out recently that he'd lost his job under suspicious circumstances, which I suspect contributed to the terrible drink problem he developed. It was so sad; he really was a good man, a loving, caring almost-step-dad to us, but when he drank he was a Jekyll-and-Hyde character. He was the boyfriend who sometimes used to get violent when he'd been drinking and after he'd threatened to kill my mum with a knife for the second time, she threw him out. It was hard though because she still loved him, but not when he drank. And he couldn't stop. I'll never forget going to see him in his little bedsit that he took in town. Mum had baked a cake for him and we delivered it. It broke my heart to see him there, but deep down I understood that it had to be that way. He eventually moved away and we never heard from him again.

Apart from her painkillers, Mum seemed fairly normal at first. Mobile, able, faculties all present. But when the deterioration started it was rapid. The cancer had got into her bones and her brain and the signs couldn't be ignored. Yet still she tried to soldier on as if nothing was wrong. Whether this was because she couldn't accept it or she was still trying to protect us by pretending there was nothing wrong, I don't know. But it was truly heartbreaking.

All her life she'd made a point of telling us that she didn't want us to see her if she'd got terminally ill and she'd go into a home or a hospice where we wouldn't have to witness or deal with it. She also stockpiled sleeping tablets, hardcore sleeping pills that she said she'd take if she were ever diagnosed with terminal cancer. Of course when it came down to it she did the opposite of everything she thought she would.

Kim, being the eldest, assumed most of the responsibility. I couldn't bear seeing Mum not being able to cope. Kim stayed with her in the night but her breathing became so impossible she almost died there and then, in excruciating pain. We all felt so terribly helpless but Kim bore the brunt of it and it was the thought of seeing Mum possibly die in the night in this shocking pain that she could do nothing about that made us think that the hospice would be better for her. Mum went along with it but she really didn't want to; she wanted to stay at home. It was a nightmare situation. When we got there, the first thing that happened was the doctor examined her and when he came out the first thing he said was, 'I don't think you have any idea how sick your mother is,' and he was right, we didn't. Meanwhile, heartbreakingly, Mum was playing along, eating what they gave her to eat and asking for things from home as though she was only going to be in there for a few days before getting better. She was that sick she was only in the hospice for a week and the day before she died I begged the staff to take her home. I could tell how much she hated it and just wanted to get her back to her comfortable little bungalow, even if it was just for a few hours. They told me that she wouldn't be able to make the journey. I knew they were right so begged them, even though I knew they couldn't, to give her more morphine – enough to kill her and put her out of the pain she was so obviously in. I stayed at the hospice the night before she went and in the morning, somehow knowing she would go, I said goodbye. The last thing I said was, 'I love you, Mummy,' and she replied, 'I know you do.' Suddenly I felt foolish and selfish. Why did I have to say that? To make myself feel better? Probably. We never really said it because we knew. Why do you need to tell your mum of 43 years that you love her? Of course you do. And she me; I never doubted it.

I couldn't bear to watch her struggling for breath anymore so I left. Got in my car and headed back to London. I could hardly drive through the tears and when I got to the roundabout that takes you onto the A2 into London from the M25 I turned around and went back to my brother's house where I sat and stared into space for about seven hours. At just after 5.30pm my brother called. She'd finally gone. Why wasn't I there? What was I thinking? She went into the unknown and I wasn't even there to hold her hand. I still hate myself for that.

Hysterical, I got back into my car and drove up the M20 to the hospice. I needed to see her but I wish I hadn't. It was good to see that she wasn't suffering anymore but seeing this lifeless shell of what was left of her after the cancer had literally eaten her away from the inside out disturbed me greatly. I don't even want to think about it.

There was an air of relief that she was out of pain, away from the horror of the illness. It was 29 September, the same day that she married my dad all those years ago.

I had no idea what to do next. Who does? You kind of go into automatic pilot. The council gave us exactly two weeks to clear out the bungalow, so we did that. I felt sad that she owned so few things. She never was a hoarder but apart from a few clothes she had nothing. Kim, who suffered badly from the guilt of her dying in the hospice, was desperate to find something, a note, an explanation – of what, I don't know. Just something. The only piece of history she'd kept was a couple of pairs of 'nylons' (stockings) the ones that she'd spent all her wages on back when she was a secretary at Unilever. I kept those, it was a lovely story that she told of her and her best friend, Berry, getting their week's pay and going into the West End to spend nearly two-thirds of it on a pair of nylons. I didn't keep much else. Just the quirky things that so remind me of her. I keep them all in a glass-topped display box now. There's a key to the door of 195 Plains Avenue with an 'H' on it, the clock she won as a finalist in the 'Daily Mirror Barmaid of the Year 1973' competition, a pickled onion grabber, a puzzle book, a crossword wordfinder and a photo of her laughing. That's my favourite thing. My mum's laugh is what I remember most now. It was infectious and her whole face lit up when she did it. It was so lovely to see her laugh and although she had a bit of a shit life at times, she definitely laughed more than she cried, something I take huge comfort in.

Dealing with the funeral was possibly the hardest part. How can you browse coffins, knowing you're choosing the box that will eventually hold and burn the dead body of the person that was your life? It was ridiculous but it happened. We chose an outfit for her and after she'd been dressed and embalmed I went to see her again. I was pleased I did because she looked like my mum again. The funeral, however, was a nightmare. Mum had requested that just her four children and a couple of very close friends were to attend and although it caused a lot of upset for her brother who wasn't invited, we carried out her wishes. It was horrendous seeing the coffin arrive; I don't think I'd ever felt such pain. None of us could possibly have spoken so I wrote something for the vicar to read out.

Mum was one of those very rare creatures that is truly beautiful both inside and out. She was the kind of person who hated no one except, for some reason, Princess Diana. She never hurt anyone and was, to her dying day, the least selfish person I have ever known.

Hers was a tough life. Against the odds she survived and succeeded in bringing up four well-balanced, strong-minded, reasonably successful, law-abiding children about whom she never stopped worrying even though we're all over 40. All of our lives we have had total respect for her, never playing truant, running away or shaming her in any way. Well, maybe once or twice.

From an outsider's view, it might look as though she had a sad life. Not so. The only thing sad about it was that she attached herself to so many unsuitable men who may have loved her at first but always ended up resenting her for her vivaciousness and popularity. Whichever bar she worked in, it was always the busiest. Her smile and laughter defied even the most miserable sod to join in.

Her happiest years were without doubt when she moved into her bungalow in Leeds. She didn't need much to make her happy, just her home, her garden, her kids and grandchildren. She loved it when we were all there together even though we'd always leave her with all the washing-up.

It was a cruel and horribly unfair hand that life had dealt her towards the end but then who ever said life was fair? What is fair to say though is that she went to her grave having achieved more in her life than any high-flying career woman. And we four are a testament to her will, courage and strength.

I hope she went knowing that she really was loved unconditionally by us all and that she truly was the greatest mum in the world.

Bye bye Mummy.

We will never forget you and we will miss you forever.

Following her death I felt like something had died in me too. I fell out with friends, didn't work, had a BUPA health check which found that my red blood cells were enlarged – 'It's what we usually find in alcoholics,' said the consultant to my horror. No surprise really, all through my mum's illness I'd used alcohol as an escape from the reality and the pain – the only time I'd ever used booze for anything other than a good time. I stopped drinking for nearly three months after that.

I'd not been at home for Christmas for some years then and I sure has hell didn't want to be at home that year, especially without her. So even though I wasn't really in the mood for one, I booked a holiday and went to Thailand on my own. When I arrived, I didn't know what I was doing there. Everything seemed so pointless. Some friends were getting married in Sydney so I booked a flight and went over there thinking a party would solve everything. It didn't. I still felt shit. So I went home and stared into space for six months and sought joy in solitude.

3 January 2004
I am discovering the pleasures of escapism. Before I didn't want to escape, I always wanted to be included which is why I watched the news and endless TV programmes that I had no interest in but felt that if I didn't watch them I would be excluded. I had to know everything, read every paper, go to every shop, listen to every radio station but in that behaviour you don't actually absorb anything at all because there's too much. So just recently, I suppose since Mum died, I've not been able to stomach any bad stuff, be it news or whingeing mates, and have taken to shutting myself away, without the TV on and just listening to music. Occasionally dancing around the flat (with all the blinds closed) naked. The joy of Eminem and me wearing nothing but Ugg boots is just too much fun to put into words.

Loose Women came back in the summer of 2004 so I picked myself up, bought a load of clothes, had my hair cut and whitened my teeth.

That series was the beginning of the huge success that *Loose Women* has become. My mum was right. It's just not fair that she's not here to share it with me.

10th June 2004
I miss my mum. She would watch Loose Women *religiously every day and then watch it again in the evening on tape. She was so proud of me. I'm taking comfort in the misguided belief that she's still watching me now and sighing with relief that at long last I've had my teeth whitened and grown my hair.*
And my name's in the paper.
And I was on the news.
And I was in the Sunday Mirror.
And I am going to be on Tonight with Trevor McDonald.
Fuck life.

CHAPTER 21

The First Time I: Experienced relationship envy

(The Single Chapter)

In October 2004, after a fine summer series of *Loose Women*, I took myself off on a long holiday. I needed it. Mum had only died the year before and I hadn't really felt like doing anything remotely pleasurable or self-indulgent, thinking, *what would be the point if I couldn't tell her about it?*

But my brother Mark was living in Southern Malaysia and I hadn't seen him since she'd gone and I felt like I wanted to be with him. We arranged to meet in Singapore where we had a few nights before heading back via Johor Bahru to Pontian where he lived.

On one of those afternoons in Singapore, we were strolling down Boat Quay, the great long row of bars and restaurants on the river that you always see in adverts for the city, and we stopped for a beer in a place called Seafood at the Pier. We sat by the water; the sun was quite low, it was about four in the afternoon. We could see the old post office, now the Fullerton Hotel, beautifully lit up across the water. It was so nice we couldn't bring ourselves to leave and before we knew it, it was dinner time and the place was filling up with eager diners. While we were sat there talking, drinking beer and ogling their food (if you ever go there, be sure to have the deep-fried river prawns with garlic, one of the most delicious taste sensations ever in the history of the world), four couples came and went and had dinner at the table next to us.

By the time the third couple sat down, Mark and I were more

than a little bit pissed and very confidently deluded that it wasn't showing. We struck up a conversation because by this time we were both budding Alan Whickers. The woman was a travel journalist from Australia and during the conversation about where we'd all come from, where we'd all been, where we were all going and what we were all doing there, I mentioned that I was thinking of going up to Langkawi, an island just off the North-West coast of Malaysia, because I hadn't been since 1996 and I was intrigued as to how different it was. She told me of a place she'd found there recently and recommended I go, it was called Bon Ton Resort.

From Singapore we went off to Johor Bahru (JB) and on to Pontian, which wasn't exactly a home from home. It was very local, no tourists and not the best place to be if you didn't have a car. Of course Mark was out at work all day, but I didn't mind. I was just glad to be there, feeling warm. Occasionally I'd venture out and walk to the shops but walking is a pretty weird thing to do in rural Malaysia and literally people would stop in their cars and stare at me. They were also fascinated because I'm a woman and I'm tall. Gigantic compared to most Malaysian women. I was there for about a week and just spent my days cleaning Mark's house, watching telly, slaughtering cockroaches and booking my next move on the internet. To Langkawi.

Mark took me to JB Airport where I flew, via Kuala Lumpur, to Langkawi. Within a couple of hours I was heading for this Bon Ton place where I'd booked myself in for two nights thinking I would just go somewhere else if I didn't like it. And, on the Aussie diner's recommendation, I'd told them I was a journalist (which was sort of true) so I could get a discount.

Driving into Bon Ton my first impressions were good. It had a small boutiquey feel and the reception was a simple desk in the restaurant area. Looking across the pool I was a bit confused. From the internet pictures it looked as though the resort was right on the sea front but there was no sign of the sea, just a swampy looking lagoon which was born out of the fact that it used to be on the beach but all the land had been reclaimed for the airport in order to accommodate international flights. I mean it wasn't ugly, but I was a bit pissed off. Then Sharm (the maître d', waiter, hotel receptionist, barman) showed me to my 'house'. And it was indeed a house – an old Kampung house from the Malay paddy fields that the owner, Narelle, had salvaged and had rebuilt in her resort. There were only five of them, all graded by colour, and mine was Yellow. As soon as I saw it I fell in love, even though there was an army of red ants on the deck and I had to crouch down to get into the tiny door. The interior was decorated in the most charming way with bright colours and a massive bed with a mosquito net all around it. The bathroom was outside on a different deck at the back and the bath was wooden, right open to the elements. I couldn't wait to get in it. Even the black ants marching all over the bed didn't put me off. I felt like I was properly in Malaysia even though I clearly wasn't alone and would have to share my bed.

I extended my stay once, then again, and again. I actually ended up staying there for more than two weeks. In fact I only checked out then because it was fully booked and they couldn't accommodate me.

I also got quite friendly with the owner, Narelle, who was really looking after me, either because she felt sorry for me being on my own, or because I'd told her I was a journalist. But a few days in and I was beginning to feel a little over-entertained. Narelle would invite me everywhere and insist on having dinner with me or make sure one of the staff sat with me while I ate. All very well-meaning I know, and I appreciated it, but I was still grieving and I did actually want to be alone. Often I would just sit on my deck writing, trying to politely avoid company, but she'd come bounding over and drag me off somewhere.

And thank God she did because it was due to one of her invitations that I ended up meeting my wonderful friends, Steve and Simon. Narelle had invited me to dinner at the Andaman, a very posh hotel on the other side of the island, with the general manager, Alison, a journalist called Joan from Singapore and her 'gay friends' who were arriving from England. She'd told me all about them – one works in travel and one works in advertising – and was convinced that I was going to know someone who knew them as they lived near me in North London in Islington.

I really didn't want to go out because I was exhausted. So I hid in my room for as long as possible thinking, 'I don't want to meet any more people, leave me alone!' But there was no escape. When it was nearly time to leave there was a knock on my door. I opened it and peered out. Steve was standing at the bottom my stairs, craning his neck; he didn't say hello, he said, 'Ooooh, yes it is her!'

'Who's HER?' I demanded.

Very apologetically he explained that Narelle had told him in the car on the way from the airport that I worked in TV and used to be married to a bloke who was also on TV. Stephen had wracked his brains to try and think who it might be and he was right. It was me – or 'her' as he put it, like I wasn't there.

The night went very, very well. I never made it back to Bon Ton and ended up sleeping on the couch in Alison's suite. The next night Steve and Simon, who were staying at the Andaman, came down to Bon Ton and they never made it home. Instead they slept in my new house, the Black house, which had two beds in it.

I have to say, it was very nice waking up with two gorgeous men in my bedroom after such a long time. Even if they were in the same bed and I was consigned to the single bed.

And from that moment on, Steve and Simon have been my best friends and, at times, my surrogate and substitute boyfriends.

Friends have always been important to me. I never had that huge extended-family thing so my friends have always been my other family really. Right from infant school, when I first met Pauline, there has always been a best friend element in my life. And I believe that it's friends, not family, that have the greatest influence on our paths and characters. Of course your parents provide you with guidance and morals and values from an early age, but it's friends that affect your personality the most. That can be the only explanation for four children from the same family turning out so completely different.

I have to say that out of all of my friends, the most instrumental in my development has to be Helen. I met Helen at South Borough when I was 11 but we didn't really become friends until a few years later. It was because of Helen that I dress the way I dress and live where I live. She was the get-up-and-go girl who had real style and aspiration and her first job was at National Magazines working for *Cosmopolitan* in London. She really inspired me and I have a lot to thank her for. Sadly we're not friends at the moment but I'm not really sure why. I know that after my mum died I fell out with quite a few people. They might not even have even done anything but I was in a very strange place. Helen and I over the years have always had ups and downs and haven't spoken for years at a time, so I'm sure we'll speak again one day.

Mitch was also my best friend for the time he was around and I learnt a lot from him, like how to relax, not stress, travel light and not have an obsession with a clean house. Scarlet was my next big best-friendship and she still is my best female friend. She's full-on, but I've had some of the best times ever with her and when we laugh it always hurts. Scarlet is 10 years younger than me so being around her always makes me feel like I'm 10 years younger too.

None of my longstanding best friends have children. I have a lot of mates that do but they have their thing going on and someone like me just doesn't have much in common with 'mums'. It's not that I fall out with my friends once they give birth but being a mum is all-consuming and friends do fall by the wayside sometimes. It's fine, I understand, and they always come back. But that's the reason why my friends have always tended to be younger than me and almost always child-free. It's definitely why I have so many gay friends. As well as Steve and Simon I have loads more. We get on well because we have the same hobbies: going on holiday, going to the pub, shopping and having fun. And because we don't have kids, we can afford to. Yes, it is shallow, but each to their own. I wouldn't dream of saying to someone who chooses to be a parent that it's 'shallow' or anything else (even if I do think it's a bit mad) but some people think nothing of judging my lifestyle, which I find odd.

Anyway, so meeting Steve and Simon really changed the way I think.

As a couple, they have the easiest and greatest relationship and for the first time in many, many years I had full-blown relationship envy. They'd actually made me think that it might be OK not to be single for once. I said out loud to them, 'If I ever have a relationship again, I want it to be like yours.'

Because theirs is one of the most compatible and accepting I have ever witnessed. And the funny thing was, hanging around with them never made me feel like a gooseberry. Gooseberry-itis wasn't something I'd ever suffered from anyway, but with these two it felt just like Simon had said, like there were three of us in the marriage. And even with friends, sometimes it can be awkward or difficult, but Steve and Simon were like cosy old blankets – I always felt comfortable with them but mainly because they're so comfortable with each other. I still do. In fact, Simon made me a little photobook of pictures that we'd had taken together, because Steve kept saying that we looked like boyfriend and girlfriend in them – he called the book *My Secret Boyfriend*. It's very funny.

To some people it might seem out of the ordinary that I was not only at their wedding but also went on their honeymoon (along with 10 other people) in 2007. Even if I wasn't invited on holiday with them I would usually turn up – 'Surprise!' – and unless they suddenly turned into Oscar-worthy actors, I don't think they minded and were genuinely pleased to see me. They were going to Thailand once and I turned up at the airport when they were checking in. Steve said, 'Ah, have you come to say goodbye?' I said, 'Nope, I'm coming with you!' Of course, they stayed for two weeks and I just went to Bangkok for three days. Then when they were in Langkawi in 2005 I turned up at the Andaman, stayed for two days and flew back! They wouldn't have minded if I'd stayed for the duration but I'm aware they need time without me too . . . though not much.

I have been happily single for most of my life, although I've had to spend quite a lot of time trying to convince people I'm not making it up. So why doesn't anyone believe me? Why have I had to justifying my happy, contented state of mind to anxious friends who, in their minds, have achieved couples nirvana simply because they are 'in a relationship' and assume that because I am not, that I must be sick, sad or lying. Or all three.

I was even the subject of an *Esther* debate programme once. The question was, 'Can you really be happy and single?' I sat there for over an hour justifying myself while almost the entire audience questioned my status. God, it was exhausting. I left there extremely happy that I was single and thinking that everyone else in that studio would have loved to have been too.

And I'll tell you the reason – it's because for a lot of women being single is not, and nor has it ever been, an option. It's easy to see why. Single women are seen as sad or as having failed. But usually only by other women. Especially if you're over 40. In fact, socially, it is almost tantamount to having a hideously contagious disease. No one invites you anywhere and if they do, they'll 'bring someone along to make the numbers up'.

I've never understood the pressure some women put on themselves to pair off – to never even consider a life away from the expected, stereotypical one that often forces the perfectly sane and sensible into relationships that then end in disaster, with what should have been their best years wasted.

I'm not sure how this way of thinking came about. I saw my mum's life permanently blighted by unsuitable men but that didn't stop me getting one or two myself. Unsuitable men are, after all, annoyingly desirable sometimes. No, I have just always been happy not conforming. But people can be so bloody patronising. I have been frowned upon sympathetically and told, 'Don't worry, I'm sure you'll find someone.' *But I wasn't worried, you moron.*

Being single and over 40 then becomes a series of questions that, no matter how many times you answer them with the same answer, get repeated over and over:

'When are you going to settle down?'

'What do you mean, you don't want children?'

'Don't you think it's a bit shallow to just go on holiday all the time?'

Er, no?

I really enjoyed holidaying alone too. In fact, some of my most exciting and interesting holidays have been taken alone. Some of the worst and most traumatic have been taken with partners/boyfriends/ husbands. Spot the couple on holiday together – they're the ones who never speak.

Of course there are downsides to being single, but they are few.

The word 'spinster'. Men get the cool 'bachelor', we get 'spinster', a word that makes you just want to spit when you say it.

The phrase: 'Oh you'll love my friend (insert random bloke's name)' then going to dinner parties to meet random bloke only to find he's four feet tall with a hump.

Shopping on a Saturday night in Somerfield and wanting to shout, 'I'm out and I'm proud to be single and shopping in Somerfield on a Saturday night!' But instead you buy two of everything, or loads of Doritos to make it look like you're having a party.

Going for dinner with couples and paying half the bill.

Spending evenings or holidays with bickering couples.

Not enough sex.

But despite these few disadvantages, I've never suffered from that Bridget Jones type angst where you feel worthless or incomplete without a man. And actually I hate *Bridget Jones* for making it OK for women to become 'desperate' winos who'd do anything, however humiliating, in order to bag the bloke.

Not that it was an *ambition* to stay single all my life; indeed, I wasn't. I thought I'd met the right one (though God only knows what made me think that) and tried marriage. I would again. But I wasn't going to put my life on hold until it happened. That's why I've always been quite cautious in relationships, never being the first to say 'I love you', if ever saying it at all.

As I've said in a previous chapter, getting married was never on my list of things to do. Having a great life was. Maybe I'd learnt (a bit) from my mum's (bad) experiences, or perhaps I'd just stumbled upon a preferable lifestyle to the one that society expects – one that I did indeed try, albeit for a brief period, which merely endorsed what I'd always believed: that I was better off single.

And while some of my single friends (the few of them that are left) are indulging in serial dating madness, spending all their time searching for the elusive Mister Right, they are bypassing life and inflicting misery on themselves with their unrealistically high expectations. This makes them boring and tiresome. On the other hand, I have a few single friends who are happy, single, have great lives and are an absolute pleasure to have around. These are the ones who've considered the alternative and taken advantage of the simple pleasures life offers, learning to enjoy them without seeing it as a stop-gap between men and to consider the single life as a choice rather than something that has to be 'handled' or 'dealt with' like some terminal illness.

Of course there's nothing better than loving someone and having that love reciprocated, but I have never needed that. And out of all the relationships I've had, I can count the number of serious ones on one hand. And none of those were ideal. So by the time I got to my forties, I was perfectly happy and prepared to be single for the rest of my life. In fact, I'd been mentally preparing myself for it as I approached the dreaded five-oh.

You see, from where I was standing (especially before I met Steve and Simon) I couldn't see many relationships among friends or colleagues that made me think that being single wasn't preferable. Most of them were always moaning about or arguing with their partners. Never having sex, or if they were, that wasn't right either. And I would have my lovely, hassle-free single life where I could go where I liked, whenever I wanted, with no approval being sought or disapproval being given.

Steve and Simon will always be my friends; they really are like part of my family. We even have nicknames for each other – we call each other 'chimp', all of us, we're all chimps – and strangely enough I now do have the same happiness they have. And the best news of all is, they love him too. He's called the shark.

CHAPTER 22

The First Time I: Had a really lucky escape

(The Tsunami Chapter)

'Oooh, I nearly died!' is one of those overused phrases that's said in response to any number of events. When Russell Brand walked onto the set of *Loose Women*, I nearly died. When I once got on a running machine and couldn't turn it off, I nearly died. And so on.

Then there are the times when I could have easily died. Like when I rode my bike down the 35-foot-high, wrought-iron spiral staircase at Week Street when I was two and cracked my head open so severely my mum thought I'd never look 'normal' again. Or when I put my head (again) through the glass in the bookcase at Plains Avenue while playing hide and seek.

And then there are the times when you really nearly die, like in a head-on collision. I nearly had one once, and although, because of a weird turn of events, we didn't actually crash, I'm certain that if we had we would both have been killed that night.

In 1994 I had a kidney infection. I was prescribed antibiotics, which I hate taking, and had to stop drinking. OK, no problem. For three months. Right. I was working at Virgin Radio at the time, a hotbed of social activity every night of the week so it would be tricky avoiding booze for that length of time. Anyway, I did it, lost loads of weight, looked the healthiest I'd looked in years, got used to it and didn't drink for nearly six months. The only difficult part was going out to the pub, to parties, dinner parties, whatever. It's not that it's difficult not to drink, but people can be quite boring if they're sloshed and you're not. I suppose if you give it up for good you get used to that, or you don't go out to parties or to places where you might encounter drunks. Anyway, I did go out and I still enjoyed myself. Mostly because I saved a load of money, not only from not boozing, but also from being able to drive everywhere and not having to shell out for expensive London taxis.

The night in question, I went to a party in West London with my friend Jack. I drove in my Fiat X1/9, a small sports car with a targa top that might as well have been made of paper for all the good it was in a crash.

I know this because about a year before, I'd had a mental block at some traffic lights where, in my head, the lights had gone green whereas in reality they were still bright red. Consequently, I put my foot down and ploughed into an innocent Renault 5 that was sitting there patiently. Well, the Renault looked like it hadn't been touched. I won't say it looked new because it was old and quite decrepit. But my shiny black, nearly new Fiat was almost written off, and it cost an arm and a leg to replace all the front panels, bumper and lights. I didn't even hit it that hard either. It wasn't funny but Chris, who was in the car with me, thought it was hilarious. Maybe it was? Anyway, that's how delicate my car was.

So Jack and I are in the car driving home through Maida Vale, which has some very wide roads, some have been made into dual carriageways to accommodate the enormous demand for parking in the streets there. So you have two lanes of parked cars and two very single lanes for the traffic going either way. The properties are five or six stories high and almost none of them are houses, so each plot might have anything up to twelve cars to park. It's a nightmare as anyone who lives there will tell you, especially late at night when everyone's home. Friends have told me of having to park in the next borough and some people are simply forced to park illegally until the restrictions start again the next day when they can then move into a vacated space.

It was late and the parked cars were bumper to bumper. We were driving up the left side of one of these dual carriageways, not fast, normal speed. Suddenly, but calmly, Jack says, 'Look, there's a car coming up our side of the road.' Some pissed or drugged-up idiot in a BMW was not only on the wrong side of the road but he didn't have his lights on either. And he was driving fast, heading straight for us and an almost certainly fatal collision.

In a split second I registered what was happening and turned the steering wheel to the left, hard into the left side of the road, where there just happened, bizarrely, to be a gap between two cars. Not one big enough to park in, but just big enough to drive directly into it and up onto the kerb, which was so high it damaged the bumper and punctured one of the tyres in the process. As we came to our abrupt halt, the BMW drove on past; he hadn't even slowed down.

If I hadn't had the kidney infection, I wouldn't have been on antibiotics, so I probably wouldn't have been sober that night and I might be dead. Of course I'm not saying I would drink and drive, but even if I'd had one drink I doubt very much I'd have been sharp enough that night to take advantage of that small space and I would defamundo not be here now.

So, in effect, it was another time when I could have died.

However, the only time when I *really* nearly died – in the sense that I genuinely had to fight for my life and survival – was on Boxing Day 2004 when the Asian tsunami hit Phuket, in Thailand, where I just happened to be on holiday. And again, an exceptional set of circumstances leading up to that morning played a part in me living to tell this tale.

For a start, I shouldn't really have been there. I'd not long returned from my five-week jaunt around Asia so it wasn't like I needed a holiday. But Thailand was where I'd spent Christmas for the previous three years and the pull was too strong, I couldn't resist it. I stuck it out in the UK until the 20th and when I could bear it no more I booked a flight. Two days later I was in Phuket with my friends who were already there – Sam and her husband Eddie (Eduardo, who I'd first been to Thailand with in 2001), Sam's daughter Amber, Eddie's extended family, and my best friend Scarlet. She'd been there with her boyfriend who'd flown home the day I arrived. Sam and Eddie were staying at the Sheraton Laguna Beach at Bang Tao Beach, further north from where Scarlet and I were staying at Patong Beach, the liveliest, loudest, most touristy place on the island – like the Benidorm of Thailand. We loved it. I still do. Our hotel was the one we always stayed in, the Casuarina Patong Garden Resort. A pretty, friendly little place that comprised about a dozen bungalows situated around a pool in lush gardens, just across the road from the beach. At the back of the grounds was a two-storey section of rooms on two floors.

Boxing Day, 9am. Early for me. I had only been in Phuket for three days but so far hadn't managed to get out of bed before midday. On Christmas Day I hadn't managed to get up at all because I was so ill. At first I thought it was a very bad hangover but as the day went on and I got worse, I was convinced I had malaria, dengue fever and meningitis all at the same time. In actual fact I'd picked up a food bug either from the Christmas Eve buffet or some of the day-old street food we'd scoffed at 4 in the morning.

It was a beautiful day so I ignored the lingering nausea and sprang out of bed, determined to get to the beach early to make up for lost time. The same beach that just two days before, we'd been lying on: sleeping, swimming, having massages, buying everything and anything from the relentless sellers that trudge up and down all day with their heavy loads. It was idyllic. By 9.30am I was sitting in the garden restaurant eating fresh papaya and contemplating fried eggs. It was peaceful, sunny, quiet and everything was normal. I remember thinking how reliable it all was – the weather, the clear blue sky – it was always there, it never let you down. I didn't get the eggs because I was feeling a bit faint, and as Scarlet started on her morning fag I went back to the room for a little lie down. Ten minutes later nothing was normal. Scarlet came running back to the room. In fact everyone was running – in the direction of the two-storey block. It was the moment when everything changed. In a matter of seconds, heaven had turned to hell.

What happened next was so mind-blowing and fast and out of the ordinary that blind confusion set in and panic took over. The peaceful breakfast scene was shattered. Blown to smithereens. First, I saw a huge deluge of water go past the window at the back of the room at breakneck speed. It looked like the gap between our hotel and the next building had suddenly turned into a river with white-water rapids. My first thought was that it was some kind of land-slip, or burst water main. I even looked up at the sky to check to see if I'd missed an almighty downpour that might have caused some flash flooding. It was the same, clear blue.

The water was at the front of the room now. Speeding past the window, gushing in under the door. I picked up some of our stuff from the floor and put it all on the bed where I stood, terrorised. Scarlet was the sensible one, she opened the window, thus avoiding the pressure that would have built up and prevented us from opening it later. I wondered how she knew to do that; it must have been a wholly natural instinct. It released a wall of water that quickly filled the room. Electrics were sparking, the stench of sewage over-whelming.

The concrete plant pot outside our room, being the highest thing around, was where everyone was perched. An old Dutch guy, his son who had just woken up and was naked, and one of the Thai staff. Scarlet joined them, I carried on panicking on the bed which by now was floating unsteadily and I was losing my balance.

I didn't move partly because I was frozen with confusion and fear, and partly because I was convinced it would just stop and go away soon. I don't know why, but I always thought I'd be quite good in an emergency. I'm quite strong and I do tend to take charge of situations when things are going wrong. But I've now realised I'm not at all. My behaviour the whole time we were in danger was that of a shaking, gibbering wreck.

It quickly became apparent that it wasn't stopping.

'Where's it coming from?' I screamed.

The Thai man replied, 'From the beach.'

What? How? But the beach is 100 metres away. More confusion. Why was my beautiful hotel with its casuarina trees, bright blue pool and festive decorations, suddenly in the sea? Moreover, why was the sea ruining my holiday and all my stuff? I still didn't get it. The notion of a tidal wave just did not occur to me.

Scarlet was screaming at me to get out of the room (how come she was suddenly the wise one?) and it began to sink in that we were in serious danger, even though I still didn't know what it was. I grabbed a mobile phone from my bag, stepped onto a chair until it stabilised and clambered out against the force of the water which was now waist high and rising.

After a few minutes it seemed to slow down. But people were shouting, 'Coming more, coming more!' We knew we had to get higher but access to the higher floor via the stairs was by now impassable with dangerous debris and chest-high water. The old guy and the naked son were in the water, forcing their way through an opening in a corrugated canopy to the roof of the two-storey section. As petrified as we were, we were in no doubt that that was where we needed to be too.

Scarlet then had her moment of madness. She went back into the room to get her computer. It was my turn to be sensible and I shouted hysterically at her to get out. She came back out having put it on top of the TV in the vain hope that the water level wouldn't reach that high.

We jumped into the filthy soup, losing our shoes in the process, and waded over. The only thing to climb up was a piece of flimsy wooden trellis that didn't seem to be attached to anything. I froze and shook with fear. What if I didn't make it up there? Scarlet was now screaming at me to move. Somehow I got up, and she followed. The man and his son pulled us both to safety.

By this time you could hear it coming. The noise was what I remember most vividly. Within seconds the second wave hit. It was more violent and more voluminous than the first and doubly terrifying. It swamped everything, bringing with it all sorts of deadly cargo. A giant, angry torrent of swirling sea, mercilessly crashing through everything that dared to get in its way, with the remains of breakfast, sewage, beach paraphernalia and most of the hotel's structure in tow. It engulfed the tiny, precarious refuge that we shared with about 20 others – mostly hotel guests but also some Thai women with babies. No one spoke. Everyone just looked around in total shock, not quite believing what was happening. The trellis we climbed up was gone, the breezeblock wall at the back of the hotel gave way. Pieces of furniture rushed by, crashing into rooms through the doors and windows. The sound of breaking glass filled the air. Through the hole in the canopy we could see a man floating, face down. Little did we know but the building below us was beginning to collapse. The force of the washed-up debris against the front of the rooms on the ground floor had shattered it. Not difficult, since it was made of plasterboard.

I have no level of fear to compare it to so it's impossible to describe how I felt right then. All I remember thinking was that a helicopter would surely come and rescue us soon, just like you see on the news, or in the movies.

Meanwhile, the Thai staff were attempting to rescue some of the animals from the small sanctuary out the back. One brought out a dead puppy. A red setter swam and swam around looking for higher ground so he could rest his legs. Another dog had found a pile of rubble and was sensibly perched on the top of it. And the two cute little poodle puppies we'd befriended were OK. Filthy but unfazed.

The fear of more waves was ever present, but after about three or four hours the water had subsided to around knee level and we decided it was safe to go. A member of the Thai fire service led us round the back of the hotel where we had to clamber over the fallen wall, through barbed wire and over electric cables. We walked past a giant washing machine that had been lifted on to the top of a six-foot wall. It didn't look like it was going to stay there for long.

We made our way out the back through an area that a few hours ago had been clearing up from the night before, a series of bars that would keep us awake until 3am. Now it was just a debris-filled swamp. Eventually we got to the Sawatdirak Road, one of only three roads that lead inland from the beach, where the water and all its cargo was piled up for at least another 300 metres. The waves' final resting place was marked by what was literally a mountain of cars. Pick-ups, vans, taxis and a tuk-tuk all on top of one another, unceremoniously shoved back by the incredible power of the sea. It looked like a sculpture.

We walked and walked and didn't look back. The searing afternoon sun burnt my skin, due to my lack of clothes, and my feet due to the lack of shoes. We had to get to higher ground. An English guy, Justin, offered us a lift in his pick-up and as we got in it was clear he didn't have a clue how bad it was. He took us to a hotel on top of the hill where we showered off the shit and cooled down in the pool. The news was on the TV and everyone gathered round in utter disbelief. I got the feeling that the people up there didn't really appreciate the devastation that had occurred at the beach below. There was an American guy who thought he was being incredibly funny making jokes about how he was going to set up an insurance stall down at Patong and sell T-shirts with 'Wave if you've been to Phuket' printed on them, to make a load of money. I just sat there thinking, 'Shut the fuck up before I drown you in the pool, you arsehole.'

I was desperately trying to get hold of my family. It was too early for my sister in the UK so I tried my brother, who was living in Malaysia at the time. There were no lines available, all networks were busy and most landlines were completely down. The news said that the tsunami had hit Malaysia and Singapore and when I finally got through to my brother's phone there was no answer. I can't describe the feeling of despair I felt when I tried again and still no answer. An hour later he finally answered. He was OK. The realisation of the danger that I was in and the relief at hearing my brother's voice was too much, and I began to sob uncontrollably. Then he started to panic. He offered to fly up but the airport was closed. There was nothing he could do, just let my sisters know I was OK. Meanwhile I tried to text back friends who had already heard the news back home. Steve and Simon were the first to text. They said, 'Call us please, we're ever so worried.' It made me cry again.

Eddie and a guy called Ted who had a hire car headed down from Bang Tao, about 40 minutes by car from Patong, to pick us up. The Sheraton had been hit but was relatively unscathed despite its proximity to the sea because of the protection given by the lagoon that absorbed a lot of the force. But they couldn't get anywhere near us because the police had blocked off all the roads to Patong. I grabbed a map, said thanks to Justin and we started to walk to where we thought they were. The tarmac was getting hotter and our feet were burnt black but we had to go on, there was nowhere else to stay.

As we stopped by the road in the shade of a car a Thai woman came up to us and offered us a cold wet towel and some water. Then she offered us her shoes. We couldn't take her shoes, we weren't coming back. The Thai people have so little yet she and at least two other Thai women offered us their shoes.

Eventually we worked out that Eddie was at least three miles away. The Thai woman then offered to take us on her motorbike but we had no money – we said we'd pay her when we got there. She looked quite hurt as she said, 'I don't need money, I help you.' And so she did. Her friend took Scarlet and I clung on to her as she tore up and down the hills towards the roadblock. The emotion of being taken to safety was too much and as we got off the bikes, we both broke down. It didn't help that we were burnt, tired, hungry and in total shock. When we finally found Eddie and Ted, and the car that would get us out of there, we almost passed out with relief.

That night I tried to relax with a drink. Of course it just made me feel terrible and later on I was so ill I was convinced the malaria, dengue fever and meningitis had all returned.

I still can't believe how lucky we were. Lucky we weren't on the beach. Lucky we had a room that was relatively near the block with the upper floor. Lucky we hadn't been out getting pissed the night before which would have meant we would have been asleep with the curtains closed and with no way out. Lucky that that guy had found a way to get to the roof. And lucky too that we had friends on the island who could put us up and lend us money and clothes. Thank God for Sam and Eddie and the Sheraton Laguna Beach.

But no thanks to the useless British authorities. When we phoned the next day, the British Embassy in Bangkok said we needed to go to the police station to register for a temporary exit visa, which we would then have to pick up in Bangkok. They also advised us to register an insurance claim with the police. Off to the police station we went. Er, no, we were told, the British Embassy had told the police to direct people to the temporary emergency office that had been set up just outside of Phuket Town. The insurance claim turned out to be a nightmare. We had to fill in a form and write a list of everything we'd lost – which was everything. It took ages. But not as long as it took for the officer to sign it off. I'm not joking when I tell you he sat there and stared at it for over an hour. Then he'd get his colleague to come over and look at it. Then another policeman in a different colour uniform would come and stare at it. We were getting hysterical; didn't they know there'd been a massive tsunami? Later on we discovered the reason for their suspicion. Apparently the Thai Police treat all insurance claims the same because lots of backpackers who don't want to go home and are short of money make up elaborate claims in order to extend their trips. Right then we probably looked like backpackers too in our dirty, minimal clothes but, then again, all he needed to do was call one of his mates down in Patong and check our story.

So, we had no passports, no money, no plane tickets and no clothes and when we turned up at the British High Commission's emergency office in Phuket, they offered us . . . cake. Yes, cake. I kid you not. How typically quaint and British, we thought, as we waited for someone to come and sort us out, confident that they'd have all the relevant information and necessary paraphernalia to get us home. Another man came and sat down, took our names and addresses, looked sympathetic and thanked us for coming in. But what about our temporary passports and can you help us with some money to get to the airport and stuff? 'Oh no, we can't do that, you have to go to the City Hall in town for that,' he said and offered us another piece of cake. The first time was cute but the second time was just bloody unbelievable. OK, I've got no way of getting home and I only have the clothes I'm standing up in. Oh well, have some cake. What? If it hadn't all been so calamitous it would have been comical. They didn't have a clue.

However, more luck surfaced with an old friend of Scarlet's. His name was Mike and he very kindly offered to go back to the Casuarina the next day to see if there was anything of ours worth salvaging from what remained of the room. In the event, the only part of the room that was left was the back wall with the safe still on it. He managed to rip out the safe, get a JCB to crack it open in the street and retrieve our passports. They were drenched but usable after we'd dried them out. He also brought some clothes that were still hanging there. They'd dried out, but even after laundering they were ruined. No sign of any of our cameras, computers, iPods, sunglasses, or, come to that, suitcases – all swept away by the merciless power of the sea.

Mike's words to us after seeing the Casuarina were, 'I can't believe you're alive.' We went back ourselves the next day, nervous and scared and as we walked towards the hotel. It was like we were in a different place. The bustling, sunny resort of a few days ago now looked like a post-apocalyptic landscape of fallen trees, wrecked buildings, gutted shops and what looked like a sandy beach where the road used to be. In fact we walked straight past the hotel because it just wasn't there. It had been almost completely obliterated.

As we stood in front of it, mouths wide open and tears in our eyes, some of the staff, now obviously jobless, were loitering in the area that was once the reception and when they recognised us they waved and smiled as though we'd just come back from shopping or something. As we approached the room, I felt a rising sense of horror. It was even worse than I remembered. Total destruction. All the furniture in the room was turned over, upside down and covered in grime. Some of our things were scattered about, filthy and ruined. The water level reached about 10 inches from the ceiling. Somehow a giant wheelie bin had found its way to the back of the room area. It was usually out in front of the hotel.

Miraculously, among the wreckage I managed to find my house keys, my favourite studded belt, which was water damaged and rusty, and a book that I was quite upset about losing on account of the fact that it had a little message in it from an old friend I hadn't seen for years. It was *Perfume* by Patrick Suskind and the message was, 'To McGiff, You smell like shit, Love Adam. Feb 95.' There wasn't much to smile about that day but seeing that message did the trick.

And that's what I left Phuket with. A plastic carrier bag with some borrowed clothes, my house keys and my book, but I can't get upset about that because so many people lost so much more.

Arriving in Bangkok, life seemed pretty normal. The only indication that anything was wrong was the presence of representatives from almost every single embassy worldwide in the arrivals hall. Once again, the British rep was monumentally useless. After asking us to sit down and offering to contact Eva Air to request a re-issue of our tickets, he then asked if we'd filled in a form (we had, in Phuket) and then sent us into the giant airport to find the Eva Air office ourselves. He didn't even offer us any cake this time.

We stayed in Bangkok for a night. We couldn't believe how unfazed everyone seemed to be. As we killed some time by the pool, there were two men, a Brit and an American, arguing over loungers. It made me so cross that I went to one and gave them both a piece of my mind. 'Don't you know thousands of people are dead and huge parts of this country have been wiped out? And you're arguing over sunbeds? Get a grip!' It also seemed weird, and somehow not right, seeing everyone at the hotel running around setting up the lobby for a New Year's Eve party. Upon finding out the extent of the devastation it was cancelled, as were all celebrations in Bangkok, I later found out.

Landing at Heathrow was another emotional moment. I was home. Would I ever go away again? I honestly didn't know. As we walked through the arrivals at Terminal 3 Scarlet's boyfriend was waiting for her; he looked beyond relieved. I didn't think I'd be bothered that no one was coming to meet me but I was. Selfish of me, yes, because at least I'd made it home, I wasn't lying in a morgue in Phuket. But still, I wanted someone to at least be pleased to see me, to comfort me.

Arriving home, I spent a week staring into space and watching Sky News – the death toll was rising by the hour. The exact final toll will never be known, but is estimated to be around 250,000. I look at that number and I can't get my head around it. It's almost impossible to comprehend that number of people perishing. So many didn't make it and I wonder how I did. And why? It makes me believe even more that whatever happens in life, when your number's up, it's up. Like your card is marked from the day you're born. It can be the only explanation. I've always been quite realistic and pragmatic about death but since that day I have thought about it even more – mainly as to how precious life is and how it can so easily be snatched away in an instant. I thought a lot about my mum afterwards too. Firstly because, in a way, it was a good thing that she'd already passed away because the stress and the worry of me being in Thailand (had she heard the news before I could have contacted her) would have killed her anyway, especially with her irrational fear of the sea. And secondly, because I wondered whether or not it was her who was helping and guiding me that day.

I'm still heartbroken by the stories of people who lost their loved ones in an instant, in such a monstrous, albeit natural, disaster. I still feel guilty that I ran home and didn't stay on to help those less fortunate than me. I feel angry with Mother Nature for wreaking such havoc on such peaceful and giving countries. But most of all, I feel gratitude to whomever or whatever it was that was looking out for me that day. And an ever bigger gratitude to all the people that helped us, some of whose names I don't even know.

It didn't exactly change my life, as I'd always lived for today and I've always tried my best to live life to the full. All it did was make me think of a whole series of 'what ifs'. What if I hadn't gone to Thailand? Might Scarlet have been on the beach on her own? Then again, if we had been on the beach that morning it might not have been a bad thing because I did happen to know (from watching so much of the Discovery and National Geographic channels) that before a tsunami or a tidal wave hits the shore the water gets sucked out for miles. This means I would have known what was going to happen and could have alerted people while making a getaway. If Scarlet had been there on her own she definitely would have been one of those people who went exploring on the empty seabed, picking up dead fishes. What if Sam and Eddie hadn't been there? How on earth would we have coped? Where would we have stayed? How would we have eventually got home? What if the Dutch guy hadn't found a resting point outside our window? What if we'd been in the underground shopping centre like so many people were?

And for that reason, while the Thais set about restoring and rebuilding their lives and livelihoods, I, rather disloyally, spent the next Christmas in the Caribbean on the easyCruise ship and hated it. I felt bad for not supporting the once thriving, but then ailing,

Thai tourist industry, but a whole new set of 'what ifs' had arisen. What if all the friends we'd made over the years perished? What if we came back and they weren't there and big fancy hotels had been built by greedy developers in place of all the small, family-owned places? What if it happened again?

In May 2006, a group of us went back to face it. It was time. I'd looked at some pictures on the internet and I could see that things were almost normal again already. However, we didn't stay in Patong for fear of being too close to the beach, with only three escape routes for the whole two-mile long beach road, so we stayed in Kata, two beaches down from Patong. The resort we stayed in was way back from the road and wasn't affected by the tsunami one bit. We felt safe there.

Happily, on arriving in Patong for a night out, we found that everything was the same. The same bars, hotels, restaurants. All a bit more shiny and new, less bedraggled than they once were, but still the same. It was still light and we walked down to where our hotel had stood. It was gone, replaced by a big block of investment holiday flats. Horrible. It was the only site we noticed that had been sold to developers, everything else looked as though it had remained. Patong Leather, the shop that will run you up a pair of bespoke cowboy boots for 80 quid, was back with a vengeance. The Irish Bar, the Australian Bar, Sailor Bar, the Bangla Road madness, the ladyboys, all back in business. We had a great night and were relieved to notice the Tsunami Warning Systems all in place and lots of familiar faces saying hello. The next day we went there for the whole day and spent it on the beach, which was nowhere near as busy as it should have been for that time of year but while that wasn't good for local business, it was good to see the beach like that. Not groaning under the weight of so many sunbeds and fat, sweaty Western sex tourists. All the regular beach sellers were still there. I can only conclude that it must have been a tad early for them on that fateful morning. In the afternoon Scarlet and I took a tuk-tuk to the place where the lady who helped us lived. We just wanted to say thank you to her for that day. As soon as we knocked on the door she remembered who we were, invited us in, we met her daughter and her English husband, had some tea and took some photographs together. She told us how difficult it had been for the whole place since the tsunami and thanked us for coming back there for a holiday. She owned a hotel next door and said they had nearly been forced to close but things were finally looking up.

That Christmas we all went back again and took part in the 'Lighting of the Beach' ceremony where huge tranches of the beach are planted with candles which are lit at dusk in remembrance of those who died. There are lantern ceremonies too where you light a petrol lantern and it sails off into the sky. It's possible that people are simply selling these lanterns for their own personal gain but all the same, whatever you do or whatever you think, it's still putting money back into the local economy. That day was very emotional and the only way Scarlet and I could cope with it was to get raging, rotten drunk, which helped us with getting all the emotion out.

I'm happy to report that the resort is completely back to normal now. The beach is busier than ever, but that's fine. I've been back four times since then and I went there again for my fiftieth birthday. I still love it and I always will, and even though I didn't die there on Boxing Day 2004, I would happily die there at any time in the future because it is possibly my most favourite place on earth.

CHAPTER 23

The First Time I: Thought life couldn't get any better

(The Where I am Now Chapter)

In August 2008 I honestly thought life couldn't get any better. I had a great job, a weekly column in a women's magazine, I had spoken at an Oxford Union debate, met Russell Brand twice, *Loose Women* had been commissioned for another full year and it was up for the TV Quick Award for Best Daytime programme for the second year running. I'd been to Dublin, Shanghai, Doha, Bangkok and had just come back from three weeks in Singapore, Langkawi and Chiang Mai.

I was also set to move to Paris. After nearly 30 years in London, I needed a change of scenery and a challenge. I wanted to shake things up a bit. I planned to commute on the Eurostar twice a week, which with the same journey time as Manchester where most of the other *Loose Women* lived, wouldn't have been a problem. I was scared but excited at the prospect mainly because I couldn't really speak French. I figured living there would force me to become fluent, something that had been on my list of New Year's resolutions for nearly as long as 'write a book' had.

The only thing missing from my brilliant life was sex. By then though, it had been missing for nearly seven years, which wasn't a huge problem for most of that time given that I'd completely lost interest in everything for more than half of it because of the grief from losing my mum.

But I'd started to get it back and was doing a lot of thinking, thoughts that usually involved either Danny Dyer or Russell Brand. I had a picture of Danny Dyer that he signed for me, up on my notice board in front of my desk at home which said, 'To Carol, don't ever forget I love U. Danny. xxxxx' It was the shot he'd done for *Cosmopolitan* magazine and he was completely naked but covering his bits with his hands. It's a very sexy shot. He's kind of perfectly formed with big shoulders, just enough hair on his chest that rather attractively leads down to his stomach and beyond. And he has the cheekiest, dirtiest grin on his face. I credit that picture for bringing my mojo back.

That, and a programme called *Sexcetera* which is an American series that looks at the different and varying sexual peccadilloes of people from all around the world. It's semi-pornographic at times but mostly the really naughty bits are covered up. You might be shocked if you watched it, like I was the first time I did. Because I'd become a bit of a prude. That first series going back on *Loose Women*, I couldn't even talk about sex, let alone think about doing it. So *Sexcetera* made it feel un-dirty again and although almost nothing in the show could be considered sexually 'normal' to most people, it made it seem that way to me.

Of course I was never going to get off with Danny, he was taken but I told the *Loose Women* and the people watching many times, if I ever do it again, I want him to look like that.

More seriously though, I was getting into a kind of panic. I was going to be 50 soon, an age which to me was the end of life as we knew it. I'd got it into my head that if I didn't get laid again before I was 50 then that would be it. And thinking about it brought back all the desire and the old familiar frisson that comes with sexual tension. I couldn't bear the thought that I might never be ravished again.

I even went on a date, an amazing feat seeing as I didn't do dates. Well, it was a sort of date. It was actually a quick drink before both of us had to go off and do something else on a Monday night. I nicknamed him Groucho Mark on account of the fact that I met him in the Groucho Club in London when I was on a night out with the girls. He kept coming over, telling me he thought it was hilarious that I talked about my ex-boyfriends on the telly, I think, secretly hoping to be one of them. Anyway, when we left, my friend Sally forced me to go over to him and snog him. Which I did. What followed just reinforced everything I hated about dates and relationships and everything I loved about being single. Even though nothing had happened there was that 'will he, won't he' air of anticipation, checking the phone, wondering if I'd bump into him. And we'd only spoken on the phone a couple of times. I turned into a ridiculous teenager. Then I narrowly missed him in the bar of the Courthouse Hotel when I was with the *Loose Women* and just as we were in the car going to a party the phone rang. Straight away I said, 'It's my boyfriend!' (which is what I used to call anyone who so much as looked at me) and the car erupted with excitement. I didn't answer it, which they were most annoyed about because they were more excited than I was that he'd called. It became a kind of sport for them, monitoring and taking an interest in my love life. I quite enjoyed it really. I even got quite courageous and texted him one weekend asking him if he'd like to come round and check out my fake watch collection (we'd talked about it briefly on our 'date'). He never replied. Anyway, he was nice but he had too much going on so it never went any further, but it was a start.

So I really wasn't looking for a relationship.

But then I met another Mark.

Loose Women series 12 finished on 7 August and we finished recording the show for 8 Friday at around 6.30pm as usual. There was a lot of excitement because we'd been on for most of the year with few breaks and we knew we were coming back in less than three weeks' time for another whole year. So the wrap party was very much needed. It was a really nice day and Jacqui, the production manager, had organised the usual Routemaster bus to take us there. I went up to my dressing room and got changed into my party frock. I hadn't made much effort, I'd just grabbed something from the last series leftovers, a silver dress from Warehouse which was quite short. No, actually it was very short. I wore it with high-heeled silver shoes. As I walked into the green room I saw two people sitting up at the bar there. I'd seen them before but couldn't think where. I thought they might be crew. The guy of the two looked very familiar. In my usual rude manner I ignored them both. Actually I wasn't being rude, I simply thought that I should know who they were and was a bit embarrassed that I didn't so I wasn't about to say, 'Do I know you?' as that would have been even more embarrassing. Anyway, so following a few glasses of champagne in the green room everyone went off on the bus. I didn't because I was going to meet Steve and Simon who were also coming to the party, which was in a club in Old Burlington Street, just off Oxford Street.

About an hour after I'd arrived, my friend Karl Lucas, who was working on the show as the audience warm-up man at the time, collared me and said, 'Carol, have you met Mark and Juliet?' It was the guy and girl who were sitting in the green room who looked familiar.

'I don't know, have I?' It's what I always say because it happens all the time that I meet people when I'm drunk and then completely forget them. 'Hi, are you having a nice time?' I was looking at Mark quite intently, I don't know if I was trying to work out where I knew him from or if I was wondering why Karl was only just introducing us. Anyway, I walked off and carried on with the party. About half an hour later Juliet came up to me again.

'I've got to tell you, you've got an admirer,' she said.

'Who, me? Who is it?'

And she pointed to Mark and said, 'Him.'

I looked over and saw Mark leaning against the wall, trying to look cool I think but still looking very chiselled and handsome. 'What, really?' I said, and immediately marched over to him and struck up a conversation. I must have been pissed. I would normally have ignored the news, not believed it, or thought whoever had said it was taking the piss.

Within an hour we were snogging, dancing and having a great time. He was very nice to look at and I thought I'd better make the most of it as he was probably pissed too and wearing his beer goggles. Everyone was interested of course, 'Ooh, look at Carol, she's pulled!' And I bloody well had!

He came back to mine that night. Steve and Simon were also staying with me and we all sat up until about 4am drinking champagne before going to bed.

We didn't have sex on the first night, mainly because everyone had had too much to drink and when I woke up in the morning he wasn't there. He'd gone and slept on the sofa and Simon had found him there, in just his shorts, with no blanket or anything. When he came back down, in his jeans, with no top on, it was like a Diet Coke moment. My beer goggles were well and truly off and he was still gorgeous. 'Get in here,' I said as I lifted up the cover; I just wanted to have him lying in my bed even for five minutes, just to see what it would be like. Then, in his hefty but soft Northern accent he said, 'You know there's a couple o' lads next door?'

I laughed and told him, 'That's not a couple of lads, that's a couple of gays, it's Steve and Simon, remember from last night?'

'Oh yeah,' he said, the penny dropping. At that precise moment they both got up and walked into my room, Simon perching himself rather coquettishly on the end of my bed (he will deny this). They were both impressed that I'd managed to get off with this handsome young man, so much so that Simon went upstairs and grabbed my camera to record the event. He works in advertising so he styled us on the bed and took a 'Liam and Patsy' *Vanity Fair* cover style picture. It's a good picture and I was glad he took it because I honestly didn't think I'd ever see him again. As Mark was about to leave, the last thing he said to me was, 'You're very sexy you know,' and I didn't say it but I thought, 'Mmmm, not sexy enough obviously, otherwise why would you go and sleep on the sofa?!?'

When he left to go to work, Simon said, 'Aren't you going to swap numbers?' (he's such a Cilla sometimes) but I was trying to be cool.

'No, he knows where I am,' because he worked at ITV, which was why he was at the wrap party.

Simon also, cheekily said, 'Ooh, it was nice of him to walk around all morning without his top on, wasn't it!' Honestly, ogling my boyfriend before he's even my boyfriend!

Later, when casually enquiring about him from someone at work,

I found out that he'd taken part in a short film I'd recorded for *Loose Women* earlier that year, playing a builder who was supposed to ogle me as I walked out of a bar in another kind of spoof Diet Coke moment. I thought he looked familiar. Apparently he was gutted that day because I hadn't even noticed him and he'd spent ages doing his hair and everything.

Eventually I plucked up the courage to ask for his number when I was on a night out with some of 'the kids'. After a few wines and a bit of encouragement from one of my favourite kids (I call him 'Babes' but his name's Steve, and he's one of the producers), I texted him. Poor Babes, he had to sit there for a full 10 minutes while I panicked because Mark didn't text straight back. When he did we all sat there analysing it for about an hour and came to the conclusion that it was positive. Phew.

I didn't see him until about three weeks later at another party at work. Once again, within minutes we were very close and we ended up staying out until about 2am talking about travel and work and where we come from (he's from Manchester). We even arranged to go on a proper date.

The only problem was, on 1 September, while getting ready for the TV Quick Awards, I dropped a really heavy wooden framed mirror on my foot and broke my big toe in three places. It didn't stop me going to the awards but afterwards, when I couldn't walk, I had to have a giant boot thing on it. So, our first date did kind of mirror Samantha and Smith's in *Sex and the City*. She had the same boot thing because she fell down a hole after freaking out when he went to hold her hand.

I wanted to see him but I was pissed off about the boot so I texted him. 'Sorry, I can't go out, I've got a giant boot on my foot and look like a right chump.' He replied, 'I don't mind staying in with you.' It was the right answer. Anyway, he came round and we went to the local pub, me with the boot on. I was mortified. I kept looking at it, perched on the little table that the staff had provided. He turned my head and said, 'I can't even see it.' Ting! Another right answer!

He stayed the night and I don't know about Ting! it was more Gong! But seriously, after so long what a relief to find someone who not only is genuinely adorable, kind, funny, gentle, generous, gorgeous, handsome, young and with all the right values but to be totally compatible in bed with, it was almost too good to be true.

The following weekend we went to one of my favourite restaurants, Gilgamesh on the Friday night, spent Saturday in the pub where his best friend, Ben, joined us then went to the zoo on the Sunday where I was doing a thing for my friend Jeremy Joseph of G-A-Y. When Jeremy was telling me that I might have to get in with the lions I was scared but Mark said, 'Don't worry, I'll get 'em for ya!' Ting! We then went for Chinese food with some other friends and secretly, when we'd all finished, he went and paid the bill. Ting, ting, ting! By the Sunday night, I didn't want him to leave.

Then, for the first time in my whole life, I had the boyfriend/girlfriend conversation and it was official. He was my boyfriend. I had a boyfriend. A proper, grown-up boyfriend. Even though he was only 26 at the time and 22 years younger than me. He was still grown-up, probably more so than me if I'm honest.

I fell in love with him quite quickly. I knew I had because I invited him to a friend's fortieth birthday party in Cornwall two weeks after our first date and while we were there, I ironed his shirt. Me. Ironing. A shirt for a bloke. No one could believe it and some of my friends took pictures of me doing it. But joking aside, I wanted him to be there because I wanted him to know my friends and I was confident that he'd get on with everyone and anyway, I didn't want to go without him. I was right; even Scarlet liked him and she's tough. But then there isn't really anything not to like about him. He's the total opposite of me! Quiet, mild-mannered, polite and considerate. When he talks to people you can tell he's genuinely interested in them and he doesn't talk about himself all the time. He loves his mum and dad and he has a taller, older, equally good-looking brother that all my friends want to meet because Mark's so perfect. Well, he's not perfect, of course he has faults like everyone else. Like sometimes he doesn't listen and he eats so fast, I don't think we've ever actually enjoyed eating a meal together – he's always finished before I've started. And, er . . . that's it. Everything else is right. We like the same music – he loves old 1970s soul, more so since he realised that all the great covers of the 1980s originated then. He found this out at one of David Gest's shows. The Stylistics were singing 'You Make Me Feel Brand New' which he thought was a Simply Red song. I put him right. And I love The Killers, Kings of Leon and Scouting for Girls. And of course we both like a drink although we rarely get drunk together because I usually get drunk first and Mark has to take me home!

It's a bit disconcerting that his mum, Marie, is only ten years older than me and looks the same age but at least she *is* older than me so it's fine! (Sorry Marie!) I get on well with his family and he spent last Christmas with mine which, amazingly, didn't scare him off, so we must be right for each other.

We got engaged twice. First in Phuket on Christmas Eve 2008, but he wasn't completely satisfied with that time because he didn't have a ring to give me. So, when we went to Paris in the January for his birthday, he secretly bought a ring and on a beautifully cold but sunny day, on the bridge in front of the Eiffel Tower, he got down on one knee and said, 'Will you marry me, again?' He didn't need to ask.

Now, anyone who knows me will probably be puking as they read that as it goes against everything I've ever said about soppy romanticism. I'm not denying it. And of course, I've got a lot of stick from people who've said, 'Listen to you, I thought you wanted to be single forever?' No, I didn't say that, I said I would be happy to be single forever if that were the case and I hadn't met anyone I wanted to spend the rest of my life with. Well, now I have. He's The One. And I know he is the RIGHT one because I've had the ultimate WRONG one.

Even as a perma-singleton I always believed in 'the one'. People, especially my *Loose Women* colleagues, are always surprised by this view and regularly shout me down with accusations of 'but you love being single, how can you believe in The One?' But I do. I've met so many people who meet someone and instantly know and most of those people have been together for years; they are not short-lived, fly-by-night relationships. The difference is, I wasn't *looking* for The One. I always said, that if you happen to meet or find them then you are very lucky but if you don't then you shouldn't settle for The One That's Not Really The One But They'll Do, or ruin your life searching for them and then being miserable because you haven't found them.

The same goes for marriage. Although I've not had great experiences of marriage, whether mine or my family's, it doesn't put me off because I believe in it. Marriage is important to me and if you feel committed and if you're in love with someone why wouldn't you want to make that commitment public?

It goes without saying that I changed my mind instantly about moving to Paris. I didn't need to go there for adventure now, it had come to me in the form of Mark and after meeting him I can now see what was happening. I was getting bored. Bored with my surroundings, bored with my life as it was, bored with everything except my job. I wasn't depressed, nowhere near it, just stagnating. I seemed to have everything I needed, clothes, gadgets, property, and there was nothing I wanted either. I didn't listen to music anymore preferring the silence. I didn't care that I wore the same New Look £5 jogging pants for weeks on end without washing them.

Mark has changed all that and has brought new interest in everything. Like where I live. I now see it through new eyes after he said, 'I can't believe you want to move away from here when you've got all this on your doorstep.' He was talking about Camden. For years I'd dismissed it as a cramped tourist hellhole and never ventured anywhere near it at the weekends. Now, I long to wander around it again, something I haven't done since my weekends were given over to writing this book.

The same goes for my flat, which I was getting tired of and didn't really live in anymore. When I first moved in people were always coming round. I had a party once, just me and my friend Lisa (a small party) and on the same night, there was another party going on on the ground floor so we decided to amalgamate. Before I knew it, there were about 20 drugged-up teenagers in my flat, dancing around to Wham, breaking glasses on the floor and continuing to dance on it. The floor was wrecked. I didn't give a shit, it was only a floor. But living on your own for a long time has far-reaching effects. I had become mildly obsessed with preserving it so I wouldn't have to do any work on it. It hadn't changed in over 10 years. All my neighbours were doing up their places because they were worn out because people were LIVING there. Mine, on the other hand was pristine (apart from the floor) and nothing was wearing out. I didn't like anyone staying the night, or even coming round lest they'd spill water on the floor. I changed nothing. I'd had the same furniture I'd had since 1980. I never did Christmas, I always went away. And there was never any food in the fridge. I was in danger of becoming so solitary I was beginning to worry that I might be found dead and covered in flies because I hadn't spoken to anyone for so long.

But now, after 18 months, Mark has officially moved in and although we kind of need more space, we're not moving. I'm still getting used to it and I'm still a nightmare: I continue to chase after him with the hand-held Dyson™ dustbuster if he's eating a sandwich but I'm sure that'll pass eventually.

There is only one problem. But, it's a problem no one can do anything about so I should take my own advice and stop worrying about it. The age difference. People are obsessed with it and I always knock it back with, 'It doesn't bother us so why should it bother you?'

Although that's not entirely honest because it does bother me. Not a huge amount but it does. When I was single I only had me to worry about, only me to please, or not. And I was kind of resigned and quite looking forward to liberating myself from the importance of appearance. Now, I have a responsibility to try and preserve what I've been blessed with after this ridiculous amount of time. I don't mind doing that but it's tough and there's a lot to live up to and even if he says he's not bothered, I owe it to him at least.

Because he has improved my life beyond recognition. Everything I loved doing alone I can't imagine doing now without Mark. Before my birthday party I flew to Bangkok on my own, I was only there for three days but it didn't feel right without him.

He even managed to make my fiftieth birthday party even more special than it already was. I had an amazing party on the banks of the Chao Phraya river in Bangkok. I'd planned it for months, all by myself and I was determined for it to be perfect. Everyone was transported to the resort, the Chakrabongse Villas, by luxurious speedboat where we had a champagne reception while watching the sun set over the famous Wat Arun, the Temple of the Dawn, followed by a beautiful Thai seven-course dinner. Then disco and karaoke until 2am. Forty people flew in from the UK, Luxembourg, Australia, Malaysia, Burma and the Philippines. I was overwhelmed to say the least. More so because everyone had made such an effort to dress up, which made me feel a bit guilty because I, as ever, was doing my Worzul Gummidge impression. My sister Kim, my brother Mark and his girlfriend Nani, my niece Emma all came and some of my oldest friends including Stuart, the MP, Scarlet, some of 'the kids' from work, Sherrie, Denise and Tim and Mark's brother Paul also attended. It was fantastic, nothing went wrong, it didn't rain, no one misbehaved or fell out and the last people left at 7.30am. But there were two highlights for me. The first was seeing my sister Kim having such a good time. She has had a rough time over the last few years with jobs and men and I've never seen her let her hair down like that; she even did some 'dirty dancing' with Simon and the aid of a chair! But the number one highlight was Mark making a speech, because he is so shy and when I have to do things like that he's almost sick with nerves on my behalf he hates it so much. He doesn't enjoy the spotlight at all so for him to get up in front of all those people, some of whom he hardly knew, must have been really difficult. He only said a few words but for me, it made my evening. It was one of the best nights of my whole life so far.

And so life did get better, it keeps getting better.

Picture acknowledgements

Most of the photographs are from the author's collection. Additional sources: 11 (bottom) © BIGPICTURESPHOTO.COM, 12 (top left) © ITV1/ Splashnews.com, 12 (middle left) © Xposurephotos.com, 12 (middle right) © TVTimes/Scope Features, 12 (bottom right) © Ken McKay/ Rex Features, 13 (top) © Splashnews.com, 13 (middle and bottom) © Press Association Images, 14 (bottom left) © Mike Clark.

Every reasonable effort has been made to contact any copyright holders of material reproduced in this book. But if there are any errors or omissions, Hodder & Stoughton will be pleased to insert the appropriate acknowledgement in any subsequent printing of this publication.

Index